LEADING

BEYOND CHANGE

LEADING
BEYOND
CHANGE

A Practical Guide to Evolving Business Agility

Michael K. Sahota
Audree Tara Sahota

Illustrations by Marc Hundleby

BK

Berrett–Koehler Publishers, Inc.

Berrett-Koehler Publishers, Inc.
1333 Broadway, Suite 1000
Oakland, CA 94612-1921
Tel: (510) 817-2277
Fax: (510) 817-2278
www.bkconnection.com

ORDERING INFORMATION
Quantity sales. Special discounts are available on quantity purchases by corporations, associations, and others. For details, contact the "Special Sales Department" at the Berrett-Koehler address above.
Individual sales. Berrett-Koehler publications are available through most bookstores. They can also be ordered directly from Berrett-Koehler:
Tel: (800) 929-2929; Fax: (802) 864-7626; www.bkconnection.com.
Orders for college textbook / course adoption use.
Please contact Berrett-Koehler: Tel: (800) 929-2929; Fax: (802) 864-7626.

Distributed to the U.S. trade and internationally by Penguin Random House Publisher Services.

Berrett-Koehler and the BK logo are registered trademarks of Berrett-Koehler Publishers, Inc.

Printed in the United States of America

Berrett-Koehler books are printed on long-lasting acid-free paper. When it is available, we choose paper that has been manufactured by environmentally responsible processes. These may include using trees grown in sustainable forests, incorporating recycled paper, minimizing chlorine in bleaching, or recycling the energy produced at the paper mill.

CIP data for this book is available at the Library of Congress.
ISBN: 978-1-5230-9346-5

First Edition
27 26 25 24 23 22 21   10 9 8 7 6 5 4 3 2 1

Book producer: Westchester Publishing Services
Cover designer: Adam Johnson

A number of the drawings were inspired by the bikablo publications, www.bikablo.com.

We dedicate this book to those committed to their own evolution, and through that, contribute to the evolution of humanity.

Contents

LEADING

BEYOND
CHANGE

PART ONE

STARTING THE JOURNEY

1 ■ An Invitation to the Extraordinary

What lies behind us and what lies before us are tiny matters compared to what lies within us.

—Ralph Waldo Emerson

Let's start with a question: Do you embody what it takes to lead the evolution of a high-performance organization? People are trapped within this underlying belief that "I've got this," and it keeps them stuck.

We have discovered an alarming secret: most of what people believe about leadership, effective workplaces, and how to create lasting change is either incomplete or outright incorrect. Even worse, even when people know intellectually what to do, they are not actually doing it in practice. And furthermore, they fail to recognize the discrepancy.

We started out looking to create high-performance teams and organizations. We wound up finding peace with ourselves. This is the unexpected impact from a shift in leadership. It is also the key to unlocking what we all desire—successful outcomes.

We have cracked the code on high performance, and it's not what you think. It's who you are. This book can change your life.

A Tale of Two Organizations

We begin with a tale of two organizations. We share contrasting perspectives of the same situation to highlight very different understandings of leadership, change, and organizational performance.

Traditional

The room was filled with a sense of dread and gloom. There was a feeling of tension in the air. The project was late, and everyone knew it. It was a big room, and there were over 40 leadership representatives from various project teams. The meeting was supposed to start at 10:00 a.m. but Mary, the vice president, had not arrived, so people were huddled in quiet conversation.

When Mary walked in hurriedly at five minutes past the hour and sat at the head of the massive boardroom table, the room fell silent. Mary spoke clearly and confidently: "We are here to get this project back on track. We have a critical deliverable in two months and have board-level commitments. Failure is not an option. How do we get this back on track?"

The group was in various levels of fear and resigned to several hours of misery. They had been to this kind of meeting before and knew how to play the game of covering up problems and finger-pointing so that someone else would take the blame. Everyone knew it was impossible to deliver everything on time and that pointing this out was a career-limiting move.

As Mary took command on the investigation of how to get the project on track, the game of charades played out.

Evolutionary

Even though the meeting didn't officially start until 10:00 a.m., Mary, the vice president, was there 15 minutes early to welcome people and connect with them on a personal level. This was going to be a big meeting with the whole project team of over 200 people, so Mary enjoyed the opportunity to meet with the new delivery team members. Some of them were surprised that Mary actually seemed to be interested and care about them as people.

At 10:00 a.m. there was an excited buzz in the room with people catching up and talking. As was typical in this organization, there was some time to connect as human beings. Between conversations, Mary noticed what the room felt like: Was it time to start yet? At around 11 minutes past the hour, Mary noticed that the sense of expectation was rising, and conversations were falling off, so she kicked off the meeting.

"Thank you so much for coming. I know there are some new people to our organization, so I want to make sure everyone understands how we do things around here.

"The purpose of this meeting is to use our collective intelligence and wisdom to create the best possible plan for this project. While the forecasts we have given to the board are important, as are our customer's needs and expectations, what is most important is that we look after each other. And that starts with making 'we' statements. We are all in this together. There is no finger-pointing or blame in our organization."

The room was crackling with excitement and energy—everyone knew this was what was needed, and they were looking forward to the challenge. Mary handed the meeting off to Kay, an expert in large group facilitation, who would guide the group though the hours ahead. Mary spent most of the day listening and learning—not only about the project but also about what she needed to do to develop the people and the organization system so that this kind of emergency meeting would not be needed again.

Patterns for Leading Beyond Change

We give you the business patterns needed to learn a new way of leading and approaching change to move from a *traditional organization*

to an *evolutionary organization*. This book will not only explain the step by step of Leading Beyond Change, it will also, more importantly, help you create the inner shift needed to unlock practical skills and techniques.

We make the audacious claim that we have created a reliable path to solve business's biggest challenges:

- How to address employee engagement, culture, and leadership challenges
- How to create business agility to support innovation and organizational survival
- How to evolve a Teal (high-performing) organization
- How to create change without creating conflict
- How to realize the promise of Servant Leadership through Evolutionary Leadership
- How to create a vibrant B Corporation or a conscious business

What to Expect on the Journey

Fully receiving this book will take you on a journey. We are talking about shifting from a static, cause-and-effect view of reality to a dynamic, emergent one. Every person, every organization, is on its journey of evolution. No matter where you or your organization is on the journey, we offer specific tools and techniques to help you on your way. Even more importantly, we offer you a space for self-reflection so that you can evolve your leadership capabilities.

Here are what some graduates of our training programs have said about the work:

And in three years, people say to me, "Oh, we cannot recognize you! You have grown so much." It's really true. I have a friend who was working with me five years ago and he said, "My God, what happened to you? You completely changed."

—P. Bourgeon

You start connecting all the things. And you can say, "Okay, if I'm the problem, what can I do to also become the solution?" How can I start working with myself? How can I use all the techniques and the tools that you are happily setting with us? Yeah, that's my biggest aha moment.

—C. Tsonis

Back then, I think it was a lot of confusion, because going from that state, from "You're done" to "No, you're not," that took me a little bit.

It's not easy, but it's so worth it. Do it. Go through the stages. Trust the process, because it's a process. It takes time, but everything will change for you. It will not only change how you show up at work. It will change how you show up as a partner, as a friend, as a family member. Everything, and I mean that . . . everything will be changed for you. It doesn't matter what you do. You are a leader everywhere. As a family member, you are a leader. It will change you. Go on that ride. It's worth it.

It turned out, it was not about the tools, and it was not about telling others to do that. It's an Evolutionary Leadership journey, and that's what it is in the end. Yes, you get tools, but you get tools to help you with that journey. You will eventually inspire people through your being.

You changed my life. One year ago, I didn't know what I signed up for, but you changed my life.

—P. Zylka

Our Journey

The book in your hands represents our life's work learning about how to evolve people and organizational systems. We have taught and consulted with thousands of leaders worldwide to help them get out of their own way to realize the extraordinary. We share something of our own unique stories to help you understand where this information is coming from and to begin to connect to the key themes of the book.

Michael

As a recovering perfectionist, I have had a lifelong passion for figuring out how to do things really, really well. Originally trained in an elite engineering program, I went on to complete a master's degree and part of a PhD in artificial intelligence around how to build autonomous robots that can operate in complex environments. When I got involved with Agile software development approaches, I learned like crazy how to actually get them working in organizations. This quest took me on a journey of discovery into culture, change, and leadership.

I realized that the only way to create a high-performance organization was to help the leaders evolve. My wake-up moment came when I realized I was a well-intentioned asshole, and that there was no way I could help leaders evolve no matter how smart I was and how much I knew. I needed to grow first. This journey took me to India to study shifting consciousness and the rapid evolution of human beings.

Life didn't deal me great leadership skills. For my own success, I have had to learn step by step how to stop making mistakes and start making better choices. That would be the alternate book title: *How Michael Stopped Messing Up and Finally Learned How to Create Lasting Success with Others*. It's hard to escape the background radiation of conditioned behaviors and patterning to show up like an adult. It's a moment-to-moment choice, and I can say it has been an extraordinary experience.

While my journey of self-evolution continues, I have seen markers of confirmation. We have given keynotes and trained thousands of leaders around the world. Early on these ideas were more controversial, yet people have a desire to create better working environments and lead successful organizational transformations—so for them these concepts make sense. We have seen the rapid spread of our approach. People we have just met tell us our own teachings without even knowing the source.

The most rewarding confirmations are the continued heartfelt stories of our students—of how every aspect of their lives has transformed. We hear about how application and impact of our work has given them peace, successful outcomes, and healthy relations. A marker of their shift in consciousness is that they are recognized as leaders and influencers, and this recognition results in promotions.

Audree

My education and career has been working with the psychology of disease as a professionally trained energetic healer. The approach was simple: heal yourself first to become a clear channel to heal others. It has been an intense personal growth journey since 1997. My passion for my own growth led me further into studying yoga, meditation, metaphysics, and professional coaching. My desire to heal others was foundationally set on a clear principle and truth—that it all began with me. The core belief of my work is that I am a transmission of what I want to see in the world.

During my career as a healer, I had the honor to be a member on a medical team. The five years I spent on this team was a crucial point in my career. It led me to further my studies of human consciousness, how pain and suffering creates psychological imbalance and physical disease. I studied in India to understand the truth of the egoic construct, its nature, and behavior. It was a deep personal journey of growth that changed the fabric of my life. My deep study and life integration led me to become initiated into advanced techniques to shift consciousness. The profound shift in my consciousness shaped my perceptions and greatly impacted the course of my reality.

Yet, how did it get me to this book? I had a hypothesis: Humanity is suffering, and the only way to change this is to change the consciousness of the society we live in. Simply put, when humanity shifts into a higher state of consciousness (i.e., inner peace, connection, abundance, and collaboration, etc.), thoughts will change and behaviors will change. The impact is a liberation of suffering that is the basis for a global "cleanup" of inequality, discrimination, poverty, pollution, and oppression. This seems impossible and overly optimistic, yet I had a plan.

The fastest way to help humanity is to go into the workplace. People work or they are in relationship with someone who works. Currently, the workplace is the most progressive mirror of truth in human behavior, perhaps even an accelerator of revelation. Humanity has not figured out how to get people to function without command-and-control behavior. This style of management creates severe damage to people. Not just physical health issues—deep psychological issues, which get perpetuated in their home environments.

What if we shifted the consciousness of the executives who govern the organizations? What if they created amazing workplaces and cared about people? Workers would be engaged, motivated, and high-performing. Products and services would be impacted by the high state of consciousness that people are in. The organizational purpose would be connected to society and the environment. The organizational focus would shift to humanity and the planet. People, planet, and profit—we can have it all. Most of all, there would be less suffering, poverty, conflict, and pollution.

So how do we get there? Read this book. Michael and I met in India, where we both were dedicated to our own personal evolutions. We both knew one thing: we are the problem, and we are the solution.

Why This Book Matters to Us

What most excites us about this work is that it is a framework—a step-by-step guide to evolving organizations to high performance, including yourself. We have combined our knowledge, our experience, and our purpose and have created the maps, models, tools, and the direction to create the extraordinary.

We are claiming the movement of Evolutionary Leadership to guide a shift in the world of work. Yet, more importantly, we have cracked the code on the "how to do it" and the "path to get there." We can say this because we walk our talk. We created this body of work through our personal experience and developed techniques based on our personal success using them. This body of knowledge may seem simple, yet putting this into practice is not for the faint of heart or for those who want it easy.

We believe that what you are reading here will continue to evolve and spread into something bigger than anyone is able to conceive. We see this with our students and clients. What we do is difficult to explain, yet those who use this work experience a profound evolution in the way they show up to life. It impacts every aspect of your life—in your personal organization and your professional organization.

This work will evolve you as a leader. You will have the knowledge, tools, and skills for this new way of working. You will evolve into someone who is showing up in extraordinary ways. You will lead in a state of deep inner stillness. The leader you evolve into will make a great impact and deliver change.

Your Turn

- As you read each story (Traditional and Evolutionary), what were your reactions?
- What kind of leader do you aspire to be?
- How ready are you to let this book change your life?

2 ■ Setup for Success

Preparation, I have often said, is rightly two-thirds of any venture.
—Amelia Earhart

Why This Book Is Needed

Organizations are facing far greater challenges in today's rapidly changing world, and despite much investment in change, they are continuing to fail at providing engaging workplaces.

Most Organizations Suck

The truth is that most organizations on this planet, from corporations to nonprofits, have terrible performances. Employee engagement, culture, and leadership are the number one issues facing organizations (Solow 2015). Large organizations that have been around for decades or even centuries are going bankrupt as they fail to compete with the fast pace of a modern world that is volatile, uncertain, complex, and ambiguous—the VUCA world.

Now more than ever, society is demanding change. Organizations are being asked to shift to more conscious business practices—to place an emphasis on taking care of customers and the environment—and to provide workplaces that support the needs of workers. People are demanding environmental responsibility and equality as they struggle with financial deprivation and untold suffering. This demand to change organizational structures is not enough. Even if the organizational desire to change is there, the understanding of how to make this change is elusive.

Change Is Hard

Attempts at organizational transformation, whether in the name of Agile, Digital, Lean, or culture, either fail outright or fall far short of lofty expectations. The whole mechanism of understanding organizational change is a broken paradigm. It's time to hit the eject button on what no longer works.

Leadership Is Lost

The truth is that those with the power to effect change are truly lost. They do not have the understanding, skills, or stable presence needed to effect real change. And it's not getting better: "While there is a $366 billion investment globally in leadership development, most organizations are not getting results" (Westfall 2019). Our view is that without a fundamental rethink of leadership, there is no hope of progress.

Humanity Is Dying

To pull out to an even wider perspective, the survival of the human species seems to be coming to an end with environmental overuse and collapse. Unless there is a global shift in how we function, adapt, and lead change, finding a way forward will likely be increasingly difficult and perhaps even impossible.

Leading Beyond Change

"Leading Beyond Change" has multiple overlapping meanings that clarify the purpose and contribution of this book.

Beyond = Business Agility and the Future of Work

It is possible to create high-performing organizations filled with energized people that are able to surf the waves of change. Whether you call this business agility, Teal (high performing), Evolutionary, or the future of work, it is possible for you and for your organization to evolve. Whether you care about the results, the people, or how to innovate, this book holds the keys to understanding where you are and where you want to go.

Leading Beyond

Are you interested in leading an organization beyond business as usual to the future of work? There is a clear set of capabilities and skills that anyone can acquire to learn this new way of leading. We show you step by step exactly what this looks like, so you can evolve your leadership.

Beyond Change

It may sound crazy, but the secret to change is to stop trying to change things. Out of this seeming paradox, a new paradigm arises for how to move beyond change to ongoing organizational evolution. With the guidance of very practical business patterns, a new future may emerge.

SHIFT314 Evolutionary Leadership Framework (SELF)™

We have created the SHIFT314 Evolutionary Leadership Framework (SELF) to create the understanding and application needed to evolve high performance. The SELF system includes the Laws of Organizational Dynamics™.

While the laws provide an understanding of the intrinsic cause-and-effect relationships, SELF provides a means and approach to apply the laws that evolve people and organizations.

While some concepts you may have heard before, many are novel to our work. For example, in the Integration of Culture, Leadership, and Org.Change model, you will discover how organizational culture, organizational leadership, and organizational change are not three separate subject areas. Instead, they are deeply intertwined, and lasting success comes from an integrated understanding that informs novel application.

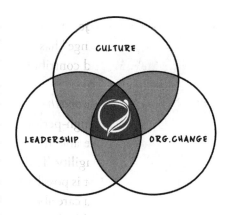

SELF—an Introduction

In this book, we share one part of the SELF. It is a collection of maps, principles, models, patterns, and tools that you can use to unlock success.

> *SELF is a practical guide for leading beyond change*
> *to evolve business agility.*

While it is about your "self," it is equally about how you can make lasting change without power, budget, or authority.

The components of SELF that we will be highlighting in the book are shown in table 2.1. Each component is represented by an icon. These icons will be used throughout the book to highlight the SELF components and provide rapid access to key information. The elements of SELF that we will be highlighting in the book are as follows:

Table 2.1: SELF Components and Icons

Icon	What	Description
	Map	Visual infographics that tell you how to get from where you are now to where you want to go.
	Principle	Principles guide effective evolution by explaining what to do or by linking cause and effect.
	Model	Analytical models that you can use to collect data and perform analysis. A frame for viewing and understanding the world around you.
	Tool	A specific practice or technique that you can use to improve results.

The Laws of Organizational Dynamics™

The SELF is ultimately an encoding of what we call the Laws of Organizational Dynamics. As organizations are composed of people and structures, the laws provide an integrated understanding of the interplay between people and aspects of organizations.

It sounds fancy, yet it is really all about the law of connecting cause and effect. Things like A → B. For example, we might illustrate with the principle: when you treat people well, they perform better.

Like the law of gravity, the Laws of Organizational Dynamics are always in effect. Ignorance of a law does not excuse one from the consequences when they break it. The whole purpose of this book is to help you understand the laws so you can be at a place of choice for what you want to create. It's up to you whether you want to follow the laws or not.

Expect Practical, Not Academic

The very first version of this book was written in an academic style, and it was boring. It has since been heavily modified, and the focus is on practical application and ease of understanding. We could easily double the number of citations—however, that's not going to help you create impact. In the event that you recognize key messages that aren't mentioned, just see that as confirmation that you are on the right path.

How to Get the Most Out of This Book

The book is divided into three parts:

- **Part One: Starting the Journey** gives you a bird's-eye view for how to evolve high-performance organizations by starting with leaders.
- **Part Two: Patterns for Leading Beyond Change.** The core of this book is dozens of business patterns that cut across seven dimensions of organizational functioning. The traps of traditional organizations are contrasted with the high-performance practices of evolutionary organizations.
- **Part Three: Integration and Application** revisits key messages and guides you through steps for application and continued learning.

Your Turn = Your Success

Throughout the book there are Your Turn questions at the end of each chapter and pattern—this is your chance to actually improve in practice. Just reading the book without application will give you an academic understanding. However, it will not have the practical results that you may be hoping to achieve. It is scientifically proven that journaling exercises increase learning and retention.

Our advice for you as you set out on this journey is to play "all in." We promise that you will get out what you put in. Why is this important?

Imagine you want to be a great soccer player. Reading books on soccer won't directly translate to success on the field. What will lead to success is application and practice. Success requires muscle memory, where new ways of perceiving and acting are integrated into your being.

Download Workbook and Diagrams Now

We have created a free package to support your learning journey, which includes:

- *Key diagrams:* Easy reference to key diagrams to orient you while you read the book and support integration of concepts.
- *Exercise workbook:* Use journaling and reflection activities to deepen learning and evolve your consciousness.
- *Tools:* Tools to go beyond the book contents to accelerate your evolutionary journey.

Download at: https://shift314.com/leading-beyond-change.

Your Turn

- What does "leading beyond change" mean to you?
- How well is culture, leadership, and organizational change functioning in your workplace?
- What connections do you already see between the topics of culture, leadership, and organizational change?

3 ■ LEADING

The Evolution of Leadership

The person who can reform themselves, can reform the world.

—Yogananda

In this chapter, we explain Evolutionary Leadership—the foundational model for the Shift314 Evolutionary Leadership Framework (SELF) and for the whole of the book. We contrast Servant Leadership with Evolutionary Leadership using the from/to pattern that forms the core of this book. While there is value in Servant Leadership, it is ultimately an interim pattern that has value. However, it is inadequate to unlock an evolutionary journey.

 ### Servant Leadership
Servant Leadership represents a powerful concept and widespread movement of the last few decades toward a more evolved form of leadership. The main focus of the approach is a move away from traditional management to a more people-centric

approach. We see Servant Leadership as an interim pattern—helpful elements in context—however, not what is needed to create evolutionary results.

While Servant Leadership is generally aligned to the concepts in this book, the specifics and details of what to focus on are quite different. An original essay from 1970 captures the essence of Servant Leadership:

> The servant-leader is the servant first. . . . It begins with the natural feeling that one wants to serve, to serve first. Then conscious choice brings one to aspire to lead. That person is sharply different from one who is leader first, perhaps because of the need to assuage an unusual power drive or to acquire material possessions. . . . The leader-first and the servant-first are two extreme types. Between them there are shadings and blends that are part of the infinite variety of human nature.
>
> The difference manifests itself in the care taken by the servant-first to make sure that other people's highest priority needs are being served. The best test, and difficult to administer, is: Do those served grow as persons? Do they, while being served, become healthier, wiser, freer, more autonomous, more likely themselves to become servants? And, what is the effect on the least privileged in society? Will they benefit or at least not be further deprived? (Greenleaf 1991)

From this passage it can be seen that many of the aspirations and goals of Servant Leadership, such as caring for people and supporting their development, are fully integrated in the models proposed in this book. At the same time, key principles such as foresight and conceptualization, while helpful qualities, are not proven out as essential attributes of high-performance leaders. Other key principles and qualities of a servant leader, such as the desire to serve, require a shift in consciousness.

Retiring Servant Leadership

One challenge with the term *Servant Leadership* is the name. High-performance leaders are not servants—they hold power and use it as needed for the benefit of the people and the organizational system. The abdication of power is not helpful. While they do *serve* people, their more important role is to model the responsible use of power. The principle of *persuasion*, a pattern of Servant Leadership, is an antipattern that derives from a limited understanding of the paradox of power. In contrast, influence is a far more helpful conceptualization.

The other key challenge with Servant Leadership is the outward focus on people and the organization. The inward focus on oneself and one's own development is a secondary or tertiary concern. For example, while growth is mentioned in the principles, it's about growing others. The only way to fully realize the desired behaviors of a servant leader is through an evolution of behaviors and ways of thinking, or a shift in consciousness to a different state of being. As such, it's time to retire Servant Leadership in favor of principles that will more directly lead to its goals.

We see Evolutionary Leadership as a natural evolution of Servant Leadership and other more conscious leadership models: keep the parts that work and reformulate the rest. It is essential that leaders focus on what is most important—themselves.

There are many valuable extensions and additions to the core concept of a servant leader that can be understood as interim patterns or ones that align with evolutionary organizations.

Evolutionary Leadership

We offer Evolutionary Leadership as a concise and precise essence of replicable high-performance leadership.

*Evolutionary Leadership is the **choice** to evolve **oneself** and develop the capabilities needed to evolve an organization.*

With Evolutionary Leadership, we see that our way of being is a transmission that impacts how we do everything. There are two dimensions to the choice:

1. *Being:* The ongoing commitment to evolve one's consciousness to a more evolved state of being.
2. *Doing:* The ongoing commitment to understand and apply the Laws of Organizational Dynamics or SELF, or better to evolve people and systems.

Anyone can be an Evolutionary Leader—it's a matter of choice. Of course, the degree to which one embodies the full principles of Evolutionary Leadership is a journey of evolution. When making the above choices, it is a natural outcome that evolutionary leaders will inspire others to become evolutionary leaders. An evolutionary leader's commitment is essential to look at the reality of our inner world and our interactions with others.

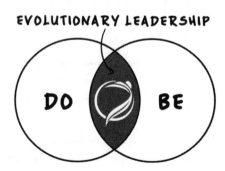

One can be an Evolutionary Leader with or without knowledge of the principles of Evolutionary Leadership. There are many case studies with leaders who demonstrated a high willingness to evolve themselves and learn how to effect positive change in their organizations. As such, our definition of Evolutionary Leadership is based on the key principles required to reproduce high performance in leaders and organizations.

Characteristics of Evolutionary Leaders

Here's a quick preview of the chapter on Evolutionary Leadership, which outlines key dimensions for personal evolution:

- *Self-evolution:* The choice to focus on one's own evolution.
- *Conscious:* Becoming more aware of how we function and the nature of our existence.
- *Being:* Operating from an increasing understanding that all doing rests on our way of being, our behavior, and our inner state. That the greatest impact we have is from who we are.
- *Overcoming the ego:* Overcoming the grip of egoic patterns that keeps us in conflict and fear.
- *Transmission:* Through a personal evolution, a shift in consciousness and evolutionary capabilities are transmitted into the organization, creating an effortless impact of evolution and high performance.

Evolutionary leaders develop very different patterns of interacting with those around them:

- *Leading by example:* Creating impact on those around us by setting a positive example and modeling behavior.
- *Caring for people:* Developing an intrinsic sense of value for other people as human beings and demonstrating this in all interactions.
- *Developing leaders:* A deepening belief in the possibility for greatness in each person and supporting their evolution not just with capabilities but with the whole of their being.

A Recipe for Creating an Evolutionary Organization
Evolutionary Leadership can be understood as a prescription or recipe
for how to create a high-performance evolutionary organization. To
manifest an evolved organization, one requires the leader creating
or uplifting the system to embody the being and doing of an evolved
leader. As the leader shifts their consciousness and integrates new
ways of functioning that reflect that level of consciousness, they will
be modeling a more evolved culture and way of being. Each interaction with other people in the organization will naturally pull them
to the new norms of the leader.

Over time, the consciousness, the structures, and the practices of
the people in the organization will reflect the leader. Of course, the
whole process can be accelerated by special training and mentoring
programs to shift consciousness and introduce more evolved practices to integrate them.

Being over Doing
Our assumption is that you are reading this book to increase your impact. The diagram shows three different approaches to evolution and their level of effectiveness on
shifting one's ability to create impact.

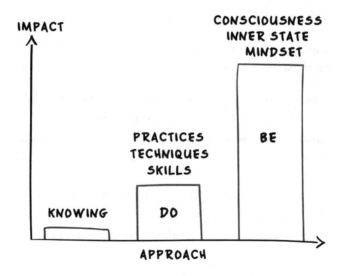

- *Knowing:* While it is important and helpful to know information, it's not that useful unless it is integrated into doing and being.
- *Doing:* As you are able to use new practices, techniques, and skills, your ability to create impact around you will increase.
- *Being:* It's about a shift in our inner state of being that can be described with words such as *mindset* or *consciousness*. Even though our doing rests our being, for many this is an untapped dimension.

It's OK if you don't fully understand what we mean immediately. The key point is that all the exercises in the book are about shifting your way of being.

Your Turn
- What do you see as the most important characteristics of high-performance leaders?
- Would other people you know describe you as meeting these characteristics?
- How does Evolutionary Leadership differ from what you currently believe about high-performance leadership?

4 ■ BEYOND

From Traditional to Evolutionary

It was the best of times, it was the worst of times,
it was the age of wisdom, it was the age of foolishness,
it was the epoch of belief, it was the epoch of incredulity,
it was the season of Light, it was the season of Darkness,
it was the spring of hope, it was the winter of despair,
we had everything before us, we had nothing before us,
we were all going direct to Heaven, we were all going direct the
   other way.

—*A Tale of Two Cities*, Charles Dickens

In the first chapter, we shared stories of an emergency meeting from the perspective of traditional and evolutionary organizations to give you a feel for the dichotomy this book is exploring. In this chapter, we continue to contrast traditional organizations and evolutionary organizations and give you a map to orient yourself as you read the book.

The whole of this book is about understanding, at a very deep level, what an evolutionary organization is and how we can show up as leaders to create these extraordinary organizations.

Beyond = Evolutionary

The good news is you probably already have some idea of what an evolutionary organization is. There are many terms that give you a sense of where we are going, such as the *future of work, Teal, reinventing work, business agility, adaptive,* and *antifragile.* We have created the evolutionary organization as a grand unification model for high-performance organizations. The model integrates and extends existing views of culture, leadership, and organizational change.

A Fundamental Rethink

In this book, we outline the integrated shift needed across many aspects of a human and organizational system to create an evolutionary organization. What follows is an examination of the contrasting views of culture, leadership, and organizational change. In this chapter, we give you the high-level summary. The details are shared in part three, "Accelerating Application."

Organizational Culture: Traditional versus Evolutionary

In traditional organizations, management governs the organization. The primary focus is on driving for results, and levels of psychological safety are so low that job stress, blame, and cover-ups are the norm. People are there to be managed and manipulated to get outcomes.

In contrast, evolutionary organizations understand that everything depends on the people in their organization. In an open and supportive environment, people can explore the root challenges, including the need for people to grow. Culture is integrated into everything that happens, rather than an afterthought. High performance is a norm.

Organizational Change: Traditional versus Evolutionary

In the Traditional approach to change, the organization is viewed as a mechanical system that can be understood to such a degree that a fixed transformation program can be defined, measured, and followed through a fixed series of steps. Typically, the solution is copied from other organizations with the usually invalid assumption that mandating the same defined solution here will actually work.

In an evolutionary approach to change, there is a good understanding of the complexity of the organizational systems and a deep surrender to need for an emergent and unfolding journey. Daily effort is needed to slowly evolve the system toward the star on the horizon. The focus is on the never-ending work to support alignment and fuel inspiration.

Leadership: Traditional versus Evolutionary

With traditional leadership, the focus is on the use of power to direct activity toward organizational goals. The focus of managers is primarily on ensuring that work gets done to meet quarterly objectives. It's all about doing the work.

With Evolutionary Leadership, the focus is on self-evolution and learning to be a powerful role model for people. The focus is around developing other leaders by supporting their growth and effective decision making. The understanding is that an evolved inner way of being is needed to unlock high-performance activity.

Integration of Culture, Leadership, and Organizational Change

An essential insight to make progress on the journey from Traditional to Evolutionary is to understand that all the aspects of an organizational system are deeply intertwined. Organizational change is deeply connected to culture and leadership.

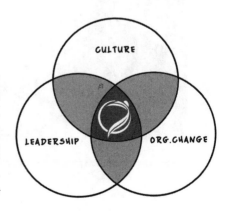

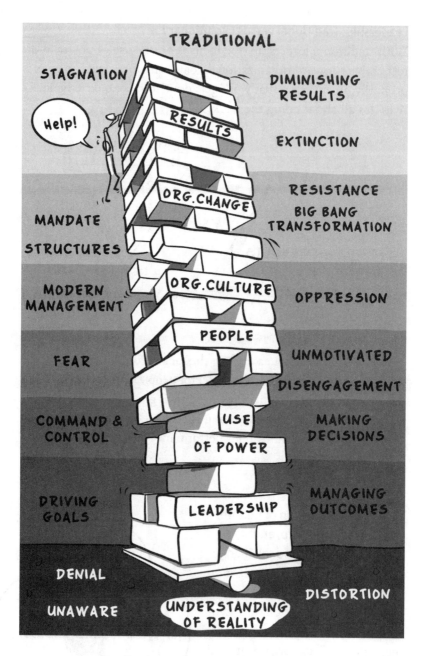

Figure 4.1: Map: Traditional (Jenga)

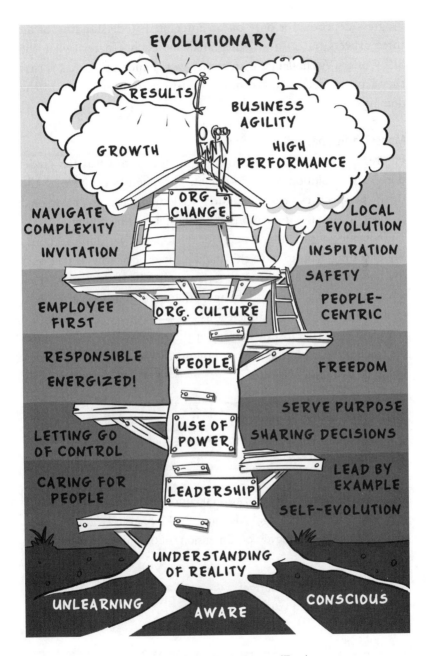

Figure 4.2: Map: Evolutionary (Tree)

Progress depends not only on an integrated understanding of all three aspects but also an integrated approach. That is what the SELF offers. A challenge with earlier works and approaches is that they have tended to focus more on just one or at best two of the domains.

Maps: Traditional and Evolutionary

Figures 4.1 and 4.2 show contrasting images and words for Traditional and evolutionary organizations. These figures go beyond the three perspectives above (culture, leadership, and organizational change) to seven key dimensions of organizational functioning.

These are your high-level maps for the topics covered in this book. We encourage you to have this page printed or nearby as you read the book so you can effectively orient yourself. In part two, "Patterns for Leading Beyond Change," there are multiple patterns to explore on each of these dimensions.

Our hope is that just by looking at them you will be able to sense the state of the evolution of your organizational system from Traditional to Evolutionary.

Download Instructions

You can download key maps for printing, such as the diagrams below. See instructions in chapter 1.

Seven Dimensions of Organizational Functioning

Both the Traditional (Jenga) Map and Evolutionary (Tree) Map illustrations have the same levels or dimensions of organizational systems:

- Results
- Organizational Change
- Organizational Culture
- People
- Use of Power
- Leadership
- Understanding Reality

The levels help clarify the nature and scope of this book. They provide an integrated understanding of key dimensions of organizational functioning. While the Traditional and Evolutionary maps have the same levels, they are different in the content and meaning. The Traditional or business-as-usual approach differs from the new ways of organizational evolution.

A key thesis of this work is that we need an integrated understanding of all dimensions to create a lasting shift in the organizational system. Our view is that while there are many brilliant works on culture, leadership, organizational change, use of power, and people-centric environments, they only form pieces of the puzzle. Here we put the puzzle pieces together through the SELF system and Laws of Organizational Dynamics.

Evolutionary Organization

An evolutionary organization is defined by the Evolutionary (Tree) Map shown in figure 4.2. It operated from an evolved understanding across all the levels or dimensions of organizational functioning. The whole of this book is a detailed explanation of what these shifts are.

The creation of an evolutionary organization is a natural consequence of leadership choosing to be evolutionary leaders. It's simply a matter of time and effort.

Your Turn

- What is closer to your organizational reality, Traditional or Evolutionary?
- What is the rate of evolution of your organization?
- When you think of your day-to-day focus and behavior, do you operate closer to Traditional or to Evolutionary?

5 ■ CHANGE

A Radically Different Journey

You can't use an old map to explore a new world.

—Albert Einstein

The journey to develop an evolutionary organization is like setting out to climb the peak of Mount Everest. Success depends on preparation, training, and a thorough understanding of what lies ahead. In this chapter, we provide three high-level maps and orientation needed to understand the whole of the journey.

Once again, we are sharing a high-level summary of the whole book. It is natural to have questions or not quite understand everything immediately. Don't worry, each element will be explained in detail later.

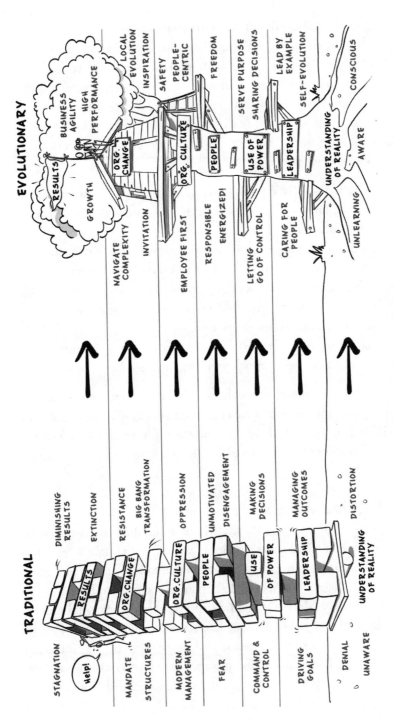

Figure 5.1: Map: Traditional to Evolutionary

Map: Traditional to Evolutionary

In chapter 4, "BEYOND: From Traditional to Evolutionary," we shared the maps for Traditional (Jenga) and Evolutionary (Tree) to illustrate the breadth of change needed to make an effective shift in organizational functioning.

Figure 5.1 shows the multidimensional shift needed for organizations to move from Traditional to Evolutionary. It can be used in the following ways:

1. Getting a holistic sense of which approach—Traditional or Evolutionary—feels closest to the day-to-day reality of the organizational system.
2. Scoring your organization (or team/group) from 1 to 10 to get a sense of where your organization is on its journey.
3. Noticing what parts of the map are discussed in your organization. For example, what parts are regularly discussed and have effective action?
4. Noticing what dimensions or levels of the map need more attention to help unlock your organization.

The more important use of the map is for you to recognize that just making a change to one or two parts of a system will not create a holistic change. Instead, there are a number of interdependent components that all need to shift to make effective progress on the journey.

Map: Reality Matrix

Figure 5.2, the Reality Matrix Map, illuminates the cause-and-effect relationships that form the fabric of organizational reality. It shows where to focus effort to create a shift in the biggest challenges that organizations face today.

The Reality Matrix is implicit in both the Traditional (Jenga) and Evolutionary (Tree) maps. Each level of the jenga and the tree rests on an earlier level. Success and results depend on all the layers beneath. Each illustration has the same levels or dimensions of reality, yet the beliefs, perceptions, and choices differ radically.

A key lesson from Lean is that the way to get results is not to focus on results but to focus on the organizational aspects that will lead to results. The Reality Matrix shows us what to focus on to ultimately create the results we desire.

The cause-and-effect relationship can be expressed top-down or bottom-up.

Figure 5.2: Map: Reality Matrix

Bottom-Up

The Reality Matrix shows how to evolve a high-performance organizational system. Look at the diagram and visit the levels starting from the bottom and moving upward:

1. Understand that reality shapes leadership.
2. Leadership shapes the use of power.
3. Use of power shapes people.
4. People shape the organizational culture.
5. The organization culture shapes organizational change.
6. Organizational change shapes results.

Top-Down

Look at the diagram and visit the levels starting from the top and moving downward:

1. Results flow from organizational change.
2. Organizational change flows from the organizational culture.

3. The organizational culture flows from people.
4. People flow from use of power.
5. Use of power flows from leadership.
6. Leadership flows from understanding reality.

It's about Impact

What came first, the chicken or the egg? Or in the case of the Reality Matrix: What dimension causes the other dimension? The truth is that there are complex interdependencies between the layers—that organizational evolution involves an integrated coevolution across all the dimensions.

> *The purpose of the Reality Matrix Map is to understand*
> *where to focus effort and unravel a complex system.*

Whether we are aware of it or not, the reality is that we are living in the matrix. The map is called the Reality Matrix to highlight that our views of what is reality and our beliefs about people and organizational functioning keep us trapped in the machine world—business as usual.

We invite a journey beyond a surface-level understanding of evolutionary organizations to go on a deeper dive into their true meaning. Our invitation is to wake up to the subtle reality of what is happening around us, and through that we realize the extraordinary.

Map: The Evolution of High Performance

The Evolution of High Performance Map describes the cause-and-effect relationship that leads to results. It's an integration of a number of the Laws of Organizational Dynamics into a high-level map to guide you as you read this book. It lets you examine where to focus in order to create the shift that you want in your organization.

The key message is that the results of the organization are a reflection of the leadership of the organization. Any substantive

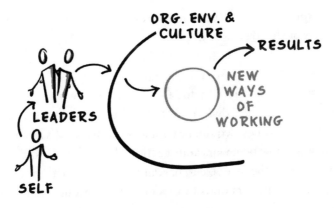

Figure 5.3: Map: Evolution of High Performance

change in the results of the organization comes from a change in the leadership.

Figure 5.3 shows that leadership evolution is the most rapid and direct means of organizational evolution.

Let's look at the causal relationship between the elements in the map:

1. Results depend on new ways of working.
2. New ways of working will only succeed where there is a supportive organizational environment and culture.
3. The organizational environment and culture depends on the behaviors and choices of the leaders.
4. The ability to develop leadership in others depends on the evolution of one's self.

For a book on organizational change, we are setting out from a very startling proposition: *The most rapid and direct means to high performance is to focus first on your own evolution as a leader and human being.*

The map can be read backward and forward. When we read the map forward, we see a powerful recipe for success:

Evolve oneself → evolve leaders → evolve the organizational environment and culture → evolve new ways of working → get results.

As we explore each of the steps, you will receive the overview of a key thesis of this book.

Evolve Oneself

The most important activity for a leader is their own self-evolution. Leaders focus on their own inner states of being and shift to higher levels of consciousness required for high performance. As leaders learn and integrate new behaviors and practices that reflect a more evolved way of working, they are able to have greater impact. The most important thing that leaders do is to model culture through their behavior. As leaders lead by example to model learning and growth, they transmit and inspire others to do likewise.

The map can be applied at any level of an organizational system. It does not require authority, budget, or permission. Each of us has the ability to influence the people around us.

Anyone in the organization can be a leader—not just management. The only requirement is the choice to evolve oneself and have passion for success.

Evolve Leaders

High-performance leaders develop other leaders around them. The primary means of evolving other leaders is by shifting one's inner state of being so that every interaction feels different. This is the transmission of Evolutionary Leadership.

Examples of one's state of being include: respect, feeling psychologically safe, caring, believing in people, curiosity, and openness. The secondary means is to lead by example where one's actions and behaviors reflect operating from a more evolved consciousness to demonstrate what's expected of people. Tertiary means is by improving the overall environment and culture so that it is conducive for learning and growth. The final means are by direct relationship through mentoring or coaching to help people develop capabilities.

Evolve Organizational Environment and Culture

While the organizational environment and culture is a cocreation by all the people, those in power have the greatest influence. The daily and hourly choices made by leadership set the tone for the organization. As the leadership evolves in consciousness and integrates new practices, they are able to effectively support evolving organizational performance.

Here we see the understanding that organizational evolution is an iterative, emergent process that starts with a profound desire to create success. Progress starts with the tension between a clear understanding of the current organizational reality and the hopes for the future. With a focus on culture, it's about evolving people first so they can effectively experiment with strategic and tactical changes.

Evolve New Ways of Working
Over time the organization will evolve new ways of working that support their new way of being. While inspiration may be taken from movements, such as Agile, Lean, Digital, and design thinking, these are explored and integrated organically in ways that fit the needs and goals of the people and the organization. It is an emergent process that unlocks the capabilities of the organization.

Get Results
The final outcomes sought by organizations, such as financial results, adaptability, sustainability, a great workplace, and navigating complexity, are wholly dependent on the evolution of work practices.

Your Turn
- How closely do the maps presented here reflect your own understanding of the laws of cause and effect?
- In your organization, what levels of the Reality Matrix get the most attention?
- What beliefs do you have that are different from the maps presented here? What are they?

6 ■ Getting the Most from Patterns

"Begin at the beginning," the King said, very gravely,
"and go on till you come to the end: then stop."
                                    —Lewis Carrol, *Alice in Wonderland*

In this chapter, we are equipping you with how to use part two of this book, which is formulated as a collection of patterns for each of the seven dimensions of the Reality Matrix.

Each pattern is designed to guide and cultivate your ability for leading beyond change. You will also receive some very powerful tools and models to unlock the doing and being of Evolutionary Leadership. Just reading each pattern without considering application will limit the benefits of using the book.

Exploring the Seven Dimensions

There is one chapter for each of the seven dimensions of the Reality Matrix. It is very important to note that we have sequenced the

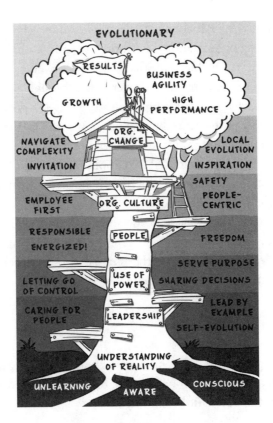

chapters in an order that is most supportive of your evolutionary journey.

As such, we will not explain the tree from top to bottom, or from bottom to top. Instead, we will jump between layers based on the complexity and sophistication of the idea.

Chapter 7, "Unlearning Reality," is the foundation of the whole book. It provides an understanding of how cognitive bias prevents us from learning as well as specific techniques to overcome them. This part is essential for your own evolutionary journey.

Chapter 8, "Getting Results," explores what organizational high performance is and how it is very different from the business-as-usual norm of the business world.

Chapter 9, "The Truth about Your Organization Culture," offers a deep dive into understanding your organizational culture and the keys to its evolution.

Chapter 10, "It's All about the People," explores the roles people play in shaping organizational performance, and it challenges even progressive views of what it means to treat staff well.

Chapter 11, "The Paradox of Power," cuts through the chaos and conflicting advice for leadership around the use of power. The secret is in learning the art of how to use power in ways that support the evolution of people and the organizational system.

Chapter 12, "Organizational Evolution," is a very practical guide to evolving an organizational system. We show you the painful traps as well as the patterns for success.

Chapter 13, "Evolutionary Leadership," details the leadership required to evolve or even participate in a high-performance organization. This chapter illuminates the essential shift in the consciousness or mindset of leaders to exhibit effective behaviors.

The Pattern of Patterns

Table 6.1 explains the different kinds of patterns that you will find in this book. Each pattern has an icon to indicate what type of pattern it is and how to think about its use.

From Traditional to Evolutionary

In this book, we share patterns in pairs to create contrast in order to highlight options for growth. *Most* of the patterns in part two of the book are from Traditional to Evolutionary. The Traditional aspect reflects low-performance organizations, while the Evolutionary aspect reflects high-performance organizations.

An example is pattern 10.3, "From Status and Domination to Equal Voice," in chapter 10. Domination of others is a guaranteed performance killer, while creating a space for people to have their voices and opinions count is essential for high performance.

From Interim to Evolutionary

Some of the "from" aspects are interim patterns found in organizations that have evolved beyond the Traditional but have not yet

Table 6.1: Types of Business Patterns

Icon	What	When to Use	Description
	Evolutionary pattern	Wherever possible	An aspect of an evolutionary organization leading to high performance. *Primary* attribute for high performance.
	Interim pattern	Secondary; adapt to context	An organizational aspect that is valuable when used in context. *Secondary* attribute of high performance.
	Traditional pattern or antipattern	Avoid	An aspect of a traditional organization that leads to low performance.

moved to Evolutionary ways of functioning. Here the patterns serve to contrast something that might be good in a specific context to something that is more universally associated with high performance.

These interim patterns can be understood as half-truths or something that is only true in a certain context.

A good example to illustrate this point is pattern 9.1, "From Customer First to Employee First," in chapter 9. Customer first is an interim pattern, as it will help an organization develop some improvement in performance. Why? It's important to focus on customer experience for many reasons. However, putting customers *first* actually blocks high performance. For some, this is a very controversial statement, which is why we have a pattern to explore this idea.

Our general advice is to be really careful when using interim patterns, since they can block higher performance.

How to Use Patterns to Evolve

Each from/to pattern gives you the opportunity to evaluate yourself as a leader as well as where your organization is in its evolutionary journey.

Your Turn = Your Evolution

The secret to getting the full value of this book is to really examine yourself and your organization as you read the patterns. Each pattern has a section called "Your Turn" for you to pause for reflection and to journal. It is scientifically proven that you will learn and retain more by taking time to actively process the information you are reading. Writing has much more value to this process than just reflecting.

Taking time to invest in journaling will support a shift in how you see yourself and how you see the world around you. This new awareness itself is the shift in consciousness this whole book is about.

Principle: Listen to the Voice of the System

Effective action requires a clear understanding of reality. We define the principle *listen to the voice of the system* to describe the act of understanding what is happening with any aspect of an organizational system: a team, a department, or the participants of a workshop. It's about taking stock of what is happening so that one can lay the foundation for intelligent action.

Tool: Readout

A readout is one way to listen to the voice of the system: to sense what is happening around you. In the case of this book, we are asking you to use it to sense where your organization is and to discover what possibility for growth is available.

We are suggesting that for each pattern, you listen to the voice of your system. We invite you to do a readout to make sense of your organizational reality. Let's do an example together for pattern 11.3, "From Command and Control to Letting Go of Control," in chapter 11. One means using command and control, and ten means letting go of control. Just draw a line on a piece of paper or use the downloadable workbook.

Where is your organization from 1 to 10 on the journey from command and control to letting go of control? As you think about this question, you might reflect on leadership behaviors as well as organizational policies and procedures.

Using the readout will not only help you integrate learning for each pattern, it will also give you a readout on how your organization is doing with this aspect of high performance.

Where Are You?

You may use the same readout in figure 6.1 to check in with where you think you are on your journey of evolution as a leader. To continue the example, consider how you show up as a leader. Where do you act more command and control, and where are the places that you let go of control?

Lookout for Leadership Edges!

A leadership edge is a leadership behavior that limits us from showing up as the leader we would like to be. It's a challenge area that blocks the outcome we desire. As you go through this book, we invite you to reflect on your leadership edges.

To continue working with the example pattern, you might notice a couple of leadership edges around moving beyond command and control:

- I have a hard time giving up control.
- I don't like to follow when others lead.
- I want to be in control so I feel more secure.

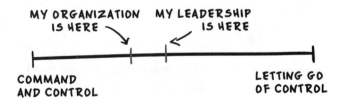

Figure 6.1: Readout

We invite you to keep a running journal of your leadership edges as you read this book. Don't worry, it's normal. In chapter 18, "Continuing the Journey," you can work through your leadership edges using the 4A's Leadership Practice. If you are curious to learn more about leadership edges right now, you can jump ahead to pattern 13.6, "From Leadership Development to Self-Evolution."

Your Turn

- What is your intention for reading this book? Is your goal to learn new information or to develop new capabilities?
- Are you reading this book more to help your organization or to evolve yourself?
- How strong (1 to 10) is your commitment to get the maximum benefit by taking time to reflect and journal?

PART TWO

PATTERNS FOR LEADING BEYOND CHANGE

7 ■ Unlearning Reality

Can You Handle the Truth?

Welcome to what is arguably the most important and the most challenging topic of this book: reality. At the bottom rung of the Traditional (Jenga) and Evolutionary (Tree) Maps is reality. It serves as the foundation of everything else.

Mastery of this chapter will unlock incredible power and ability. And yet, not everyone is really ready for that. If you let it, application of this chapter alone can radically change your life.

We ask that you slow down and really take in each of the patterns in this book to ask yourself: Could you have some mistaken assumptions? Could what's happening around you be different from what you think it is? Is it possible the fastest path to unlocking your success is to detect and unlearn invalid beliefs? Is it possible that you play a much bigger role in the challenges you face?

You take the blue pill, the story ends, you wake up in your bed and believe whatever you want to believe. You take the red pill, you stay in wonderland, and I show you how deep the rabbit hole goes.

—Morpheus, *The Matrix*

PATTERN 7.1: FROM DENIAL TO DISCOVERING REALITY

KEY POINTS

- The greatest challenge organizations face is the unwillingness to consider uncomfortable data and related conclusions that disturb the status quo.
- Our perceptions are our model of reality and are often not as accurate as we assume.
- We can improve our model of reality by investigating our assumptions.
- Embracing reality requires an ongoing practice to question assumptions and improve models of reality.
- Organizations and leadership that choose to embrace reality can more effectively solve challenges.

DENIAL

A central challenge faced by organizations is a denial or unwillingness to look at the reality of what is happening and why.

The biggest challenge is not that the information is absent, it is that it is getting ignored. "We don't act on what we know. Virtually every medium to large organization showcases the success it has had with self-management, quality improvement efforts, partnerships, autonomous operations, and giving superior service to customers." (Block 1993).

So the problem is not discovering information, it's about the willingness to look at what it is present.

Consider the effectiveness of a person or organization when in self-deception, denial, minimization, or distortion of reality. The choices and actions are going to be based on a distorted understanding of what is happening and a mismapping of cause and effect. As a result, the choices will not be very effective. This is why we are rarely ever able to create lasting solutions for all but simple situations.

Which plans will be more successful—plans based on half-truths and lies, or plans based on the reality of the situation?

The result of widespread and recurring denial is that nothing of any consequence really changes. Of course there are transformation programs, initiatives, strategic plans, and reorganizations, yet the core way of functioning in an organization still remains unchanged. A key step in creating lasting change requires taking the "red pill" to look at the uncomfortable truths of what is happening.

A related symptom is that most organizations do not track the effectiveness of changes that have been made, either through quantitative or qualitative metrics. Or even worse, they use metrics that are meaningless in relation to the actual stated purpose of a change.

 REALITY

The core challenge we face, both as human beings and as organizational systems, is that *reality is not what we think it is*. The truth is that none of us really fully knows what reality is. Our beliefs shape what we perceive.

Take, for example, this drawing of a woman. How old is she?

The Woman. Source: Wikipedia

Perspective is the Achilles heel of the mind.
—Dee Hock, *One from Many*

The image is ambiguous and can be interpreted as a young woman or an old lady (Covey, 2004). We see what we expect to see based on our beliefs and perceptions. As human beings, this happens to us all the time when we misunderstand a text, an email, or what someone says.

 MODEL: REALITY DISTORTION FIELD
From a neurolinguistic programming perspective, the human brain cannot possibly store all its incoming sensory data. As such, the three basic functions of the mind are to:

1. generalize
2. distort
3. delete information (Bandler and Grinder 1975).

Thus, we operate on a generalized, distorted, and incomplete model of reality. The most accurate way to describe our mind is as a reality distortion field.

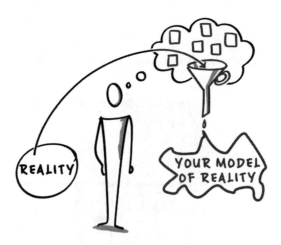

The challenge we face is that we interpret reality based on our existing beliefs about the world. So what we perceive is *our model of*

reality and not reality itself. All of this is an automatic, seamless process that happens in our unconscious. We have no conscious awareness of the raw information that does not make it to our conscious awareness.

Reality is not what we think it is. *Confirmation bias* is the related psychological term that, in our opinion, grossly understates the challenge we face to create useful models of reality. Reality of an organizational system is the key to unlocking its potential for success.

 PRINCIPLE: DISCOVER REALITY TO UNLOCK SUCCESS
Understanding reality is a critical key ingredient for success. When we understand reality or the truth of a situation, we have the possibility of coming up with effective actions. When our actions are based on a clearer understanding of reality, they will be able to address the real challenges and are likely to have some positive impact. The effectiveness of efforts will be much higher than those based on a lower-fidelity model of what is happening.

Success requires that we know what reality is—what is happening within ourselves and within the organization. In the book *Good to Great*, a key foundation of success is the willingness to "confront the brutal facts" (Collins 2001, 13). This applies not only to looking at our organizations but also, more importantly, to looking at ourselves as leaders.

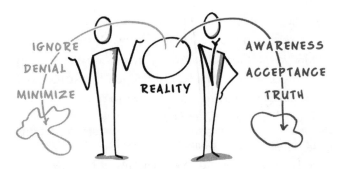

In *The Grand Design,* it is proposed that there is no model that actually reflects reality—what we have is "model dependent realism" (Hawking and Mlodinow 2010).

> *All we can do to really learn the truth of reality is to constantly test our models and seek new ones.*

At each moment we have a choice—take action based on our current model of reality, or invest time in learning what reality *actually* is. The purpose of this chapter is to help you understand the importance of discovering reality and how to hack your brain so you can operate more in this reality.

How to Discover Reality

Why is it so difficult for us as human beings to become fully conscious of the reality we live in?

Our minds are designed around two key assumptions that limit our ability to function:

1. The model of reality we have in our head is the actual reality.
2. Other people have the same model of reality that we do.

> *All models are wrong, but some are useful.*
> —George Box

At Bridgewater, the largest hedge fund in the world, the quest for discovering reality is supported through a focus on seeking truth and choosing radical transparency (Dalio 2017).

Question Your Own Models

The biggest challenge we face is our default assumption that the thoughts in our head are reality. As we saw, this is not the case. So success relies on our humility to recognize that we do not really know what reality is. Our best success is to let go of existing models and beliefs that have low fidelity—to be open to new ideas that shatter our existing beliefs and understandings.

Investigate Other People's Models

The secondary challenge is our often invalid assumption about other people's models of reality. Of particular importance for success is the discovery of what other people's views of reality are. A keen interest in others' perspectives gives us a powerful means to overcome our own tacit assumption that other people believe the same things that we do.

Are You Ready for the Red Pill?

Are you ready to take the red pill and see how deep the rabbit hole really goes?

Dee Hock speaks eloquently about the challenges and benefits of discovering reality:

"We can attempt to understand and change our internal model of reality. That is the least common alternative, and for good reason. Changing an internal model of reality is extremely difficult, often terrifying, and always complex. It requires meticulous, painful examination of beliefs. It requires fundamental understanding of consciousness and how it must change. It destroys our sense of time and place. It calls into question our very identity. We can never be sure of our place or our value in the new order of things. Changing our internal model of reality requires an enormous act of faith, for it takes time to develop, and we require time to grow into it. Yet that is the only workable solution" (Hock 2005, 201–202).

YOUR TURN

- Where are the disconnects between what you believe and what other people believe?
- Where do these disconnects get in the way of making progress?
- How open are you to the possibility that your model of reality is incorrect? 1 . . . 10

Zen Koan: "A Cup of Tea"
Nan-in, a Japanese master during the Meiji era
(1868–1912), received a university professor
who came to inquire about Zen.
Nan-in served tea. He poured his visitor's
cup full, and then kept on pouring.
The professor watched the overflow until
he could no longer restrain himself.
"It is overfull. No more will go in!"
"Like this cup," Nan-in said, "you are full of your
own opinions and speculations. How can I show
you Zen unless you first empty your cup?"
(Kaufman 2017)

PATTERN 7.2: FROM LEARNING TO UNLEARNING

KEY POINTS

- Our brains are designed to prevent us from learning new information.

- Most of what happens with people and organizations is shallow learning with no real questioning of one's assumptions about reality.

- Keeping an open mind means keeping two possibilities in mind at the same time and waiting to make a decision.

- Unlearning is about discovering invalid assumptions about reality.

- The most valuable learning is unlearning—replacing low-fidelity models of reality with more accurate ones.

LEARNING ORGANIZATIONS
In *The Fifth Discipline* (2006), Peter Senge introduces the notion of a learning organization. Conventional wisdom is that organizational learning is required for an organization to adapt to its evolving market needs and surroundings.

More specifically, the production capability of an organization will only evolve to the extent that organizational learning takes place. "Organizations learn only through individuals who learn" (Senge 2006, 129). So to create a learning organization, we require individuals who learn.

The default assumption people have about themselves is: "Yes, I am open to learning."

People believe they are ready to let go of crystallized thinking. When questioned, one might list out evidence: "I learn new skills, I attend webinars and go to conferences. I learn from my coworkers. I am constantly learning."

Let us return to the zen koan about the professor. Is it possible that we, like the professor, have no space in our minds, and that to truly learn we need to empty our cup?

UNLEARNING
Unlearning is the evolutionary step beyond typical learning. Or alternatively, we might understand unlearning as the most important kind of learning.

MODEL: UNLEARNING ASSUMPTIONS
Unlearning can be defined as letting go of our assumptions or models of reality that are not serving us.

Successful learning often requires you to unlearn first—to let go of what you know and to embrace the teaching as a beginner. As illustrated in the previous pattern on discovering reality, letting go of what we know can be incredibly challenging. It requires a commitment and an ability to overcome the traps of the mind so that you can learn rapidly.

PRINCIPLE: UNLEARNING IS THE MOST POWERFUL FORM OF LEARNING
Although this special kind of learning—unlearning— is a lifelong skill, it is essential to apply it to discover the full value of this book.

Although this book may touch on familiar concepts,
it offers an invitation to go deeper.

In particular, some of the concepts introduced in this book are the opposite of conventional wisdom and societal norms. Gaining the full value of this book requires a level of openness—or willingness to unlearn—beyond the usual.

Beware: "I Know This"

Be careful not to fall into the trap of, "Oh, I know this." We know from our experience in training people on this content that there are small nuances that make huge differences. One gentleman reported, "You were just talking about material that I already know, but then everything changed." So please look for what's different, not just for what is the same.

Model: Local Optimization Trap

Knowing information and finding success through it is actually a huge barrier to continued growth. Why? We will need to unlearn what already works for us. As the saying goes, "Good is the enemy of great." It is human nature to get caught in a local optimum: we find something that works well enough.

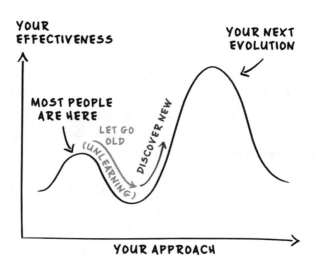

What got you here may not get you where you want to go. To move to even higher levels of success requires letting go of the old (unlearning), and the effort and openness to discover what is new and might work even better.

 PRINCIPLE: THE BRAIN IS DESIGNED TO AVOID LEARNING
It is important to understand from a neurobiological perspective that our brains are designed to stop us from learning. What? How can that be? Let's take this step by step. First, a question:

Is your brain designed to:

1. find a valuable/correct answer, or
2. find an answer as soon as possible?

I first became aware of the answer decades ago when reading *The Man Who Mistook His Wife for a Hat and Other Clinical Tales*, where I learned that the human mind is designed to confabulate (Sacks 1985). *Confabulate* is a fancy word for lie. Or make stuff up. Yes, the mind is designed to make stuff up—not to find reality or truth or helpful models. What is even more hazardous is that we believe that we are rationally thinking and that our models are true.

The answer is: *2. find an answer as soon as possible.* Surprise! Your brain—the one you are using now to read these words—is not designed to give you the correct answer.

*The brain is designed to stop thinking
as soon as possible.*

From an evolutionary perspective, it makes sense to minimize thinking. The brain consumes a high level of energy in the form of blood sugar. Our body is designed to preserve blood sugar. Hence, our brains have a clear goal: to stop thinking as soon as possible. That is why we get to the first possible answer. It's an ancient optimization made for survival that inhibits our ability to achieve our fullest potential.

It takes very little thinking or blood sugar to recite one's list of assumptions or data about reality—that is why it is so easy to stay within our existing assumptions. When we choose to explore what reality is and begin to question assumptions, that takes more energy, so the brain will tend to avoid it.

CONFLICTING IDEAS

The challenge faced in reading this book is that we will present alternate models of reality that are likely to challenge your existing beliefs and understandings. How will your mind react when you read something challenging? What's the fastest possible answer?

Consider figure 7.1. Your beliefs and models of reality are indicated as squares. It has taken you your whole life to select and construct these models. Some of them are directly related to the topics of this book: organization performance, leadership, and organizational change.

These beliefs are deeply intertwined and serve as your foundation to how you approach the world. We might even say that these are well protected and stable, since your functioning depends on them.

The reason you are reading this book is that you believe that we have a different understanding that is valuable. Our models are depicted as triangles.

Figure 7.1: Navigating Conflicting Ideas

What happens when there is a conflict between a square (your model) and a triangle (our model)?

Your mind will get you to stop thinking as soon as possible using the smallest amount of blood sugar. It will take you to the quickest answer that supports your existing models. You might think things like: the model is inaccurate, it doesn't apply to my situation, it can't work in practice. Your mind might even go on the attack: How do they know? What data do they have? Where is the proof?

CHOOSE TO QUESTION REALITY

What would it mean to "empty your cup," as described in the zen koan? It would mean that you come to explore ideas with openness, with a willingness to question your assumptions, your models of reality. ("How do I really know if what I believe now is true?") And a willingness to be curious about other people's models ("Could they be true? Is it possible? Do I have irrefutable proof that they are wrong?").

What would it mean to let go of your square? It would require rewiring all the neural networks associated with that square. This will require a huge amount of effort, blood sugar, and an ongoing process over time to permanently rewire your brain. We call this unlearning the most powerful and valuable of all learning.

It is the most valuable learning, since we are able to identify invalid beliefs or models about the world that are leading to faulty thinking and thus faulty actions.

> It's not what we don't know that hurts.
> It's what we know that ain't so.
> —Will Rogers

CAN YOU OVERCOME YOUR MIND'S LIMITATIONS?

Your mind will fight really hard to make up any reason to reject new ideas that don't conform to your existing worldview. That is its nature.

Are you ready to choose to focus attention to overcome the limiting nature of your mind? The following passage captures the imperative and challenge we face:

"It is our individual perspective, the view from our internal temple of reality, that constantly discolors and distorts our perception, blinding us to how things might become, or conceiving of, they ought to be. When everything changes around us and it becomes necessary to develop a new perception of things, a new internal model of reality, the problem is never to get new ideas in; the problem is to get old ideas out. Every mind is filled with old furniture. It's familiar. It's comfortable. We hate to throw it out" (Hock 2005, 107).

The question to consider is: What is your level of desire to create more successful outcomes? Is your desire for success strong enough for you to invest in examining your existing beliefs? Perhaps even beliefs that you have held for your entire career or even your entire life?

It is possible, and the remainder of this pattern is dedicated to explaining how to support an ambition to question models to improve outcomes.

TOOL: NAVIGATE CONFLICTING IDEAS
We offer a key piece of advice to overcome this challenge:

The test of a first-rate intelligence is the ability to hold two opposed ideas in mind at the same time and still retain the ability to function.
—F. Scott Fitzgerald

We are inviting you to interrupt the desire for your mind to come to an answer right away—to use your intelligence to keep *both* mental models alive as possibilities. To embrace the truth that you don't know *for sure* what model is a higher fidelity representation of reality.

When you are confronted by something in this book, you can ask yourself the following question: Is it possible

that the author's model is valid? Our invitation is to take the time to try out and test new models before discounting them.

The 100 percent guaranteed way to know you have fallen into the traps of the mind is that you are 100 percent sure in your own model of reality.

The secret to getting a more accurate model of reality is the willingness to question your own beliefs.

Unlearning in Practice

It's not about deciding in a specific moment which model is better. Our invitation to you is: put effort into understanding alternative models or reality—what the triangles are. How can you rationally reject something without fully understanding it?

So, what might happen by the end of this book? Consider the future when you are challenged or even confronted by the information you read here.

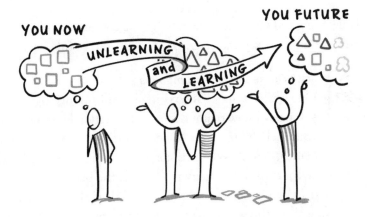

You may have a mix of existing models (squares) that are validated by this book. You may have existing models that have been replaced with higher-fidelity models of reality from this book (triangles). It may also be that your existing models have been replaced with entirely new creations (wiggly blobs).

The biggest danger in unlearning is hanging on to existing models and decorating them with elements of new models. Usually what happens is that the new model is not really ever understood but instead distorted from the lens of the existing model.

The greatest learning from this book will come from shedding existing models of reality that are inaccurate or have low fidelity or low utility in creating the outcomes you desire. The way to get the greatest value out of this book and to become a lifelong unlearner is to be willing to question everything.

If you are really lucky, you will have your existing models of reality shattered so that you can jump to increased levels of performance and success based on more accurate and useful models.

What we are inviting you to consider is not easy. In fact, it may be one of the hardest things you have ever undertaken.

> *We are our ideas, concepts, and perceptions. Giving up a part of our internal model of reality is worse than losing a finger or an eye. It seems as though part of us no longer exists.*
> —Dee Hock, *One from Many*

Unlearning and the success that it brings is a choice. It's not for everyone. However, it is a key characteristic of highly successful leaders.

 Tool: Question Your Assumptions
One way to unravel an existing belief is to investigate how you really know that it is true—to question how you know your beliefs are true. One evolutionary organization, Semco, describes their version of these practices as follows:

"If we have a cardinal strategy that forms the bedrock for all of these practices, it may be this: Ask, Why. Ask it all the time, and always ask it three times in a row. . . . It means putting aside all the rote or pat answers that have resulted from what I call '*crystallized*' *thinking*, that state of mind where ideas have so intensely hardened into inflexible and unquestionable concepts that they are no longer of any use. Employees must be free to question, to analyze, to investigate and a company must be flexible enough to listen to the answers. Those habits are the key to longevity, growth and profit" (Semler 2004, 5).

Of course, when you take this to the logical endpoint of continuing to ask "why," you may realize that there is nothing that you know that is definitely true. For practical purposes, it's best to ignore this awareness until you are ready to explore the deepest levels of reality.

Time Is Your Ally

A key practice for maximizing unlearning is to evaluate models *over time*—to test which ones (existing or new) are more accurate and useful. The basic observation is that you don't need to resolve a tension between models right away. The question is then: To get to the greatest learning, how long to keep a tension open? One second? One minute? One hour? One day? One week? One month?

Our advice is to leave the decision about what to do about the tension until later on. Wait until you fully understand the triangle.

Triangulate

When surveying land, triangulation is the use of multiple measurements so that they can be integrated to make accurate inferences. The patterns in the book are deeply interconnected. What we have seen in practice is that every individual is unique, and that what may unlock one person's perspective is different from what may unlock another's. Once one pattern clicks and you have an obsolete model collapse, it may lead to a domino effect where there is a cascade of realizations— an aha moment where the conflict releases into the joy of discovery. So the advice is to wait until you learn other models and research in this book that can be used to triangulate reality.

Tool: Keep a Tension Journal

If you are determined to maximize your learning, start an unlearning journal or log to keep track of the places where you can feel the tension between your existing beliefs or models and those that we share in this book. It could be five columns:

- *Topic Area*—What area of reality the model pertains to.
- *My Current Model*—The current model that you believe. Summarize your beliefs.

- *SELF Model*—The model we are proposing. Summarize your understanding.
- *Related Concepts*—What other book patterns are related to this model?
- *Resolution*—Make note of how long you kept two opposing ideas in mind for. What was the resolution?

YOUR TURN

- What concepts in this book are in conflict with your assumptions?

- Is your assumption that your model of reality is correct? How can you tell that you are right?

- How long have you practiced keeping two opposed ideas in your mind? How long do you think it will take to become proficient at this activity?

- What are the topics where you tend to get into arguments or conflict with others? Is it possible that your ideas are incorrect? What would happen if you were ready to let go of your ideas?

---

*When we are no longer able to change a situation—
we are challenged to change ourselves.*
—Viktor E. Frankl

PATTERN 7.3: FROM THE PROBLEM IS OUT THERE TO THE SOLUTION IS IN HERE

KEY POINTS

- Rarely do we consider ourselves in the equation when understanding what is happening.

- We are not aware of the role we play in what is happening around us.
- The practice of self-awareness creates a powerful window to new solutions.
- A willingness to investigate what we believe about ourselves and how our behaviors shape outcomes to unlock powerful new solutions.

THE PROBLEM IS OUT THERE

The default mode of functioning for a human being in our culture is to assume that the problem or the challenges we face are external to us. We collect data, the facts, and different perspectives so that we have all the right information to make a decision or take action.

When reading the patterns about discovering reality, we may primarily assume they are about the external reality of the situation we are in. Similarly with the pattern for unlearning, we may focus on considering a challenge to our models when confronting the Laws of Organizational Dynamics: culture, leadership, change, and so on.

Applying the patterns of reality and unlearning, while challenging, yields great benefits.

And yet, the greatest value of this book comes from a deeper investigation—the models we hold about ourselves.

THE SOLUTION IS IN HERE

When you are interacting with another person or an organization, how you show up matters. In fact, how you show up is likely more important than what you do or say. To quote Jerry Weinberg (1986), "Everything counts!"

The whole of who you are shapes every outcome: who you are as a person, your values, your thoughts, your emotions, as well as your conscious and unconscious actions.

On a daily basis, you may notice people who are not aware of how they are behaving and the impact they are having on you and the others around them. It could be someone speaking too long so that others tune out. It could be someone coming late to a meeting. It could be someone having an emotional reaction to an idea.

Both your conscious and unconscious behaviors are shaping the success that you are able to create. The default mode of thinking is that "the problem is out there." When the outcome is not what we hope for, we look for the problems outside of ourselves. It is easier to look externally than to choose to investigate internally.

Agile teams and other learning-oriented cultures are famous for having regular retrospectives to evaluate their work and people working together with an eye to improve the functioning of the team.

The usual scope of investigation and learning is on how to make changes to what is happening out there and experimenting with doing things differently. While this is valuable, there is a deeper investigation needed to unlock high performance.

We don't act on what we know.

—Peter Block

PRINCIPLE: I PLAY A ROLE IN WHAT'S HAPPENING AROUND ME

What if the biggest challenge is not out there but inside you? What if, when confronted by a situation, you were open to examining how you were contributing to it?

The greatest value of this book is to apply the patterns of discovering reality and unlearning to yourself.

*That means investigating the models and
beliefs you hold about yourself.*

Each of us carries an identity: we have a name, a body, a gender, etc. We can list out all of our characteristics: what we are good at, what we like, what we don't like. We also hold beliefs relevant to how we show up in the workplace: I listen to people, I care about other people's opinions, I have really good ideas that are ignored, and so on.

TOOL: INVESTIGATE YOURSELF
What happens when you apply the pattern of discovering reality to yourself? You realize that the model you have of who you are is not who you actually are.

The model of how you show up and behave is not how you actually show up and behave. And your success depends on having a high-fidelity representation of the reality of you.

We embrace the possibility that we played a part in creating the problem, and inquire what we can learn so we can grow from it.
—Frederic Laloux

When you are part of the solution, you hold a willingness to explore your role in what is happening. You are open to exploring your actions, behaviors, and unconscious patterns.

UNLEARN BELIEFS
The pattern of unlearning is invaluable when applied to ourselves. We are open to considering alternative models of how we behave. Think for a moment—how do you react when confronted that you may be doing something wrong or that you have an unconscious behavior pattern that is causing challenges?

To create a more accurate model of the reality of how you are impacting the environment around you, all you need is a willingness to be curious about new ideas. You don't need to immediately agree with challenging ideas. The secret is to apply unlearning to yourself.

Note what model you hold about yourself. Spend time understanding what the alternate model is. Keep an open mind: Could it be true? Is there at least a 1 percent chance it is true? If so, keep both ideas in mind as possibilities, and collect additional data to triangulate.

How Successful Do You Want to Be?

Self-investigation is not easy. In fact, it can be downright uncomfortable.

The question to ask yourself is: How successful do you want to be? If you are happy with all the outcomes that are happening around you, then why bother? The only reason to invest in self-investigation is that you are interested in creating higher levels of success.

Assess Your Own Behavior

As you read the patterns of the book, we invite you to be open to exploring how you really show up—your leadership edges. How do you interact with people? How do you approach organizational change? How do you show up as a leader?

The greatest value of reading the book will not come from picking up something new to try, it will be from realizing that something you are doing now is not working.

Our greatest hope is that you will realize how you have been the problem and how you can be the solution.

To get a related perspective on this topic we recommend the book *Leadership and Self-Deception* (Arbinger Institute 2010).

YOUR TURN

- When you think about your default mode of operation, are you usually looking at how to resolve challenges outside of yourself, or are you looking at your inner state and functioning?

- How often do you consider how you are contributing to the challenges around you?

- How open are you to discovering how you really show up?
  1 . . . 10
- How open are you to the possibility that you are the problem?
- Do you see places in your life where you can examine how you are part of the problem and how you can be part of the solution?

---

8 ■ Getting Results

Beyond Organizational Survival

Let's jump to the other end of the Traditional (Jenga) and Evolutionary (Tree) Maps to look at Results. Most organizations want higher performance and some level of business agility. The patterns in this chapter provide a stark outline to illustrate the key dimensions in which traditional organizations differ from evolutionary ones.

If your organization is functioning anything like a traditional business, then you are getting a fraction of the possible levels of performance. Survival is optional, and most organizations are not set up to thrive. This chapter serves as an invitation to examine how your organization stacks up against human potential.

Everything should be made as simple as possible,
but no simpler.
—Albert Einstein

PATTERN 8.1: FROM "WE ARE OK" TO THRIVING IN A COMPLEX WORLD

KEY POINTS

- Organizations are failing at a faster and faster rate. Survival is optional.

- Organizations are experiencing challenges with disruptive technology, adapting to the competitive market, and attracting and retaining top talent needed to succeed.

- Thriving in a complex world requires the organizational capability to rapidly adapt, change, and deliver.

- Organizations need to develop evolutionary capabilities to be able to *evolve*.

WE ARE OK

If your organizational performance is OK, then chances are that your organization will not survive. It's just a question of time.

ORGANIZATIONAL LIFESPAN IS DECREASING

The average company lifespan is decreasing. The average lifespan of companies listed on the S&P 500 Index is going down. Companies are increasingly going out of business, while the rate of change itself is increasing.

IT'S A VUCA WORLD

VUCA has been used to describe the landscape and volatility of the business for the past twenty years. *VUCA* is a term coined by the U.S. Military in the 1990s to characterize the world:

- *Volatility*—There is a high rate of change.
- *Uncertainty*—There is a high level of uncertainty of what is happening right now and of the future.
- *Complexity*—Situations are so complex it is a challenge to respond effectively.
- *Ambiguity*—Decisions often have to be made in the face of incomplete or conflicting information.

Consider how each term applies to the global business environment organizations face. What is interesting is the *internal landscape* of an organization. The trap most fall into is that they delude themselves into thinking that VUCA does not exist, including within the internal environment of the organization. They create structures and processes that pretend the world is stable, certain, analyzable, and clear. The trap continues within teams, departments, and the structures of culture, hierarchy, and competition among peers. This puts employees and the whole of the organization at a disadvantage, since they are no longer able to acknowledge the reality of the situation—employees need to be skilled at working though all aspects of VUCA.

ORGANIZATION SURVIVAL IS OPTIONAL

"Survival is optional, no one has to change" is a famous quote by W. Edwards Deming, speaking to organizational survival. Organizations need to evolve in order to survive. Some will. Some won't. Hence, the survival of any one particular organization is optional. Companies that are unable to or repeatedly choose not to invest in developing a new way of working are going extinct. It is important that your organization is set up to thrive and able to compete against certain large global organizations or the latest innovative start-up that has energetic and passionate people.

THRIVING IN A COMPLEX WORLD

Evolutionary organizations have developed a high level of capability. They are able to evolve and adapt in the face of the complexity of the changing world.

EMBRACE VUCA

Embracing a VUCA world is like learning to surf the waves instead of trying to make them go away. High-performance organizations not only recognize the nature of what is happening, they design their organization to respond to what is happening now and are able to respond quickly to the unknown future—not some notion of what should happen.

For example, there are many companies who have embraced VUCA by moving to adaptive planning, distributed flexible budgeting, and transparency to support rapid adaptation. The beyond budgeting movement came from the realization that annual plans and annual budgets simply did not make sense in a VUCA world (Hope and Fraser 2003).

ORGANIZATION SURVIVAL IS BASED ON ORGANIZATIONAL EVOLUTION

Evolutionary organizations are in a constant state of evolution. Products and services are evolved to meet new needs. Ways of working are improved. People develop, grow, and are inspired to innovate. Organizational survival is a side effect of the ongoing evolution of the organization and its people.

*If your organization has some sort of "transformation program" such as Agile, Digital, etc., it's probably missed the understanding that the real game is about developing **evolutionary capabilities** for ongoing evolution— that's what this book is about.*

Evolutionary capabilities are what supports the ability to navigate complexity.

 MODEL: NAVIGATE COMPLEXITY TO SURVIVE
Volatility, ambiguity, and uncertainty can be understood as dimensions of complexity. So the key question is:

Figure 8.1: Ability to Navigate Complexity

Where is your organization in its ability to embrace and thrive with complexity?

Figure 8.1 shows the relationship between an organization's ability to navigate complexity and its survival rate. As the ability to work with complexity increases, so does survival rate. It is not, however, a linear scale. There is a tipping point or threshold where an organization begins to materially work with the complexity or reality of the situation.

YOUR TURN

- How well is your organization able to respond to volatility? Uncertainty? Complexity? Ambiguity?
- How well do your organizational budgeting and planning processes support adaptation? What's getting in the way?
- Is your organization ready to compete against the best in the world? Is it set up to thrive in the future?
- How will your organization be able to respond if a well-funded, highly innovative start-up enters your marketplace?

Every company is organized based on a certain premise of human nature.

—Chip Conley

PATTERN 8.2: FROM TRADITIONAL MANAGEMENT TO KNOWLEDGE WORKERS

KEY POINTS

- Modern business practices are based on the underlying premise that workers have no brains.
- Many organizations fall into Traditional structures that inadvertently oppress workers and reduce performance.
- The knowledge worker paradigm provides an alternate understanding of how to unlock worker capability.

TRADITIONAL MANAGEMENT

Most organizations in the world operate based on the principles of scientific management created by Frederick Winslow Taylor in the late 1800s. The principles' main objective is to increase the economic efficiency of organizations by optimizing worker productivity levels (Taylor 1911). What we see in the business world today—modern management—is largely based on Taylor's principles created in the context of industrial labor, primarily steelwork.

The underlying assumption of scientific management is that workers have no brains and need to be managed. When we hold the belief that workers have no brains, we create organizational systems that can function with workers that do not have brains.

Figure 8.2 illustrates the key structures created to support scientific management. Each structure is designed on the assumption that workers have no brain. Each structure is designed to compensate for and mitigate the perceived lack in the workers. Consider your current work environment as you review each component of our modern organizational systems.

Let's walk through this diagram and model step by step:

Figure 8.2: Traditional Management

1. The manager has a brain. Success depends on the manager.
2. Workers have no brains. They are lazy, unmotivated, dumb brutes who merely perform standardized work that is given to them.
3. To overcome the lack of brains in the workers, the manager will:
   a. Create processes and procedures that define standardized work.
   b. Measure the quantity of standardized work produced.
   c. Create plans to direct and organize the workers so they know what standardized work to do when.
   d. Motivate the workers with a carrot and stick.

Each structure radiates the underlying assumption to workers: *you have no brain.* From morning until evening, workers are constantly exposed to a work environment that at the deepest levels reminds them again and again that they have no brains.

What we have experienced from a metaphysical perspective, is that your thoughts create reality. The underlying assumption of workers is like background radioactive waste—you can't directly see it, and it will make you ill when you are exposed to it. This model of management is a key contributing factor to worldwide levels of stress, illness, depression, and disengagement.

 KNOWLEDGE WORKER

The knowledge worker paradigm presents a system of work that is a stark alternative to modern management.

The term was first coined in 1959 by Peter Drucker in *The Landmarks of Tomorrow.* He suggested, "The most valuable asset of a 21st-century institution, whether business or non-business, will be its knowledge workers and their productivity" (Drucker 2009).

Although the term was originally intended for white-collar workers, it is clear that it applies equally to most job categories. For example, the Toyota production system places manufacturing line workers at the heart of their innovation and improvement efforts.

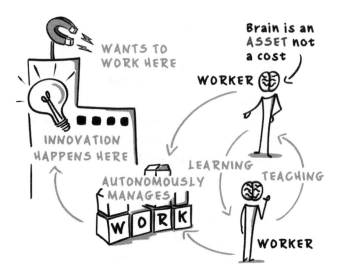

Figure 8.3: Knowledge Worker

The underlying assumption with the knowledge worker model is that *workers have brains*. Figure 8.3 illustrates the knowledge worker model:

1. All workers have brains.
2. Workers' brains are assets or sum up the value of an organization.
3. Workers learn and teach each other to develop their capabilities.
4. Workers want to come to work.
5. Workers autonomously manage the work.
6. Innovation is a natural side effect and intrinsic to doing the work.

The knowledge worker model is not intended to be literally taken as a blueprint for creating an organizational system but rather to highlight key principles that support and are helpful for capturing the full ability of workers to contribute.

 PRINCIPLE: BELIEVE IN PEOPLE
Management beliefs about workers and the ensuing organizational choices lead to a self-fulfilling prophecy.

"A self-fulfilling prophecy is the socio psychological phenomenon of someone 'predicting' or expecting something, and this 'prediction' or expectation coming true simply because the person believes it will and the person's resulting behaviors aligning to fulfill the belief" (Wikipedia 2021b).

Once we believe workers need to be managed, the structures created will shape people. Over time, people who are independent and responsible become unmotivated and disengaged. Each time someone is told what to do, every meaningless report, every uninformed leadership decision, all support the notion that people's intelligence and experience doesn't really matter.

What if beliefs about workers were different? What if management believed in people's independence and creativity?

Imagine what your workplace would be like if everyone believed in the intelligence and capability of workers. If every moment was seen as an opportunity to celebrate people's capabilities and help them evolve further. Imagine if the leaders see their role as creating an environment for greatness to happen rather than telling people what to do.

YOUR TURN

- What policies, procedures, or other governance structures would lead people to feel like they don't have a brain?
- How do people feel the organization treats them? What impact do you think that has on productivity? How well is your organization set up to fully unleash people's talents and capabilities?
- How much freedom do workers have in guiding and directing work?
- How do you think things would change if management fully believed in people's independence and creativity?

Culture is the fuel that feeds High Performance.
—Audree Tara Sahota

PATTERN 8.3: FROM BUSINESS AS USUAL TO HIGH-PERFORMANCE ORGANIZATIONS

KEY POINTS

- Business as usual = low performance.
- The modified Laloux culture model offers a lens to understand the evolution of high-performance organizational culture.
- The highest levels of performance emerge as people are fully engaged and act like adults.
- High performance stems from a shift in behaviors, culture, and consciousness.

 ### BUSINESS AS USUAL

Organizations that operate like "business as usual" are at the lowest levels of organizational performance. They frequently match many of the antipatterns shared here: denial, "we are OK," modern management, low engagement, ignoring culture, and so on.

Organizations may avoid recognizing this reality by benchmarking themselves against similar types of organizations. Although these issues are widely recognized as the number-one challenges facing organizations today, there is little or no material progress (Deloitte 2019).

If your organization is anything like "business as usual," it means your organization is operating far from its potential.

 ### HIGH-PERFORMANCE ORGANIZATIONS

There are many ways to define *performance* and many ways to realize it. As such, there is no single way to define what constitutes a high-performance organization.

We define a high-performance organization as one that substantially outperforms its peers with market and customer outcomes and is sustainable over time.

The scope and focus of this book is on the patterns that are:

1. Common to many high performance organizations
2. Possible to replicate

HIGH PERFORMANCE IS POSSIBLE FOR YOU

There are also people with unique abilities, such as Steve Jobs or Elon Musk, who provide the genius to create great success. There are also companies at just the right time and just the right place with the perfect product. These are great examples of high performance. However, they are typically not sustainable over time.

An even greater barrier is that they are not replicable! It is pretty much impossible for most of us to execute or become a visionary like Steve Jobs, but it is possible for anyone to apply the patterns in this book to become more effective.

REINVENTING ORGANIZATIONS

In *Reinventing Organizations: A Guide to Creating Organizations Inspired by the Next Stage of Human Consciousness* (2014), Frederic Laloux examines 10 organizations with breakthrough performance.

He presents a simplified version of spiral dynamics focused on organizational systems demonstrating the historical path of evolution of increasingly high-performance work systems. The focus of the book is on the organizational structures needed to support a high-performance (Teal) way of working that reflects the last stage of human development.

The original model Laloux uses is from spiral dynamics and can be described as the "theory of everything" that speaks to the evolution of human beings. It speaks about higher levels of consciousness affecting functioning (high performance) as a reflection of individual and collective behavior (Beck and Cowan 2005).

REINVENTING ORGANIZATIONS–AN ADAPTATION

The SELF Evolutionary Culture Model is a model that speaks to the essence of the high performance of an evolutionary organization. We modified and extended the work of Frederic Laloux to offer a deeper understanding of the evolutionary path of organizational performance.

 Model: The SELF Evolutionary Culture Model
The SELF Evolutionary Culture Model is illustrated in figure 8.4.

As the consciousness of an organization evolves to more effective cultures, the levels of organizational performance follow. This gives an organization the ability to navigate complexity and realize business agility.

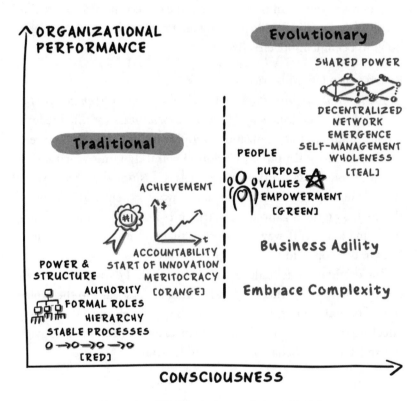

Figure 8.4: SELF Evolutionary Culture Model

We might understand these as stages of evolution of how we as human beings have organized ourselves over the course of history. Each stage contains innovations for how we may organize ourselves to create higher and higher levels of performance.

Centralized Power and Structure (Red)

Red cultures are focused on the effective use of power and structures to govern an organization well. A command-and-control structure emerges from a clearly defined hierarchy so that everyone has a clear role and level of authority. The establishment of stable processes allows top leadership to control the function of the organization.

A good historical example is the Roman Empire, which was able to scale across large distances and time delays using these key innovations.

Note: We have collapsed the Red and Amber from the Laloux stages of evolution to make a clearer model to improve diagnosis and application.

Achievement (Orange) = Machine

Orange is about traditional business or modern management. Orange organizations focus on achievement—bigger and better. Product innovation is key: How do we improve our products? What projects do we need to increase efficiency? With Orange, leaders create plans and hold people accountable for results. As leaders begin to share power with workers, the performance and economic results improve.

Since the focus is on results, a meritocracy is formed based on who actually delivers. The organizational metaphor is that of a *machine*—people see the organization as a mechanical system to be fixed and changed. Orange has been present as a way of working for perhaps one hundred years with the advent of the modern organization. Examples include almost all large organizations that follow traditional management values and practices.

More Advanced Cultures Include Earlier Innovations

Note that each culture stage includes elements of the earlier cultures where they serve the organization. For example, organizations that operate from an Orange worldview or paradigm, will include many Red approaches, such as formal roles, hierarchy, and so on.

We are considering an evolution where every point on the journey will embrace the elements of each culture system. As one reflects on this model, there can be a vision of a global template where each culture system builds on the next like a Russian doll, one inside the other. The key difference is that the culture systems will be adapted to reflect the shift in consciousness to a more evolved way of working.

People (Green) = Family

With Green, the focus shifts to create a healthy environment for the people working in the organization. Green organizations have *family* as a guiding metaphor. A clear organizational purpose is used to create alignment around goals so that workers can be empowered to make decisions. There are explicit shared values that guide behavior and decision making with leaders who walk the talk.

In a Green organization, the hierarchy will be shifted to the background so that it doesn't get in the way of people working together to find solutions. Example organizations include Southwest Airlines, Zappos, and Ben & Jerry's.

Shared Power (Teal) = Adult

Our adapted metaphor for Teal is defined as that of an adult (rather than an organism). People who act like adults take responsibility for their own behaviors and are capable of self-management. As such, this high level of maturity provides a unique ability to shape an organization where it has the illusion of no structures, yet the organization is firmly held and embraces all cultures at the same time.

Under these conditions it is possible for an organization to function with shared power and distributed decision making. Of course, acting like a full adult requires a shift in consciousness where the ego no longer has a tight grip on people's behaviors.

In our adapted model for Teal, the key characteristic is that there is shared power in organizations. When there is shared power, there can be a decentralized network for decision making so that the organization can respond rapidly to the needs of a VUCA world. A key consequence of this way of working is that there will be an emergent, cocreated response to running the organization. No one person is in charge, so the future will emerge.

Using the Model

The SELF Evolutionary Culture Model can be used to sense what elements of each stage are present in an organization. In science, a mass spectrometer is used to sense what atomic elements are present in a test sample. In a similar vein, the culture model can be used to sense how much Red/Orange/Green/Teal is in an organization.

It's very rare for an organization to just be at a single stage of evolution. Reality is much more complex and messy.

Transcending Culture Stages

It is important to understand that each successive culture stage encompasses earlier stages, so that innovations from earlier stages may be present in organizations that operate primarily at a later stage. It may be the case that an innovation is used from a different consciousness in later stages. Hierarchy is one example of this, but it could apply to any innovation.

A challenge with human beings is not to "throw out the baby with the bathwater." When presented with this model, there is often a tendency to want to move away from Red and Orange. This is a trap. What is more helpful is to use whatever innovation will serve the organizational purpose. For example, is it helpful to have a stable process for payroll? The answer is usually yes, as this will support people's psychological safety.

High-performance organizations at later stages use the innovations with a different consciousness in a way that supports organizational functioning. There is nothing inherently unhelpful about hierarchy or authority. Overreliance and low-consciousness uses of these innovations are what contribute to low performance.

Hierarchy is a naturally forming construct within living things, including human beings. We find hierarchy in nature—it is how and what we do with hierarchy that can create low-performance organizations.

THE JOURNEY TO EVOLUTIONARY ORGANIZATIONS

Many advocates of change advocate abolishing the hierarchy in favor of a flat organizational system. They assume—in our view, mistakenly—that the hierarchy is the root of the problem.

Hierarchy Is Not the Problem

Although many Teal organizations have dissolved the hierarchy in favor of autonomous teams or groups, some key examples of this way of functioning continue to have a hierarchy. In fact, the largest case study from Laloux's book *Reinventing Organizations* (2014)—AES—had a hierarchy. So do many other Teal-like case studies, such as Semco and David Marquet's *Turn the Ship Around* (2012).

> *It is a commonly held myth that hierarchy needs to be eliminated to operate with the highest levels of performance or Teal way of working. This does not hold out in practice.*

Although it can be helpful to change structures such as hierarchy to support a shift in ways of working and being, it is not strictly required. The key requirement seems to be that any negative impact of misuse of power due to hierarchy is overcome.

The final element of Teal is that of wholeness. This speaks to welcoming the whole person (mind, body, heart, and spirit) to work, so the organization can benefit from all the capabilities of the people. In some cases this may also speak to using the faculties of stillness and intuition to sense beyond the logical mind.

Principle: Organizational Performance Follows Consciousness

The performance of an organization is a reflection of the level of consciousness. The model shared here illustrates an understanding of the shift in consciousness toward more advanced stages of functioning. As power is increasingly shared, the focus is on creating an environment where people can contribute to their fullest potential. It's not just about changing structures and processes, it's about a shift in the mindset or consciousness of the people in the organization.

In *Mastering Leadership* (2015), Anderson and Adams reach similar conclusions to Laloux from the perspective of leadership development—a shift in consciousness is required to reach higher levels of organizational performance. They argue that "consciousness must evolve to a high level of complexity to meet the complexity of today's business challenges" (38). The model they present—egocentric, reactive, creative, integral—can be roughly mapped to the stages of the modified Laloux culture model.

On close inspection, other culture models such as the Competing Values Framework point to the exact same conclusion: "The highest performing leaders have developed capabilities and skills in each of the four quadrants" (Cameron and Quinn 2011, 54). High performance comes from transcending and integrating these culture quadrants—this is essentially what Teal culture represents.

It's about the People

The key factor in organizational performance is the evolution of the people. As people evolve and are able to operate at a higher level of consciousness, the organizational results will follow. A simple rule that captures the essence of the model is:

Energized, learning people = high performance

From an organizational perspective, a very simple pattern for high performance emerges: if you treat people well, they will perform better. Although the concept is simple, the challenge is that much regressive conditioning in the behaviors of leaders negatively impact employee experiences. On top of that, business as usual is so different from high-performance cultures that this simple pattern is anything but obvious.

Principle: Business as Usual = Low Performance

Anything that resembles business as usual or traditional organizations is low performance. In the whole scale of organizational systems, those resembling normal businesses represent the lowest levels of performance. It is only more people-oriented environments that are able to reach the highest levels of performance.

High Performance Is a Nonlinear Journey

Sometimes people mistakenly interpret the stages as belonging to a sequence: I am at Red, first I go to Orange, then I go to Green. However, it is not linear. There is no sequence. We can see that the development or evolution of organizational culture is a journey.

The most important dimension is the consciousness or mindset of the people in the organization.

As the consciousness of the people in the organization evolves, so will the organizational performance. As the organizational environment improves and people in the organization begin to fully show up as responsible adults (Teal), then the organization will be able to benefit from sharing of power to create higher levels of performance. This is a journey.

Green and Teal are rough approximations of reality to orient to one's journey. Every high-performance organization is unique, so there is no target. There is no "let's go Teal." Instead, what we invite is a shared desire to invest in evolving the organizational culture to one where engaged and motivated workers produce amazing results.

Myths of High-Performance Organizations

There are a lot of myths around what is required for high performance. These are often touted by futurists as *the solution*. As we are looking at a highly complex problem, it should be clear at the outset that there is no one solution.

Here are some items that are *not required* to create high performance:

- Elimination of hierarchy to create a flat structure or network
- Explicit core values
- Shared ownership with employees
- A specific salary and payment structure
- A specific kind of organizational metaphor, ideology, or framework such as Holacracy, S3, and so on

While some of these elements may be helpful at the right time in a specific context, their treatment as universal solutions is hazardous.

In contrast to a universal solution, SELF gives you the building blocks needed to unlock your organization based on your unique context.

YOUR TURN

- What aspects of your organization seem like Traditional (Red/Orange) cultures?
- Use the SELF Evolutionary Culture Model to sense what stages are present in your organizational system. Identify what percentage your organization is for each stage/color. For example, Red—40 percent, Orange—50 percent, Green—10 percent.
- Is the focus in your organization more around the structures, or is it around the people and consciousness?

---

9 ■ The Truth about Your Organizational Culture

Most people and organizations are either unaware or in denial of how toxic or limited their organizational culture is. And the way to win the game of high performance is through an evolution of culture.

When looking at the Matrix of Reality Map, we see that organizational change depends on culture, people, the use of power, and leadership. Since the role of a manager is to change the organization to get better results, a thorough understanding of all these aspects is needed to make effective and lasting change.

In this chapter, we contrast traditional and evolutionary organizations in their understanding and shaping of organizational culture. More importantly, we share a powerful model to diagnose culture and serve as the foundation for evolving culture. Creating a language and way to perceive and understand culture serves as an important foundation of leading beyond (traditional) change.

Customers will never love a company until Employees love it first.
—Simon Sinek

PATTERN 9.1: FROM CUSTOMER FIRST TO EMPLOYEE FIRST

KEY POINTS

- Looking after your customers is good business. Putting customers before your employees is a trap.
- Engaged employees create happy customers, which results in funds to support operations.
- An employees-first strategy is key to developing a high-performance organization.
- A shareholders-first strategy impairs the healthy functioning, growth, and survival of an organization.

CUSTOMERS FIRST

In the past decade there has been a large focus on customer-first strategies, such as customer experience, user experience, and customer net promoter score (NPS). All of these are important and valuable. Looking after customers is essential to serving the purpose of the organizations. *The trap is in putting customers first.*

Serving customers depends on the employees. If you do not have happy employees, how can they create happy customers? As such, customer-focus and financial-focus are secondary to the care and support of the employees.

EMPLOYEES FIRST

A lot of companies say they put employees first; however, in practice, business concerns such as profits or product launch deadlines may often override intentions.

PRINCIPLE: EMPLOYEES FIRST

Richard Branson is famous for starting dozens of successful businesses. His simple formula is, "Clients do not come first. Employees come first. If you take care of your employees, they will take care of the clients." He stands among dozens and dozens of business leaders who have independently identified elements of the virtuous cycle.

John Mackey, founder and CEO of Whole Foods Market, says, "Business is simple. Management's job is to take care of employees. The employee's job is to take care of the customers. Happy customers take care of the shareholders. It's a virtuous circle" (Conley 2007, 217).

In *Peak: How Great Companies Get Their Mojo from Maslow* (2007), Chip Conley describes the following relationship: "Creating a Unique Corporate Culture → Building an Enthusiastic Staff → Developing Strong Customer Loyalty → Maintaining a Profitable and Sustainable Business" (220). The key to high performance, then, is to focus on the development and care of staff. *Employees First, Customers Second: Turning Conventional Management Upside Down* (2010) by Vineet Nayar documents HCL's strategy for shifting the focus to employees.

 MODEL: VIRTUOUS CYCLE FOR BUSINESS
The virtuous cycle integrates and simplifies the proven reliable wisdom for creating a high-performance organization.
We define the virtuous cycle as follows: engaged employees → happy customers → healthy operating cash flow that in turn is used to support the employees. The emphasis in our model is on taking care of the employees.

The pattern is present across many high-performance organizations. Of course, organizations may achieve success through innovation or genius, yet performance will be limited by the functioning of its workers.

Consider figure 9.1, which illustrates the virtuous cycle. Where do managers and executives have the most influence to improve the flow of the virtuous cycle? For sure, providing funds to support operations, initiatives, and learning is important. However, the greatest impact on employees is the nature of the interaction leaders have with them. Other patterns we will explore in great detail are

Figure 9.1: SHIFT314 Virtuous Cycle Model

about how employees are treated within an organization by leaders directly and by the system as a whole.

As organizational leaders, the place where we have the greatest ability to influence what is happening is with the employees. That's the starting place for evolutionary leaders.

Shareholder First Is a Trap

In low-performance organizations, cash flow is diverted from healthy operations to support shareholder dividends needed to boost the stock price. Employees do not have the tools and support needed to create products and services that fully satisfy customer needs. The inferior products and customer experiences then lead to reduced revenue, which in turn leads to further pressure on cash flow.

Of course, it is important that shareholders benefit from the profits of an organization. However, healthy organizations limit shareholder payouts to *excess cash flow* that is not needed for operations. Operations come first. Shareholders second. This ensures the long-term viability of the organization. There has been a recent shift in understanding that putting shareholders first is damaging to company health. It is reported that "America's top CEOs say they are no longer putting shareholders before everyone else" (Wartzman 2019).

MODEL: HEALTHY ECOSYSTEM
An extension of looking after employees is to look after other stakeholders outside of the organization. Many high-performance organizations also create and maintain a healthy extended ecosystem for the organization. We see this as a key component to B Corporations (conscious business). It turns out it's not just good business but good *for* business, as it builds positive sentiment for the organization. Figure 9.2 shows the key elements.

Partners—Organizations develop long-term relationships with partners that share a similar set of values. It's not about who can produce the lowest-cost part, it's about what partner will best support delivering value for the customer.

Society—All our employees and customers live in society. Organizations that take care of the needs of society tend to perform better. It could be because of the positive

Figure 9.2: SHIFT314 Virtuous Cycle and Healthy Ecosystem Models

sentiment. It could be because of increased alignment with employee and customer values and ethical morals. Being a good corporate citizen is actually good business.

Environment—Organizations that look after the needs of the environment tend to have better economic returns. Conceptually, one might understand it as follows: all employees and customers live on planet earth, so when an organization acts responsibly, it creates positive sentiment.

With regard to the healthy ecosystem, Laloux describes green culture as having the following perspective: "Businesses have a responsibility not only to investors, but also to management, employees, customers, suppliers, local communities, society at large, and the environment" (Laloux 2014, 34).

For some time now, there have been movements such as the triple bottom line: social, environmental, and financial. One variant is: people, planet, and profit. There is also a growing interest in the creation of B Corporations that are both socially and environmentally responsible.

YOUR TURN

- In your organization, do customers, employees, or shareholders come first?
- What are the consequences of the current prioritization?
- How much more productive do you think your organization would become if employees were fully supported?

Dehumanization, although a concrete historical fact, is not a given destiny but the result of an unjust order that engenders violence in the oppressors, which in turn dehumanizes the oppressed.

—Paulo Reglus Neves Freire

PATTERN 9.2: FROM OPPRESSION TO ENABLEMENT

KEY POINTS AND SUMMARY

- There are different worldviews or beliefs that leaders have about people working in an organization.
- Theory X and Theory Y represent contrasting models: one of unmotivated people, and the other of motivated ones.
- Theory X and Theory Y models can be used to assess the health of an organizational system.
- The view held by leaders about the intrinsic nature of people shapes leadership behaviors and ultimately shapes outcomes.

Of particular importance in determining the level of effectiveness of an organizational system are the beliefs that people hold about one another. In this chapter, we explore the views that leaders hold around workers through the Theory X and Theory Y model.

MODEL: THEORY X AND THEORY Y
In the 1950s and 1960s, Douglas McGregor from MIT Sloan School of Management created contrasting models of Theory X and Theory Y for describing worker behavior (McGregor 1960). Table 9.1 contrasts the response from a worker based on various different dimensions of behavior.

LISTEN TO YOUR SYSTEM
This model can be used as a diagnostic tool to understand your current organizational environment by asking the questions: How do workers behave? Are they more like Theory X? Are they more like Theory Y? Does it depend on the individual worker?

Table 9.1: Theory X and Theory Y

	Theory X	Theory Y
Attitude	Dislike work. Avoid it.	Take an interest in work. May like it.
Direction	Unambitious: prefer to be directed by others.	Ambitious: capable of directing own behavior.
Responsibility	Avoid responsibility.	Seek and accept responsibility.
Motivation	Unmotivated. Need to be motivated.	Are intrinsically motivated.
Supervision	Need supervision and control.	Self-direction and self-control.

What Is Your Model of Reality?

Let's consider the question: Do Theory X and Theory Y workers exist in the workplace?

Perhaps we experience workers that act in a particular manner at a particular time or in a particular situation and differently in other situations. It may be true that we can assess a particular individual as operating more one way than another—for example, mostly Theory X or mostly Theory Y.

Yet, the answer is no. Theory X and Theory Y are judgments or generalizations made about people. They are labels that simplify and distort the reality of human behavior. It is inaccurate to say workers are Theory X or a particular person is Theory Y. So Theory X and Theory Y are models of possible human behavior. The purpose of exploring them is to examine what the beliefs held by your organizational system are.

OPPRESSION

When leaders in an organization believe people function like Theory X, then they will create organizational structures designed for Theory X workers. They will behave in ways that treat workers like Theory X workers. In turn, this will encourage workers to act like Theory X.

THEORY X EXAMPLE

Let us make a very concrete example of this. It comes to a manager's attention that different teams are using different technology solutions to solve similar problems. The manager is concerned that the lack of consistency may impact long-term performance. With a Theory X belief set, the manager may convene a group of technical leads and architects to make a decision for which one technology solution will be mandated for all groups to comply with.

ENABLEMENT

When leaders in an organization believe people function like Theory Y, then they will create organizational structures designed for Theory Y workers. They will behave in ways that treat workers like Theory Y workers. This in turn will encourage workers to act like Theory Y.

THEORY Y EXAMPLE

A manager with a Theory Y mindset might notice the same problems and then ask the teams to work together (perhaps through creation of a task force or working group) to find a good balance between the interests and needs of each team. They might also explore the balance between short-term costs and long-term benefits. Out of this, they might publish an architecture decision outlining what the strategy is for using one, or possibly multiple, technology solutions. In some situations, it might turn out that one solution will work well, or it might turn out that multiple solutions are a better option.

Through a single decision or response, we can see how a manager will support the creation of Theory X or Theory Y behaviors.

LEADERSHIP MINDSET SHAPES REALITY

Figure 9.3 shows the mindset or beliefs that leaders hold about workers will shape the reality of what is happening in the organization. As explored in the chapter on reality, we will only see what we expect to see. As such, the expectations or mindsets of the leaders are the hidden foundation of all organizational systems.

Figure 9.3: Leadership Mindset—Theory X and Y

YOUR TURN

- What does your current organizational environment indicate about the underlying assumptions about how workers behave—Theory X or Theory Y?

- When you consider your professional career, have workers shown up more as Theory X or Theory Y? What are the workers in your current workplace like?

- Look at leadership behaviors in your current organization: What does this imply about the underlying beliefs about workers—Theory X or Theory Y?

- Reflect on moments in your life when you experienced a Traditional style of leadership. How did you show up? Theory X or Theory Y?

If you do not manage culture, it manages you, and you may not even be aware of the extent to which this is happening.

—Edgar Schein, professor,
MIT Sloan School of Management

PATTERN 9.3: FROM IGNORING CULTURE TO UNDERSTANDING CULTURE

KEY POINTS

- Most organizations ignore culture because the preconditions for effective action are not met.

- Organizational culture is the wibbly-wobbly thing that connects everything—primarily the consciousness and the structures.

- Culture can be understood as the collective sum of all the people in an organization—their identity, values, beliefs, and behaviors

---

 IGNORING CULTURE

Many organizations ignore culture altogether or only provide superficial efforts to effect change. Although the maxim, attributed to Peter Drucker, "culture eats strategy for breakfast" is generally accepted, it is far easier to create progress with strategic activities rather than delve into a topic as nebulous as culture. When culture is ignored, problems never really get solved, and while organizations jump from reorganization to reorganization, transformation program to transformation program, nothing of any real consequence changes.

It is not humanly possible for us to comprehend, quantify, or model something as complex as organizational culture. Many argue that it is a nebulous, real, and very important entity, yet it cannot be seen, measured, or quantified. For example, Google avoided talking about culture and instead shaped it through a weekly all-hands meeting with the founders and other informal mechanisms to establish the Google Way of working.

Is Culture Invisible?

There are some business leaders that suggest that culture is invisible—it cannot be directly understood or changed. We present an alternate view: culture can be understood with the right models to see it. Several models are presented throughout this book.

Figure 9.4 depicts the elements of an organizational system. Tactics and strategy

Figure 9.4: Culture Iceberg

are above the waterline. They can be directly observed and analyzed so changes can be readily made. This fits nicely with Traditional thinking.

Culture is like the part of the iceberg—90 percent—that is below the waterline. It is not readily visible, and this makes it more challenging and difficult to observe, understand, and influence.

With 90 percent of the weight, it is a powerful force dominating strategy and tactics. Real, lasting, sustainable shifts in organizational performance can only come from culture. Of course, lasting change requires working at all three levels so the tactics and strategy support the culture. The starting place is organizational culture since it will guide effective strategy and tactics.

The Peril of Ignoring Culture

Most change programs for Agile, Digital, Lean, innovation, and so on are, at their root, seeking to create a change in the culture of the organizations through tactics and strategy at the mid and bottom levels of organizations. Culture is outright ignored or given some token treatment. Ignoring culture leads to the very high rate of failure of transformation programs to achieve their desired results—up to 90 percent failure in our experience. Edgar Schein captures the essential role played by culture: "If you do not manage culture, it manages you, and you may not even be aware of the extent to which this is happening" (Schein 2010, 20).

Prerequisites for Examining Culture

For an organization to address culture in a meaningful way, it would need to meet several important preconditions:

1. It is prepared to confront the reality of what its culture is and how it impacts success.
2. It needs to have an understanding of how to investigate culture.
3. It has to take time to really investigate what forces are shaping the culture within the organization.
4. It must have some way of effectively shaping the culture going forward.

*We argue that ignoring culture is actually appropriate
for most organizations, since they do not meet
basic prerequisites for working with culture.*

The purpose of this pattern is to make clear an understanding of what culture is, while the whole of this book is to investigate and shape culture.

UNDERSTANDING CULTURE
Evolutionary organizations have a high level of awareness of their organizational culture. It is seen as the fabric that holds everything together. Understanding it is the starting place for evolution.

FOUNDATIONS OF ORGANIZATIONAL CULTURE

How we behave *is* culture. We dive deeper into the reality of culture. When there is a crisis or emergency, the way an organization responds defines what the culture really is.

A simple and concise definition of culture is by William Schneider: "How we do things around here in order to succeed" (Schneider 1999, 10).

The most detailed and comprehensive explanation and exploration of organizational culture is in *Organizational Culture and Leadership* (2010) by Edgar Schein. It outlines three levels of culture:

1. Artifacts
2. Espoused beliefs and values
3. Basic underlying assumptions (24)

Schein provides the following guidance on understanding culture: "Unless you dig down to the *basic level of assumptions*, you cannot really decipher the artifacts, values, and norms. On the other hand, if you find some of those basic assumptions and explore their interrelationship, you are really getting at the essence of the culture and can then explain a great deal of what goes on. This essence can sometimes be analyzed as a paradigm in that some organizations function by virtue of an interlocking, coordinated set of assumptions" (Schein 2010, 53).

The patterns in this book are structured so you can examine the key assumptions and beliefs held within your organization. We offer a detailed map for exploring different aspects of organizational functioning.

 MODEL: SHIFT314 CULTURE MODEL
We created a culture model out of the need to not only understand what was happening in organizations, but also how to intervene effectively. Now called the SHIFT314 Culture Model, it is used within the SELF to analysis culture systems.

The view taken in this book follows the perspective of Don Box: "Remember that all models are wrong; the practical question is how wrong do they have to be to not be useful" (Box and Draper 1987, 74).

The SHIFT314 culture model introduced in this book is an abstraction of a complex reality. We have carefully created the model based on its utility in increasing organizational performance. We agree that while culture cannot be quantified or fully understood, we can use models to understand what is happening and to create actions to influence the system in a positive direction.

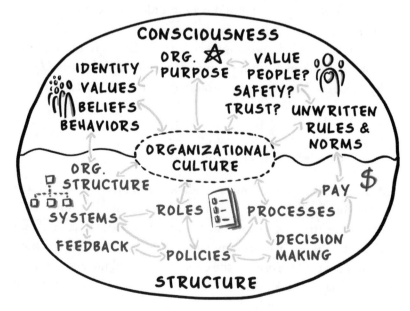

Figure 9.5: SHIFT314 Culture Model

We offer two definitions of culture in the SHIFT314 Culture Model—a formal one and informal one.

Culture is the dynamic emergent cocreation of the unifying fabric of organizational reality.

Or the more people-friendly definition:

Culture is the wibbly-wobbly thing that connects everything.

Consider figure 9.5—organizational culture is the undefined blob in the middle. It cannot be directly described. However, its nature can be determined by triangulation of the elements that form culture. Key elements that shape culture are shown in the diagram. There are, of course, many more elements since culture connects everything.

We know from quantum physics that at the very deepest layer of reality, everything is interconnected by the Higgs-Boson particle. Every element of culture is connected to every other element of culture. The arrows linking the elements illustrate that they are all interrelated and connected. It is a web of cross-linking and supporting elements. The web they weave together defines the organizational culture. The interconnectedness of everything makes changing culture a complex undertaking.

The SHIFT314 Culture Model can be used as a lens to triangulate an understanding of organizational culture. It provides a powerful tool to listen to the voice of the system to understand what is happening inside an organization.

There are two parts in the diagram: consciousness (or mindset) and structure. The structures are easier to understand since they conform to artifacts we can point to in the material world around us.

Structures

The structures of an organization are the tangible elements that are part of the 3D material world. Every element can be examined to discover what the underlying beliefs and assumptions in the culture are (Schein 2010). Below we extend the work of Schein to identify key areas of analysis.

As cultural anthropologists, we could simply observe these elements to infer what the culture of an organization is. For example, we might ask the following questions:

- *Organizational structure*—Is there a hierarchy that shows importance and power?
- *Roles*—Do people have clearly defined roles that limit how they can contribute? Can people easily create new roles to meet new business needs?
- *Systems*—Are these chosen to serve business needs or to reduce costs and standardize? Do they enforce behaviors or foster innovation?
- *Policies*—What rules do we have for people? Are they seen as Theory X or Theory Y?
- *Processes*—Are our processes designed to support the needs of customers and staff? How much process do we need? In what areas? Do they follow modern management or foster knowledge workers?
- *Decision making*—How are decisions made? What kinds of decisions can people make without approval?

For example, the policy for purchasing and expenses is revealing of the underlying assumptions in the organization. In most organizations, people are not allowed to spend any money without approval from their manager. Not even one penny. This indicates that employees are not trusted to make even small financial decisions.

> Structures exist in nature, it would be a poor assumption that disregarding structures can lead to high performance. In a higher-consciousness system, structures provide stability and have the flexibility needed for high performance.
>
> —Audree Sahota

Consciousness

The Consciousness aspect of the SHIFT314 Culture model represents the energetic and less tangible elements of culture. It could alternatively be referred to as the mindset or worldview. One might understand this as the feel or vibe of an organization. It's all about the people and how things flow. Consciousness is a reflection of both conscious and subconscious aspects of a human being.

Elements that reveal the consciousness of an organization are:

- *Organizational purpose*—Is there one? Do people feel connected to it?
- *Safety*—How much psychological safety is there for people?
- *Trust*—How much are people trusted? In what areas?
- *People*—To what extent are people valued as human beings with intrinsic value?
- *Unwritten rules and norms*—What are the sacred cows and taboo subjects? What is acceptable behavior?

The most important element is the people. The consciousness of each individual contributes to the overall consciousness of the organization. We introduce an adaptation of Dilts's logical levels to capture the essence of people in the context of culture (Dilts, Hallbom, and Smith 2012). Namely:

- *Identity*—How do we see ourselves as people?
- *Values*—What are our values?
- *Beliefs*—What do we believe to be true about our organizations, work in general, how we are seen, and so on?
- *Behavior*—What we say and do is the most concrete manifestation of culture. How we think about ourselves and our organizations will show up in every single meeting. Not only in how it is conducted but in what is noticed and what people choose to say (or more importantly not say). Are people showing up as Theory X or Theory Y?

It's about the People

Culture is such an important topic that we now offer a third and overlapping definition of culture:

The collective behavior of all the people in the organization is the culture.

Culture is ultimately about the people. At the end of the day, when we reduce a system to its essence, it is about how people behave. It's

Figure 9.6: SHIFT314 Culture Manifestation Model

about conscious and unconscious behaviors that together shape expectations and promises of the future.

Using the SHIFT314 Culture Model
Figure 9.6, the SHIFT314 Culture Model, is used to provide a bird's-eye view of the elements that shape culture in an organization. Some organizations are very focused on consciousness and use these elements as the primary way to shape functioning in the organization, as in people-centric. Other organizations focus on the structures as the primary way of understanding and running the organization, as in process-centric. We offer an integrated balanced view of culture.

YOUR TURN

- How deep and active is the focus on culture in your organization?
- Look at the elements of the SHIFT314 Culture Model—what elements get more attention in your organization? What elements get less attention?
- What elements would benefit from more attention?

Every Leader Is A Culture Officer
—John Stix

PATTERN 9.4: FROM VALUES ON POSTERS TO "CULTURE FOLLOWS LEADERSHIP"

KEY POINTS

- Values programs tend to be harmful since they avoid an investigation of the real cultural challenges and usually fall into the trap of hypocrisy.
- The behaviors at the bottom of the organization are a reflection of behaviors at the top of the organization.
- Organizational culture is a reflection of leadership behaviors.

VALUES ON POSTERS

Values programs constitute one of the gravest challenges to the evolution of organizations today. It's not that focusing on values is a challenge per se, it's the business-as-usual mindset that is used to define and promote them. The first key challenge is that they usually fail to achieve their objectives in any material way. The second key challenge is that it then gives the pretense that the culture problem is actually being addressed and prevents effective action.

As can be seen from the patterns of discovering reality and understanding culture, the starting place for evolving organizational culture requires a thorough investigation and understanding of the current situation. Once one has an understanding of the root causes and an understanding of the laws of organizational dynamics, it is highly unlikely that a values program would be an appropriate early game move.

To avoid the damage of hypocrisy,
top leaders must live and model the desired
values of an organization.

The word *hypocrite* is used for someone who asks someone else to do something that they themselves do not do. When leaders in organizations ask subordinates to follow values that they do not fully embody themselves, the essential trust and respect needed for an organization to function is lost. We would argue that most values programs in organizations are solidly in this trap.

CULTURE FOLLOWS LEADERSHIP

Let us consider the relationship between the culture of an organization and its leadership. In particular, what role does the management of an organization have to play in terms of the level of performance of an organization? Management by definition has the ownership and accountability of the organizational performance. They are 100 percent fully responsible and accountable for the organizational culture. As such, the organizational culture is ultimately a reflection of the management of an organization.

How Leaders Impact Culture

To fully understand the impact that leaders have on organizational culture, it is helpful to understand what Schein refers to as the "primary embedding mechanisms" for organizational culture:

- What leaders pay attention to, measure, and control on a regular basis
- How leaders react to critical incidents and organizational crises
- How leaders allocate resources
- Deliberate role modeling, teaching, and coaching
- How leaders allocate rewards and status
- How leaders recruit, select, promote, and excommunicate (Schein 2010, 236)

The above list is helpful for creating awareness of how culture is influenced. Of course, the primary interest of this work is the *leadership behaviors* that will lead to high-performance culture. The importance of leadership behaviors is clearly articulated in the quote by Schein: "The only thing of real importance that leaders do is to create and manage culture" (2).

PRINCIPLE: CULTURE FOLLOWS LEADERSHIP

While the culture of an organization is arguably the cocreation of all the people working together, it is ultimately the responsibility of leadership. Schein argues that "culture is ultimately created, embedded, evolved, and ultimately manipulated by leaders. These dynamic processes of culture and management are the essence of leadership and make you realize that leadership and culture are two sides of the same coin" (Schein 2010, 3).

PRINCIPLE: CULTURE INFLUENCE VARIES WITH POWER

Culture of an organization is the integrated sum of all the individuals. But due to differences in power, people will have a different impact on the culture based on their level in the hierarchy. The more senior the person, the greater their impact on the overall culture. So mathematically, the formula would be more like a weighted sum where we multiply each person by 10^L where L is the level of the manager. In figure 9.7, you will see that the number assigned to the level of influence varies based on level and power.

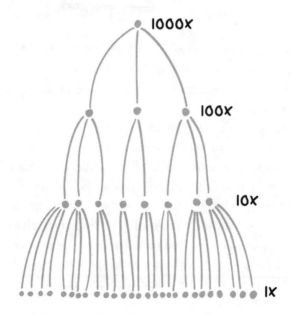

Figure 9.7: Culture Influence Varies with Power

*If you are not at the top, don't give up! We will show
you how to generate authority and influence as well as
make local shifts in culture.*

MODEL: CULTURE IS A FRACTAL

Figure 9.8 illustrates a typical organization. Each small triangle represents a person in the organization, while the large triangle represents the output or performance of the organization. The output is a collective result of the actions of all the people in the organization—both workers and managers. We can see how the collective behavior or culture shapes the organization's results and ability to function.

When asked who is responsible for the success and achievements of the organization, most managers will happily take credit. When asked who is ultimately responsible for the existing challenges, most managers will acknowledge that at the end of

Figure 9.8: Culture Is a Fractal

the day, they hold ultimate responsibility. Although, at this point most will highlight circumstances beyond their control that excuse them from full responsibility.

Glenda Eoyang, one of the founders of Human System Dynamics, observed that organizational systems are fractal: when we zoom in to see what is happening at one scale, it is just a fractal of what is happening on a broader scale. The culture we see at the bottom of the organization through productivity and worker behavior is a reflection of the behavior of management. To create high-performance behaviors at the bottom of an organization, we need high-performance behaviors at the top of the organization. To create a high-performance culture at the bottom of an organization, we need high-performance culture at the top of the organization.

What happens at the bottom of an organization is a fractal
of what happens higher up.

—Glenda Eoyang and Royce J. Holladay.
Adaptive Action: Leveraging Uncertainty in
Your Organization

PRINCIPLE: THE CONSCIOUSNESS OF THE LEADER IS THE
LIMIT OF AN ORGANIZATION

When Michael was working as a consultant, he noticed a
pattern with leaders. The limit for his success helping the
organization move to higher levels of productivity was ultimately
limited by the consciousness or mindset of the most senior leader
involved in the change effort. This pattern applies at any and all
levels of the organization.

When observing Teal organizations, Laloux noticed a pattern and
shares the insight shown in figure 9.9.

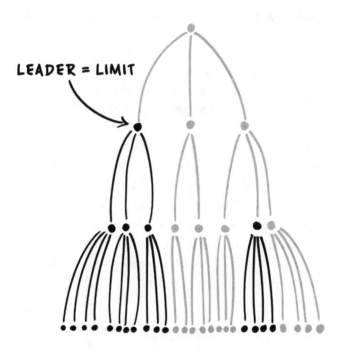

LEADER = LIMIT

Figure 9.9: Consciousness of the Leader Is the Limit of an Organization

The general rule seems to be that the level of consciousness of an organization cannot exceed the level of consciousness of its leader.

—Frederic Laloux, *Reinventing Organizations*

As such, the level of performance of an organization is a reflection of the level of consciousness of the leadership. It is not possible for a leader who is operating from a low level of consciousness to create an organization that operates from a higher level of consciousness. Leaders can support the evolution, or they can downgrade or devolve an organizational system: "The pull of leaders toward their stage of consciousness goes in two directions: they can pull 'back' practices from later stages, but they can also exert a strong pull 'forward'" (Laloux 2014, 41).

In a similar vein, Robert J. Anderson and William A. Adams argue, "The leadership system is the central organizing system that determines org performance" (Anderson and Adams 2015, 115). They see leadership culture as the core generator of the organization's culture.

It's Not Anyone's Fault

One might understand the purpose of this book as a means to support leaders in understanding the ways in which they are inadvertently promoting a regressive, low-performance culture. We do not see the gap as a failure of the people in management positions in organizations.

Ninety percent of what happens in an organization is a reflection of the system. When we take good people and put them in a business-as-usual environment, low-performance traits are developed and encouraged. Our invitation is to have compassion for yourself and other leaders. It's not any one person's fault that things are the way they are. We invite you to make a different choice for your own leadership.

Values Programs Require Modeling

Values programs will only work to the extent that all the leadership of the organization actually role model the values.

The spirit of an organization is created from the top. . . . For it is character through which leadership is exercised; it is character that sets the example and is imitated.

—Peter Drucker, *366 Days of Insight and Motivation for Getting the Right Things Done*

The only thing that really matters is that the top management leads by example with respect to a set of values. When they are able to act as a model, they may then invite their direct reports to follow suit or explore what shared values they see as important to create success.

Tool: Cocreate Values for Yourself

One successful way to use values is for a group of leaders to cocreate a set of values *for themselves*—not for anyone else.

This will support the leaders to grow themselves to be exemplary in how they model the values. Leaders may then also call each other out to rise to their best selves. It is best if the leaders keep this as private work for themselves rather than broadcast the values. As leaders "walk the talk" with new behaviors and exemplify the values of the organization, people will automatically start to follow them.

Of course, a set of values that are cocreated by a group of people create a powerful attractor for those people to orient their behavior. It is helpful for a group of people to hold shared values, as this will support organizational coherence. This practice is illustrated in the Increasing Freedom pattern through the example of cocreating house rules. Zappos is a great case study illustrating how values can be cocreated in an organization (Hsieh 2010).

YOUR TURN

- If you have a values program at your organization, to what extent do you see all levels of leadership modeling the behaviors?
- Do you see any disconnects between behaviors and expectations at different levels of the hierarchy?
- What mix of Traditional and Evolutionary behaviors do you see organizational leadership modeling?

---

10 ■ It's All about the People

Your people are your culture. Success comes through people. No change program or leadership activity can be truly effective without a thorough understanding of the pivotal role people play in all endeavors.

The shift in focus from customer first to employee first with the Virtuous Cycle fuels the growth of high performance. And when it's neglected, fuels stagnation, wasted, and outright negligence in supporting the most important assets of an organization, human potential.

Each pattern highlights the damaging or inadequate approaches that traditional organizations take to interacting with people. These are contrasted with how evolutionary organizations create passion and motivation to unlock the full potential of human beings.

The greatest asset of a company is its people.
—Jorge Paulo Lemann

PATTERN 10.1: FROM ATTRACTING TALENT TO CARING ABOUT PEOPLE

KEY POINTS

- The challenge of attracting talent is really a challenge with the workplace environment and culture.
- An essential part of creating a great environment for people is to treat them well in all aspects of their work experience.
- It is essential that managers hold the worldview and behaviors related to a deep respect for human beings.
- High-performance organizations focus substantial effort on creating a great work environment.

ATTRACTING TALENT

Many organizations today face the challenge of attracting talented workers. Highly skilled, educated people who have the needed work experience are in short supply. Companies often encounter stiff competition in hiring the people they need to not only operate but also to grow.

MILLENNIALS DEMAND CHANGE

Millennials (or Generation Y) are those born from the early 1980s to early 2000s. Their view of the world and how they function differ significantly from earlier generations. In particular, they create a unique challenge, since millennials do not function well in organizations following conventional business practices. Their tolerance for oppression in the workplace is very low. Many would prefer to be underemployed doing what they love rather than working in low-quality work environments. For many businesses, there is a real challenge with attracting and retaining bright, motivated workers.

High-performance organizations effectively include
the creative energy and passion of millennials.

SURFACE EFFORTS DON'T LAST

Most business-as-usual organizations attempt to address attracting talent through surface efforts that don't last. Surface efforts might include setting up an office in a hip location, offering job perks, renovating the office in a certain style, or marketing the company as progressive using buzzwords such as *Agile* or *Digital*.

While these efforts may be successful in initially recruiting workers, the real measure is the retention of top talent. Most people today know to look up workplace reviews using sources such as Glassdoor and LinkedIn to see what is really happening. While they may be initially persuaded that "change is in the air," the hiring promise will be broken unless the company actually delivers on providing a great work environment.

Instead of marketing how good your workplace is,
focus on just being a good workplace.

CARING ABOUT PEOPLE

Great companies attract great workers. When you have an amazing workplace, people will want to come work for you. If there is a problem attracting talent, the real problem is a poor work environment. It's really about the culture. The work environment that employees experience is a reflection of the culture of the organization.

The real problem is an ineffective culture that does not treat people well. The challenge of attracting talent is just a surface problem.

PRINCIPLE: CREATE AN ENGAGING WORKPLACE

The shift is to focus on creating an environment that is supportive of people—not only in making sure they have what they need to serve the organization but that their needs as a human being are met. People want to contribute. They want to be successful. They want to be recognized and appreciated.

People are also diverse—there is a myriad set of reasons that motivate human behavior. As such, there is no such thing as a perfect culture or environment, since the suitability depends on the people it holds. So there is an integrated bidirectional relationship between people and the organization.

At the same time, there are general patterns for the treatment of people that hold for high-performance organizations. Edgar H. Schein noted the following for healthy culture systems: internal direction, intrinsic value of human beings, true commitment to values, authentic public image, clear core purpose, respect for partners (Schein 2010, 174).

RESPECT PEOPLE

If we were to narrow down one key factor, it would be that management holds an inherent respect for human beings. John Paul Getty, a self-made billionaire who turned around dozens of businesses to become high-performing, states this clearly: "In dealing with employees, it is essential that they be given recognition as human beings, as individuals" (Getty 1986, 82).

Again, it's not about having a rewards or recognition program— this is a shallow cover-up. A similar report comes from the Gallup Engagement survey statement: "My supervisor, or someone at work, seems to care about me as a person" (Buckingham and Coffman 1999).

Respect for human beings aligns to the patterns shared with evolutionary organizations where the focus is on the well-being of people. The antithesis is traditional organizations where there is a machine paradigm and people are treated as human *resources*.

The whole of this book can be understood as the antipatterns and patterns for treating people well.

WELCOMING THE WHOLE PERSON

As organizations move to higher levels of consciousness, they invite the whole person to work: mind, body, heart, and spirit. Some organizations access untapped potential by supporting people more fully through workplace programs, such as yoga and meditation. Others create spaces for meaningful connection as human beings. This is a key aspect of high-performance organizations identified in Teal organizations (Laloux 2014).

It's Up to Management

It is management's responsibility to create a supportive and engaging environment for its people. "The primary function of management is to obtain results *through people*" (Getty 1986, 79). As such, the single most important element of work is how people experience their relationships. Does management interact and make decisions in ways so that people experience a deep level of respect and care?

It's not just a skill or a technique. It's managers holding a worldview of people being valuable and having this integrated into every behavior and choice. It's about seeing workers not as Theory X but Theory Y. In environments where management is able to create a great environment, workers really flourish.

It's Not HR's Job

One of the biggest traps modern organizations have fallen into is the delegation of looking after people and morale to human resources (HR). Peter Block outlines this challenge clearly: "The process of managing people, just like managing money, is everyone's job. . . . Human Resources (HR) has evolved into a caretaking and enabling function whose assignment is to take responsibility for the morale and emotional well-being of employees" (Block 1993, 147). Through no fault of their own, HR departments are put in the impossible position of solving the employee and culture problems. Both are fully owned and cannot be delegated away by management.

INCLUDE JOY AT WORK

A key theme in high-performance cultures is creating a great place to work. Not to attract talent. Not because of profits. Not for success. Instead, a common theme is that leaders create joy at work because *it is the right thing to do.* For sure, this totally flies in the face of business as usual, but it's hard to argue with success.

Green and Teal environments are ones where people really enjoy coming to work. One thorough reference is Dennis Bakke's explanation of a Teal-type culture in *Joy at Work: A Revolutionary Approach to Fun on the Job* (2005).

Semco is another great example of how success follows from creating a great environment and really looking after people. The company has generated over 20 percent growth per year for more than two decades through a simple focus: What if everyone loved what they did? Ricardo Semler explains this in his book *The Seven-Day Weekend: A Better Way to Work in the 21st Century* (2004): "To keep turnover low, we put mechanisms in place at Semco that remind employees to 'make sure that you are where you want to be, and make sure that this is what you want to do.' Because if they're not sure, we'll bend over backwards to find a completely different area or completely different type of work for them. . . . This is not from altruistic motives. It's purely selfish. Unless we click with a worker, unless he clicks with something he is passionate about, our productivity won't be high" (78).

The evolutionary purpose of the organization increases the meaning and purpose in people's lives. Are people happy and motivated by the work they do and the products and services the organization delivers?

Another metric is how people feel about those they work with. In high-performance environments, there is a deep respect and strong interpersonal relationships among people. Gone are the facades or the workplace masks in favor of real connection.

Healthy environments get strong responses to the Gallup 12 metric, "I have a best friend at work." Having not just friends but also best friends is a natural outcome of an environment where people treat each other well.

IT'S NOT A COUNTRY CLUB

Some fear that a company will turn into a country club where people are loafing around and nothing gets done. Of course, when we examine this fear, we may immediately see that it comes from the belief that people are more like Theory X and are unmotivated and unambitious. If the problem really were a country club problem, it would be for the entitlement that creeps into the senior layers of hierarchies, not what happens with workers.

Instead, what we see when people are treated with respect and dignity is that they become more involved, and they take more interest and responsibility. They want to contribute out of a sense of connection and belonging.

YOUR TURN

- How able is your organization to attract and retain top talent?
- How much effort goes into creating a great environment for people to work in?
- To what extent does the leadership in your organization demonstrate a deep level of respect for people as human beings?
- Where can you do a better job looking after the experience of the people around you?

---

*No one can put in his best performance unless he feels
secure. . . .Secure means without fear, not afraid to express ideas,
not afraid to ask questions.*
—W. Edwards Deming

PATTERN 10.2: FROM FEAR AND STRESS
TO PSYCHOLOGICAL SAFETY

KEY POINTS

- Fear and job stress in typical workplaces impair the abilities
  of people to function at their best.
- Psychological safety ensures the blood flow needed by the
  frontal cortex to support thinking and access to intelligence.
- Equal voice results in everyone contributing to make the
  best decision possible.

FEAR AND STRESS IN THE WORKPLACE

First, what is fear? The word *fear* is defined as: "an unpleasant often strong emotion caused by anticipation or
awareness of danger" (Merriam-Webster, n.d.). At its extreme, fear is a crippling debilitating emotion. The term *fear* is not
a single point but a spectrum with various levels of intensity. Consider these synonyms for *fear* that indicate increasing levels of fear:
concern, nervous, worry, anxiety, alarm, dread, and *terror*.

When we pause to examine the workplace, we may realize that
fear shows up much more frequently than we may have otherwise
noticed. For example, in typical workplaces, it is not uncommon for
people to dread meetings, to be alarmed by decisions others have
made, to have worry or nervousness about a presentation or outcome
of a project, or to be afraid of getting feedback on one's performance.
The polite way to talk about it is to describe it as stress. Fear is the
cause of stress in the workplace.

Varying levels of fear indicate that people are sensing danger in
their workplaces. The alternative is that people feel psychologically

safe in their workplaces. Of course, we can observe an impact on the health and well-being of our people since stress leads to disease. But what is the impact of people's emotional and psychological states on their abilities to function?

THE NEUROSCIENCE OF FEAR AND SAFETY

David Rock's work with neuroscience highlights the need for psychological safety in the workplace (Rock 2009). All kinds of fear are caused by our anticipation of danger or threat.

Let's look at what happens in our bodies when we are under physical threat. As mammals, we are designed for fight or flight. For example, when we experience a threat, blood rushes away from nonessential systems for long-term health (such as digestive systems, waste processing systems, etc.) and into our muscles, heart, and lungs. This allows bodies to take immediate and capable action. It is a reasonable strategy for survival on the plains of Africa in our distant past.

YOUR BRAIN IS A LUXURY

It takes a high amount of blood glucose to support the functioning of our frontal cortex: the seat of our intelligence, creativity, and reasoning. However, in the design of our nervous system, it is considered nonessential when we experience a threat and go into fight or flight. It requires blood glucose to operate. When we experience fear and feel unsafe, the following things happen:

1. Blood flow to the frontal cortex decreases.
2. The glucose needed for functioning decreases.
3. Our intelligence decreases.

From our bodies' perspective, the frontal cortex is a luxury item that gets dropped when the available blood sugar drops.

PHYSICAL AND PSYCHOLOGICAL FEAR IS IDENTICAL

Fear is fear. Fear at work is the same as fear of a lion. The same regions of the brain (as shown in MRI brain scans) are activated in a psychological threat as in a physical threat. The human brain has the same physiological response to a psychological threat as a physical threat—a reduction to the blood flow and ability to function. One example of this is how we may respond to an annual performance review at a typical company. The level of fear triggered in most people is the equivalent of being taken behind the building and mugged by eight burly thugs.

Human beings require a high level of psychological safety for the frontal cortex to operate at its full potential.

When our environment is unsafe or has low safety, all the intelligent, highly educated, and skilled workers recruited into the organization are significantly degraded in their abilities to function.

 PSYCHOLOGICAL SAFETY
But what is psychological safety? Amy Edmondson defines *psychological safety* as "a belief that the work environment is safe for interpersonal risk taking" (Edmondson 2018, 8). Given that Edmonson is considered a world-renowned researcher and expert, we will make the rather startling claim that the above definition is somewhat narrow and inaccurate.

PSYCHOLOGICAL SAFETY IS THE ABSENCE OF FEAR

We offer an improved definition:

Psychological safety is an inner state of being where one does not experience psychological fear.

The first improvement is that psychological safety applies in all contexts in which human beings operate: work, home, friends, finances, physical well-being, and so on.

The second improvement is to see safety as much more than just beliefs. As a human being, while our sense of safety is "all in our heads," it's not just about our cognitive processes. It's about our unconscious patterning that is connected to psychological safety. This is essential to get to a deeper understanding that can unlock benefits.

In our own personal experience, we have been in situations where we know and believe that the environment is safe, while at the same time experiencing extreme fear. The reason for this is that our unconscious processes ultimately determine our experience of reality, not our cognitive understanding. This is based on the unconscious pattern matching described in chapter 7. Further comments on this topic are made below.

THE IMPORTANCE OF SAFETY: GOOGLE'S PROJECT ARISTOTLE

Google is considered, from many perspectives, to be a high-performing organization. In the interest of creating even higher levels of performance, Google created Project Aristotle. Their mission was to discover what made Google's top teams the best of the best (Duhigg 2016). What were the conditions that enabled not just high performance typical at Google but the very best performance in the world?

After one year of research, the team's findings were: *nothing*. They couldn't figure it out. The teams had different practices and ways of working. They couldn't find anything in common with all the teams. However, they didn't give up. After another year of research, they came to a conclusion. There were two key factors in common with all the top-performing teams. While there are many important factors for high performance, there are two that are *most* important. The first factor is psychological safety. The other is what we define as equal voice.

PRINCIPLE: PSYCHOLOGICAL SAFETY IS THE CORNERSTONE OF HIGH PERFORMANCE

All the top-performing teams observed on Project Aristotle have a high level of psychological safety. It is only when we feel safe that we can give our full attention to the task at hand. We will feel comfortable with asking questions, making decisions, and challenging others. When we are safe, we can take risks, run experiments, and work toward audacious goals and game-changers. When we are safe, we can be extraordinary and create the extraordinary. It's a place of learning and growth.

When we feel unsafe, we won't speak up when things are going wrong. We will avoid decisions and instead play it safe. Instead of asking for help when we are stuck, we will cover up our weaknesses. When we are unsafe, we protect ourselves and experience stagnation.

The topic of psychological safety is not new. Deming spoke about the topic of psychological safety decades ago: "No one can put in his best performance unless he feels secure. . . . Secure means without fear, not afraid to express ideas, not afraid to ask questions"

(Deming 2000, 59). In *Artful Making: What Managers Need to Know about How Artists Work* (2003), an exploration of high performance in theater, authors Robert Austin and Lee Devin articulate the need for a secure workspace as follows: "Willingness to work at risk is vital in artful making, in part because exploration is uncomfortable. Exploration requires a willingness to supply partial answers, to float trial balloons, to look goofy, and to get things 'wrong'" (117). As Dan Mezick poignantly states, "Psychological Safety is made fresh daily" (Mezick 2012, 61).

MODEL: PSYCHOLOGICAL SAFETY SPECTRUM

Psychological safety is not a checkbox or an attribute—it's a spectrum. At one end there is fear, and at the other end is full safety or the complete absence of fear. A safety assessment is really a fear assessment. On closer examination, people experience different forms of fear throughout the day. One might examine both the intensity levels and frequency of fear to determine where on the fear-safety spectrum a particular individual or group sits. The secret to understanding and shifting safety is to focus on its root: fear.

Figure 10.1, the Psychological Safety Spectrum model, can be directly used as a readout (from 1 to 10) to investigate the level of

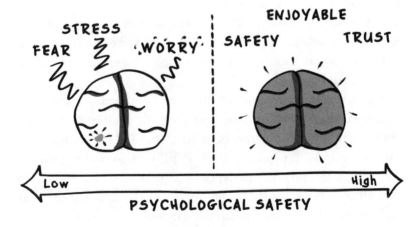

Figure 10.1: Psychological Safety Spectrum Model

psychological safety within an individual or organizational group. As it is directly connected with brain function, physical well-being, and performance, it is of high value in exploring and evolving.

CREATING PSYCHOLOGICAL SAFETY

Let us return to our definition: psychological safety is an inner state of being where one does not experience psychological fear. The first key point is that safety is an inner state of being. It's not only about our reality, it is also about how we experience our reality and the meaning we ascribe to it. It is perception and physical reaction. As such, there is an external dimension and an internal dimension.

External Dimension to Safety

It is possible to increase people's experience of safety or reduction in fear by engineering the environment around them to avoid triggering fear. In other words, to create a supportive, caring environment. In fact, the patterns in this book outline the various dimensions to creating an environment that supports people's psychological safety.

Internal Dimension to Safety

There is an internal dimension to psychological safety that is based on the makeup of an individual. While we may engineer an environment that is very supportive and safe, people may still experience fear. Based on people's conditioning, they may misinterpret external cues to perceive danger when there is no danger. This is primarily based on early childhood patterning and can be best understood through a thorough understanding of people's emotional systems (Sahota and Sahota 2018).

The development of a robust inner sense of psychological safety requires inner growth work to clear away the conditioned perceptions of the past. Elimination of *all* fear is beyond the constructs of the egoic mind—it requires the ego to fully let go of the identity it has created around these perceptions. It is not necessary to eliminate all fear. High levels of inner resilience are sufficient to create high-performance individuals and organizations.

The internal dimension of safety fully constrains the outer dimension. We can only support the psychological safety of others to the extent that we feel safe. To increase safety levels in an environment, it is important for leaders to work on both the internal and external dimensions of psychological safety. When there is a conscious decision to improve psychological safety, there will be a direct effect on the well-being of performance and desired outcomes.

YOUR TURN

- What do you think would happen to performance if people experienced greater levels of psychological safety?
- Do people routinely ask for help from other team members and groups?
- Are failures used for learning and growth or for assigning blame?
- What role do leaders play in fostering or impairing psychological safety?

Listen more than you talk. Nobody learned anything by hearing themselves speak.
—Richard Branson

PATTERN 10.3: FROM STATUS AND DOMINATION TO EQUAL VOICE

KEY POINTS

- The ego's need for status and domination deter the effective functioning of people working together.

- Equal voice is a space where people and their contributions are valued. It is a key characteristic of high-performance environments and essential for making effective decisions.
- Listening is an essential practice.
- Equal voice can be implemented immediately in meetings and decisions to get better outcomes and shape culture.

 STATUS AND DOMINATION

Human beings are social animals. There is a constant behind-the-scenes game being played out called the status game. Who has higher status? Who is lower? How can I dominate others to elevate my status so that I can feel more secure?

Looking at the unconscious behaviors played out by the ego is the last thing anyone really wants to do. However, it is essential for one to understand the damaging effects of status and domination in the workplace.

Egoic behaviors are subtle within us, as quiet moments that seem like normal expressions of the self.

"When I can dominate others, I will feel good." Of course, I won't admit this to anyone—even to myself. My propped-up sense of importance will soften my insecurities so that I have the subjective experience of greater safety.

This may happen by sitting at the head of the table, speaking first, or by using up more airtime in a meeting than everyone else. It might be by coming late to a meeting so people have to either wait or restart the meeting.

For our ego, this is a win. However, when we look at the impact on the others around us and the environment that gets created through these behaviors, we soon realize we are creating a loss.

Every small win for our ego creates an even larger loss in multiple other people. When they lose status and sense of safety, the blood supply to their cortex will drop along with their ability to contribute.

Domination of others and the playing of status games is the default low-consciousness mode of functioning where the ego is running the show. The whole notion of status and "I am better than you" is the *opposite* of the earlier pattern of caring for people, which consists of deep respect and nurturing the well-being of others.

EQUAL VOICE

Equal voice is the term we use to denote the situation where everyone's contribution is welcome and there is an opportunity to contribute. To coin a phrase: "No voice gets left behind." Equal voice takes us directly to the perspective that people matter. It is the antithesis of status games and domination. Instead, equal voice elevates the status of all individuals and nurtures equality.

GOOGLE'S PROJECT ARISTOTLE

The main finding reported from Google's Project Aristotle was around the importance of psychological safety (Duhigg 2016). The other important finding is much less reported, since it is hard to describe exactly what is going on. It's not that it's less important, it's just that it's harder to get a handle on it. In the original research, it was described in one way as conversational turn-taking. Another was about connection at a personal level.

MODEL: EQUAL VOICE

Equal voice is a space where people and their contributions are valued.

Equal voice captures the essence of the second trait found in Project Aristotle. When there is equal voice, people can challenge each other's ideas, cocreate, and discover the most effective solutions.

Just to clarify, we are defining the term *equal voice*. Project Aristotle identified several elements related to this concept; however, they were not labeled as a single distinct item.

In a meeting, equal voice means that everyone has an opportunity to speak and to contribute. With other forms of decision making, people's ability to contribute could be expressed through a survey, interactive simulation, voting, or internal online forum.

In high-performance organizations, everyone can and does contribute to making the best decisions possible. In contrast, it is not possible to get to the best decisions when people withhold important information.

Consider the alternative to equal voice that is typical of Traditional workplaces. Here we may see decisions being made without consulting or advice from those who can improve the decisions. We may see people not speaking up with ideas because there is no opportunity or there is insufficient safety to do so.

It can be said that safety and equal voice travel together. Where we see one, we see the other. Therefore, at some level they are inseparable. We are simply using these concepts to point to an underlying reality that is beyond words.

BENEFITS OF EQUAL VOICE

1. *Better decisions*—The most direct and obvious benefit from equal voice is that there will be more information to support better decisions.

2. *Psychological safety*—The act of creating a safe space where people can contribute their ideas supports the overall sense of safety.

3. *Develop leaders*—Inviting people to contribute ideas gives them an opportunity to participate in leading the organization in a safe way.

EQUAL VOICE DOES NOT MEAN EQUAL DECISION MAKING

Let us be very clear here: equal voice is *not* equal decision making. As the leader you may still retain the decision-making authority or optionally share it with others. As leaders, we can get the benefits of equal voice without giving up decision making. As long as the decisions respect the input of people and serve the purpose of the organization, the question of who actually makes the decisions is less important. With equal voice, we start the journey toward high-performance ways of functioning, such as cocreation and distributed networks for decision making.

LISTENING

Listening is the basic requirement for creating equal voice. "Listening is not a skill; it is a discipline. Anybody can do it. All you have to do is shut your mouth" (Drucker 2004, 113).

Let us consider: Why is it so hard to fully listen? One reason is that our conditioned pattern of listening has been hijacked. We have been trained to listen without really connecting or fully listening. We half listen while there is a dialogue going on in our heads, problem solving, judging the person, thinking about other things, or the "me-too" thoughts that are spinning through our minds.

Another point to listening is that we tend to speak instead of listening. Speaking demonstrates our status and supports our abilities to dominate others. Listening is a form of humility and elevates the status of others. One key challenge is that many leaders are not even aware that they are not listening well.

One telling pattern seen in leaders who are committed to evolve and grow themselves is a powerful capacity to listen. Listening allows us to discover new information and unlearn incorrect information that has been blocking our success. It allows us to connect with one another as human beings and develop relationships. It supports better decisions. As Deming describes the most capable manager: "He listens and learns without judgement on him that he listens to" (Deming 1994, 128).

EQUAL VOICE IN MEETINGS

A powerful way to make immediate shifts in performance is to use strategies to support and foster equal voice.

Tool: Listen First, Speak Last

The act of creating a space where others share before you do is a powerful way to support equal voice. As a leader, you may convene a meeting and set the stage for the problem to be solved or the opportunity to be explored. After that, invite your team to share their thoughts. Once everyone has shared, then you may add your ideas.

Equal Sharing before Discussion

It is important to note that questions and discussion are deferred until after everyone has shared. It is all too easy for an objection or opinion to be disguised as a question.

Of course, whether people really share or not is a function of their level of psychological safety. It will not be possible to fully neutralize the damaging effects of hierarchy in one fell swoop.

Share in Reverse Seniority Order

When juniors share first, they are not constrained by what the more senior people have said. There is more space and possibility for them to share their ideas and perspectives. Once the more senior people speak, there may be little to say other than, "I agree with such and such idea" or "Yes to this idea, and here is another thought."

By sharing in reverse-seniority order, the more senior people are elevating the status or importance of the junior staff. This signals the willingness of senior staff to listen and the invitation and importance of junior staff to contribute.

Tool: High-Performance Meeting Protocol

Creating and supporting equal voice in meetings is fairly straightforward to understand—everyone talks in turn and everyone else listens. Most meetings don't work like this and are anything but equal voice, so we will give some concrete practices for how to have highly productive meetings:

1. Introduce the topic/problem/challenge.
2. Have people share in reverse-seniority order.
3. One person shares for a maximum time box (thirty seconds, one minute).
   a. No interruptions.
   b. No questions.
   c. No challenges.
   d. No disagreements.
4. Then the next person shares.
5. Repeat until everyone has shared.
   a. People may pass if they wish. This may be because they have nothing of value to contribute or because they do not feel safe.

EQUAL VOICE IN ORGANIZATIONAL DECISIONS

Imagine you are making some decision in your organization. It could be because you hold a position of authority in the hierarchy or because of authority of a function. If you are really interested in making the best decision possible, the only way to tell a good decision from a poor one is to get feedback. Are you ready for the truth?

To get clear feedback, one might send out a survey or share a potential decision via an internal forum. You might share the planned decision, key data, and reasoning. You might ask for an approval rating (e.g., Likert scale or thumbs-up, thumbs-down, etc.) and for comments and advice to improve the decision quality.

EQUAL VOICE = EGO CONTROL

Equal voice is a simple practice that takes the hidden games of status and domination from the shadows and puts it on center stage where it can no longer hide. Mastery of equal voice requires a journey of self-development and the letting go of ego to develop the same level of consciousness and related function that is required for creating high-performance environments. With equal voice, we overcome the desire to be the smartest person in the room and instead create space for other people to lead and share control.

The actual practice is simple: "Shut up. And listen." However, it is easy to underestimate how strong a grip the ego has on our behavior.

YOUR TURN

- Whose voices have the most importance in your environment?
- How would a shift to equal voice impact the quality of the decisions in your environment?
- Where do you see a willingness (or not) to let go of egos and importance to make the best decisions for the organization?
- How good are you at supporting the equal voices of others?

If you treat people well, they will perform better.
—Michael K. Sahota

PATTERN 10.4: FROM DISENGAGEMENT TO ENGAGEMENT

KEY POINTS

- Lack of employee engagement in most organizations is a key contributor to low performance.
- Most organizations distort and misapply surveys because they are missing the preconditions for effective action.
- Treatment of the Likert scale response of "neutral" as a 0 will create a more accurate view of reality.
- Increasing engagement is only feasible when leaders are ready to evolve first.

DISENGAGEMENT IS THE NORM

For decades Gallup has undertaken groundbreaking research on worker engagement. There is a worldwide challenge with employee engagement, with 87 percent of employees not fully engaged at work (Harter 2017). Deloitte reports 87 percent of management report the issue as important or very important (Solow 2015).

The mass levels of disengagement represent staggering economic waste due to low levels of productivity. It is also a massive human waste with people whose work lives are lacking in joy and meaning.

While the understanding of this challenge has been clear for over two decades, not much has really changed. Current efforts to solve the employee engagement problem have generally failed to address the challenge in any material way. In this section, we will unpack why that is and what to do about it.

ENGAGEMENT

The level of performance in an organization is a reflection of the levels of performance of its workers. Workers who are fully engaged will produce the highest levels of organizational results. They will enjoy coming to work, too. Without engagement, organizational structures, technology, and strategic plans are of little consequence.

UNDERSTANDING GALLUP12 ENGAGEMENT

In the late 1990s, Gallup launched a massive research project to determine what employee survey questions would lead to a high-performance workplace (Buckingham and Coffman 1999). They looked for statistical links between survey questions and key business outcomes such as productivity, profitability, retention, and customer satisfaction. Out of 100,000 questions, they were able to identify 12 candidate questions through a combination of focus groups, factor analysis, regression analysis, and concurrent validity studies. These were validated in 1998 through statistical analysis with financial data from 2,500 business units at 24 different companies.

Table 10.1: Gallup 12 Engagement Questions

Does the mission/purpose of my company make me feel my job is important?	Does my supervisor, or someone at work, seem to care about me as a person?
Are my coworkers committed to doing quality work?	Do I have a best friend at work?
Do I have the materials and equipment I need to do my work right?	In the last seven days, have I received recognition or praise for doing good work?
At work, do I have the opportunity to do what I do best every day?	This last year, have I had opportunities at work to learn and grow?
In the last six months, has someone at work talked to me about my progress?	At work, do my opinions seem to count?
Do I know what is expected of me at work?	Is there someone at work who encourages my development?

The 12 questions are named "employee engagement" and are the source of the industry term.

Imagine asking the staff at an organization the Gallup questions shown in table 10.1 (Buckingham and Coffman 1999). Which questions are the most important indicators of high performance?

Twenty Years Later: Nothing Has Really Changed
Twenty years after Gallup completed their groundbreaking research and published it, what has changed? We might find workplaces have gotten a little bit better, but overall they haven't changed much.

How can that be? The Gallup12 is a statistically proven metric that reveals the level of performance of an organization and what specific things to focus on to improve performance. Any reasonably intelligent, motivated manager will:

1. Measure the engagement score.
2. Resolve the challenges to improve working conditions.

What's even stranger is that most large organizations use an on-line engagement survey (usually Gallup12 or some variant) to support an improvement in organization performance. Something has gone very wrong.

ENGAGEMENT SURVEYS: THE DEADLY TRAPS

Let's look at where use of the powerful tool for measuring engagement has gone wrong. We have discovered the following traps that block organizations from using employee engagement surveys effectively. Below we share the highlights, as there are too many traps to report them all here.

1. Influence Staff and Distort Data

One key challenge is the coercion that may take place around completing the survey. In some organizations, people are so disengaged that they don't even bother to complete the survey. Rather than observing high disengagement as the actual result, various countermeasures are deployed that distort the real (optional) responses. For example, making the survey mandatory, repeated reminders, or asking managers to track how many of their people have completed in their group. Even worse, when well-intentioned management creates metrics, targets, or bonuses for improved results, it is no longer possible to get a clean read of the system. Instead, there is typically direct and indirect coercion. Sure, numerical scores will increase, but this will be an artifact of the manipulation rather than a real change in people's work experience and behaviors.

2. Changing the Survey

With the goal of increasing scores and without any real ability to change what is happening in the organization, many change the survey to create the appearance of better results. Questions that score high may be added to uplift the real scores. Questions that score poorly are removed. Another key challenge is too much neutral in the result scores, and some will remove the option of "neutral" in the spirit of getting the real answer while actually distorting the data further.

3. Reporting on Incomplete Information

The data almost always looks better than it actually is. When the response rate is less than 90 percent or 95 percent, we might consider the data to be reasonably accurate. But what about a 60 percent response rate with an average engagement score of 3.5? Is the average really 3.5? What about the 40 percent who did not respond? All the people who are uninterested, unmotivated, overworked, and so on—what scores would they give? If we estimate the 40 percent who did not respond at an average engagement level of 2.0, then the real average is 3.0, not 3.5. The quality of the result is grossly overstated.

4. No Change

The real killer for employee engagement surveys is that nothing really changes. There is no management action to resolve the challenges people face. Even worse, the challenges are assigned to the workers to solve when the problem sits with management. Then apathy sets in, and people stop responding to surveys.

5. Not Looking at the Real Data

The ultimate challenge with most surveys is that people are not looking at the real data. Managers get aggregated, synthesized data where they no longer can observe the real data. Even if they can see the real data, the way it is reported is highly misleading.

SAHOTA INNOVATION FOR ANALYZING THE REAL DATA

Let's look at the details of running an employee survey to see where most organizations go wrong with the actual data.

We start with a question such as, "At work, do my opinions seem to count?" So we can accurately measure the result, a Likert scale is used to test for agreement. It looks like this:

"At work, my opinions seem to count."

Please select your answer:

1. Strongly disagree
2. Disagree
3. Neutral

4. Agree

5. Strongly agree

Imagine each manager gets a report demonstrating how they scored on each question. At a typical business-as-usual organization, a manager might get a 3.4 in one area and a 2.8 in another area. The 3.4 score might then be celebrated as a "strength," and the 2.8 as an "area for improvement." Performance at this level is often considered acceptable.

Consider for a moment an employee responding to a question with "neutral."

Q: Do I know what is expected of me at work?

A: Neutral

Q: Do I have the materials and equipment I need to do my work right?

A: Neutral

Where are you going when your car is in NEUTRAL? Nowhere!

Where is your organization going when people's engagement scores are neutral? Nowhere! Neutral reflects a very low level of performance. Yet, it gets counted as 3 out of 5. We interpret 3 out of 5 as: not bad. We can live with that. Could be better, but it's not terrible.

 Tool: Evolutionary Scoring for Likert Scale

The Sahota innovation is to make neutral = 0. In hindsight, it seems obvious that it would make sense to have the numerical scale match the meanings of the results. Mathematically, it's fairly straightforward—one just subtracts 3 from all the responses.

As shown in figure 10.2, neutral is now represented by the number 0. The scores for different responses will now be:

1. Strong disagree→ −2

2. Disagree→ −1

Figure 10.2: Evolutionary Scoring for Likert Scale

3. Neutral→ 0
4. Agree→ +1
5. Strongly agree→ +2

Remember the example with the typical manager? Let's look at the truth of their scores:

Traditional (False) Scoring	Evolutionary (True) Scoring
3.4	0.4
2.8	−0.2

Anything below a 1 = "agree" is in the "needs attention" category. A score of 0.4 is a poor score—nothing to celebrate. Unfortunately, scores below 1 are routinely celebrated as "strengths." A score of −0.2 makes it clear there is a cause for immediate attention, investigation, and support.

Model: Employee Engagement = Management Scorecard
The title of the book that shared these research findings
is *First, Break All the Rules: What the World's Greatest
Managers Do Differently* (Buckingham and Coffman
1999). The title is very revealing of the key findings and implications for what it takes to create high performance. The research reveals that business as usual is in fact low performance, and that high
performance comes from managers who operate very differently
from the norm. In fact, the startling result is that *most performance
is a function of the immediate manager*, not the organization!

A better term than *employee engagement* for the survey is *management scorecard*. While the situation does have to do with employees, and while it does measure engagement, the results are a
reflection of the management of the organization. When managers
shift perspective to understand that this is *their scorecard* for creating a healthy environment for workers, the focus shifts to the actions and behavior of the manager, and the possibility of change is
birthed.

How to Increase Engagement

The desire in organizations to increase engagement is often well
intentioned and noble. The challenge is that the necessary preconditions to effectively act on employee engagement data is usually not
present. The heart of the challenge is that a real change in survey
results requires a real change in the behavior of managers. Without
the conditions, skills, and education that is needed to achieve this,
people try to manage through the situation, and then these various
forms of traps emerge.

The first step is not to get the data. That's a trap.

The starting place is to create the conditions where collecting the
data will yield to a positive outcome. Some of the key items to focus
on to create the right preconditions are:

- Develop a shared understanding of the link between
  people and performance.

- Invite a genuine desire with management to care for the people in the organization.
- Support leaders' abilities to develop new skills and shift their consciousness so they can model people-oriented behaviors.

In fact, most of the patterns in this book can be understood as a way to move from disengagement to engagement. For example, the shift from status and domination will decrease engagement while equal voice will increase engagement.

YOUR TURN

- Which of the five engagement traps have you seen organizations fall into?
- How has overly optimistic reporting (neutral = 3) impacted the ability to effect real change in your environment?
- What is the level of desire and commitment with leadership to actually make a better work environment?

Give a man a fish and you feed him for a day; teach a man to fish and you feed him for a lifetime.

—Maimonides

PATTERN 10.5: FROM STRENGTHS DEVELOPMENT TO SELF-DEVELOPMENT

KEY POINTS

- While strengths development is useful, self-development is essential for unlocking high performance.

- Self-development is not just about developing skills and knowledge but more importantly about working through limiting beliefs and behaviors.
- People may choose to focus on self-development since they want to become better people or because they may want to be successful.
- A culture of self-development is needed for organizations to evolve.

STRENGTHS DEVELOPMENT

The focus in many books, leadership training, and conventional business wisdom is to develop the strengths of people.

While we wholeheartedly agree with the value in developing people's capabilities and talents, this is only part of the truth. It is certainly not the be-all and end-all that it is often represented as.

Everyone has strengths and weaknesses. This is normal. When we only focus on strengths, we limit the scope for the growth of human potential.

Ray Dalio outlines the four choices that are possible when observing weakness:

1. Deny it.
2. Work on it.
3. Find ways around it.
4. Change your goal (Dalio 2017, 160).

The strategy implicit with only developing strengths is option 3, to find ways around the weakness.

The choice to work on weaknesses or challenges is key to developing high performance. While strengths development has a place, it is secondary to working on weaknesses.

SELF-DEVELOPMENT

In high-performance organizations, a holistic view of success is taken so that the focus moves beyond developing strengths to the heart of high performance—evolving beyond our challenges and limitations. It's about developing people as human beings. While this includes developing skills, knowledge, and abilities, it also includes working through challenges and developing new behaviors. Effective self-development includes all aspects of a human being: identity, values, beliefs, and behaviors. It's all about a shared choice to grow as human beings.

PERSONAL GROWTH = ORGANIZATIONAL GROWTH

Organizational growth is a reflection of personal growth (Sahota 2013b). The evolution of the culture and capabilities of an organization is only possible through the evolution of the people in the organization. The evolution and performance of an organization is wholly constrained by the development of people. Furthermore, we are speaking to a wider view than just actions and behaviors to include: identity, values, and beliefs.

PERSONAL DEVELOPMENT IN PRACTICE

The most thoroughly articulated explanation of the importance of individual growth can be found in *An Everyone Culture: Becoming a Deliberately Developmental Organization* (Kegan and Lahey 2016). They argue that in organizations, the development of staff is an essential element in the development of a high-performance organization. We will explore the expression of these concepts through two high-performance organizations documented in this book, NextJump and Bridgewater.

 PRINCIPLE: FOCUS ON SELF-EVOLUTION
Another peak organization is NextJump, where they realized that it is more productive to have people who want to learn rather than experts who aren't interested in growth. At NextJump, the concept of "better me" signals a company-wide culture of personal evolution: a shared commitment to showing up as a better person. "Better me signals the importance of constant improvement. . . . When you visit the company's headquarters, it's clear that the consistent work on self-improvement extends to supporting healthy lifestyles, in addition to transcending the mind-

set you bring to the office" (Kegan and Lahey 2016, 20). Here, they speak of the mindset of individuals as the key to high performance. The whole belief system came from the realization that it is better to have less experienced staff who want to grow than to have experienced staff who have no interest in growth.

At NextJump, a core belief is that the key to individual performance is to develop challenge areas. Everyone in the organization has a backhand—an area where the person has challenges or struggles that interfere with their performance. Problems in the organization are not only seen as external but also as a reflection of inner limitations. At NextJump, every problem is there to "solve you"—to help you discover and evolve your inner world (Kegan and Lahey 2016, 139).

Pain + Reflection = Progress

Bridgewater, the largest hedge fund in the world, describes a system of developing staff that operates on similar principles to NextJump. Even though conceptually similar, it is very different in terms of language and implementation. Every person has a "baseball card" that tracks key characteristics so that people know how to navigate effectively in meetings. Each baseball card has "rely-ons" (strengths) and "watch-out-fors" (challenge areas) (Dalio 2017, 547).

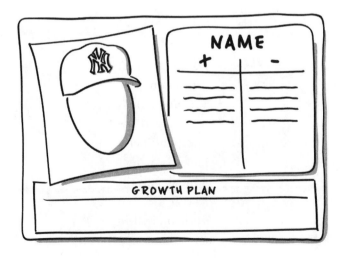

Similar to "solve you," Bridgewater describes "probing" as a way to look into the deeper why of a person's behavior. This may take the form of an "after action review" to learn about the person (Kegan and Lahey 2016, 50). The high level of truth and reality of our inner world that is needed for growth can be challenging for us as human beings. To remind and orient people to the necessity of this approach to development, Bridgewater uses the phrase: "Pain + Reflection = Progress" (Dalio 2017, 152). This translates to: the pain of our personal limitation plus the choice of reflection leads to progress and personal evolution.

YOUR TURN

- Where does your organization focus individual development efforts: toward strengths or toward challenges?
- To what extent does your organization provide the time, space, and support for people to work through challenges?
- How willing and ready are people in your organization to look at areas of challenge?

---

11 ▪ The Paradox of Power

The paradox of power refers to the seeming conundrum: how to use power effectively while at the same time enabling the power of others. The seeming dilemma—either using power or giving it away—is the paradox. And high performance emerges from coming to understand and transcend the paradox of power.

The whole of the journey from traditional to evolutionary—in all of its aspects—can be understood through the lens of effective use of power. There are many traps on this journey, from the wholesale abandonment of the hierarchy to creating too much autonomy before people are adequately prepared. Whether you are coming from a more traditional management mindset or a seemingly progressive one, be prepared to have your beliefs challenged and hopefully recalibrated to an understanding that will serve as the foundation for how you may approach leadership and organizational change.

With great power comes great responsibility.
—Stan Lee, *Spider-Man*, Marvel comic,
August 1962, vol. 1, no. 15

PATTERN 11.1: FROM EXERCISING POWER TO LEADING THROUGH INFLUENCE

KEY POINTS

- The key organizational challenges of a traditional organization come from the overuse and ineffective use of power.

- Leading through influence is generally far more effective than using authority and power.

- The essence of leading is to evoke or bring about people who choose to follow willingly.

- The simplest strategy is to treat everyone like a volunteer.

EXERCISING POWER

Most organizational systems today exhibit a high level of use of power and authority to forward goals and activities.

The typical consequence of Traditional management, with its addiction to command and control, is to dominate others, consequently fostering low levels of engagement and Theory X workers.

Power exists as a tool or mechanism for impacting a system. As a tool, power is neither good nor bad. It just exists. It can't be gotten rid of. The choice we face is how will it be used and what choice will lead to positive consequences.

The word *leadership* is used in the Traditional business environment to mean a variety of different things:

- The people in charge of the organization—managers or executives
- The people with authority or power
- The act of directing and guiding people.

For the most part we have a sense of what real leadership is. We recognize that in business-as-usual organizations, the word *leadership* is used for anything but the real thing. We do our best and carry on without fully recognizing the painful loss of true leadership.

 LEADING THROUGH INFLUENCE
Leading through influence is the ability to energize and build interest in an outcome without using authority, power, status, or any form of manipulation. It is a more complex skill—hence the name *the paradox of power*. It also demands an evolution in consciousness to internalize the understanding so that one can embody the change through action and behavior.

THE PARADOX OF POWER

Successful leaders are able to get things done in a very different way than with the direct use of power. We define the *paradox of power* as a shift in understanding and consciousness that allows one to understand the nuances of the effective use of power. Understanding the paradox of power allows one to achieve far more than one's formal status or authority—these people are called *influencers*. Executives and managers who use influence over power are able to achieve great things.

While navigating the paradox of power is the focus of this chapter, it is interlinked and touches many other patterns, such as the effective use of power and how to influence change without the direct use of power. The antipatterns highlight the specific and categorical damage that can be created through the ineffective use of power.

USE POWER SPARINGLY

This is a simplified principle that captures the essence of how to lead through influence: stop using your power. A more nuanced and accurate summary is to only use power as a last resort, and even then use the least amount of power possible.

Deming identifies that effective managers avoid the use of authority: "He has three sources of power: 1. Authority of office, 2. Knowledge, 3. Personality and persuasive power; tact. A successful manager of people develops Nos. 2 and 3; he does not rely on No. 1. He has nevertheless obligation to use No. 1, as this source of power enables him to change the process . . . to bring improvement" (1994, 126).

What we are speaking about here is the right balance. In some situations, no power or only a very small amount of power is needed. In other situations, strong and effective use of power may be required. Some managers make the error of abandoning all power in the name of autonomous teams or a misunderstanding of what Servant Leadership really means.

PRINCIPLE: LEADING IS AN EMERGENT PHENOMENON

To fully clarify what it means to lead through influence, we need to clarify an understanding of *leading, leader*, and *leadership*.

Of course, one might simply define a leader as a person who leads others and leadership as the act of leading. This then begs the ques-

tion: What does it mean to lead others? Related to this is the very practical question: How can one tell if one is leading? It's easy. Check to see if there are followers. Hence the following definition:

leader = a person who has followers

In the book *One from Many: VISA and the Rise of Chaordic Organization* (2005), Dee Hock provides the following insight to clarify this topic: "*Leader presumes follower.* Follower presumes choice. One who is coerced to the purposes, objectives or preferences of another is *not* a follower in any true sense of the word, but an object of manipulation. The terms leaders and followers imply the continual freedom and independent judgement of both. A true leader cannot be bound to lead. A true follower cannot be bound to follow. The moment they are bound, they are no longer a leader or follower. If the behavior of either is compelled, whether by force, economic necessity, or contractual arrangement, the relationship is altered to one of superior/subordinate" (47).

Let us consider what it means to lead others when people have a choice about whether to follow or not. The following passage about Morningstar describes a Teal way of working with shared power and conscious leadership: "Leadership in a self-managed environment is different, however. The source is definitely not position, title or hierarchy. *The only indication of a leader is whether someone has followers or not.* In a self-managed environment, leadership is earned, not granted. Generally speaking, the person earning a position of leadership is the person with the most experience to bring to bear on a particular problem or situation. Positions of leadership in self-managed situations aren't permanent. They revolve, depending on who has the most ability to deal with a situation, and whether people trust that person enough to follow him or her" (Kirkpatrick 2011, 91).

We make the following definitions to clarify the true meaning of the terms *leader, lead,* and *leadership*:

leader = a person who has followers
lead = to evoke followers
leadership = behavior that evokes followers

When we attempt to lead and no one follows, that is definitely not leadership.

We use the word *evoke* to capture that effective leadership will manifest or result in followers. The people who choose to follow are accepting an invitation to follow. They are not created by the leader. It is in fact the other way around: through the act of following, they create the leader.

To move to a high-performance organizational system, it is required to have leaders who lead—we refer to this as leadership leadership. Success hinges on leadership that actually leads. In business as usual, there is often a complacency and acceptance of managers and executives in positions of power who fail to lead.

Leading is an emergent phenomenon of a group of people. A leader may attempt to lead, yet success is measured by whether people willingly choose to follow. As such, leading, being a leader, or leadership is an empirical result that depends on what happens in practice. Further, it is a dynamic phenomenon—one can be leading one moment and not in the next.

> True leadership is the ongoing attention to one's
> choices and their outcomes.

Treat Everyone Like a Volunteer

Let us return to the practical situation where someone is a manager and wishes to grow to become a leader who leads. A key phrase that provides guidance for managers to:

> Treat everyone like a volunteer.
> —Peter Drucker

Volunteering is optional. A volunteer is someone who voluntarily chooses to participate. With volunteers, people can no longer rely on power or authority to influence behavior. When one treats everyone like a volunteer, one has no alternative but to act like a real leader or fail.

On one occasion when we were visiting with an executive vice president at Google, we discovered how he had learned this very same lesson when he started working there. After a successful career in management roles at start-ups and other organizations, this VP joined Google. At that time, Google employees had the freedom to change projects, and there was so much demand, they did not have to put up with bossy business-as-usual managers. Soon a few engineers left the team rather than work for this VP. This created a wake-up moment. The VP had a choice—to fail, or to learn a new style of leadership. He chose to reinvent himself to act like a true leader.

A similar wake-up moment occurred for David Marquet in the case study *Turn the Ship Around* (2012). As the captain of a submarine, he was in deep trouble. He and the crew knew he was incapable of giving effective orders. They all knew that they would fail to return the submarine to active duty if Marquet kept making decisions. He had a choice—to shut up and relinquish power or to fail in his mission. Marquet understood that relinquishing power would require that he learn a completely new approach to leadership. He chose to reinvent himself to act like a true leader, and through this act he created such passionate followers that they achieved the highest audit score in the history of the U.S. Navy. The true engagement needed for high performance requires real leadership.

Most managers in organizations do not have the benefit of such a clear choice: to fail or to grow. In most organizations "good enough" is the repeated choice that leads to Traditional (Red, Orange) culture systems and the performance that goes with them.

TOOL: FOUR KARMAS

We have modified a Buddhist teaching called the four karmas to create a tool to guide interactions with a person or a system. These four options illustrate the different uses of power. Each successive level can be seen as using more power.

1. *Peace*—Create peaceful relations. Support psychological safety.

2. *Enrich*—Give the person or system what it needs or wants. This can be education, financial support, or emotional support.

3. *Energize*—With energize, we put our will and our desire into what should happen. This is where we may share what we see and what we think would be valuable. We invite people to support, join, or follow us. Participation is optional.

4. *Destroy*—Destruction can be used to oppress or liberate. In its healthy usage, we understand that new creation may require destruction and may use power for the ultimate good of the person or system.

With every situation, one can use the four karmas to evaluate alternative patterns of interaction. High performance comes from using the right level of power to support the people in each unique context.

From the perspective of the four karmas, the only real use of power is for destruction, conscious destruction. As an enabler of change, it is important to be conscious at each moment where we are operating to ensure we are using the most effective move for the given situation.

It is typical for our human conditioning to see destruction as a negative use of power. This can lead to a false sense of humility or a suppression of thoughts and behavior that can lead to a retainment of unhelpful structures or team members. Many leaders choose to avoid destruction for the sake of trying to be fair or a being a good leader. In these situations, we can choose a new perspective, where destruction is for the good of a system and for the good of individuals. Of course, when there is a shift in consciousness or mindset, the power of destruction when using the four karmas looks very different. Growth and transformation are a normal outcome from the positive use or conscious destruction.

YOUR TURN

- If you did not have any title, role, or authority, who would still come to your meetings or agree with your ideas?

- Do people follow you because they believe in you or because of your authority?
- During your day-to-day interactions, what karmas do you tend to operate in?

When people feel that what they are doing serves a higher purpose, they are more motivated to perform at their best.

—Brian Tracy

PATTERN 11.2: FROM SERVING GOALS TO SERVING PURPOSE

KEY POINTS

- While goals are helpful to create alignment, their dominance adversely impacts performance.
- Objectives and key results (OKRs) don't work unless you have the right culture.
- People will become more engaged when they have a meaningful purpose.
- Purpose is more important than goals.
- Leaders who are able to set aside personal interest and ego to serve purpose inspire people and earn the right to lead.
- The responsible use of power to serve a shared purpose develops a healthy culture.

SERVING GOALS

In most traditional organizations, goals shape the focus and structure of organizational activities. Frequently, top leadership commits to specific outcomes and metrics with the board of directors. These are usually formulated as a strategic plan with cascading sets of objectives or subgoals for various groups, departments, and teams. In this process, groups are frequently given different and often conflicting goals that lead to organizational tension and conflict.

Communication plans are made to get middle managers and workers to understand what is needed of them, and yet there is little hope that people might actually be excited. Often a whole system of management by objective is in place to measure conformance and compliance. The workplace becomes increasingly meaningless, and low levels of employee engagement lead to low productivity. Even worse, the ability of the organization to adapt to the changing world is blocked or hampered by the typical annual planning process.

OKRs—Oh No!

OKRs is a system created at Google to seemingly avoid the trap of top-down goal creation. Each OKR consists of an object or goal that is created by the team or subgroup. In Google's context, they define a key result that is a stretch goal—something ambitious and challenging—so that the team has a chance to push the envelope and deliver the extraordinary.

When there is a high level of psychological safety and space to learn from failure, then these structures will work. It is a great example of how Google made goals useful in their context. OKRs will only work in very evolved organizations.

What happens in more traditional organizations is that OKRs are misinterpreted, misconstrued, and used very much in the same way as Traditional goal management. Suddenly, it's the top leadership defining or guiding the OKR creation. Without psychological safety, talking about stretch goals doesn't make sense—people will just play it safe.

The key challenge is that OKRs are designed to act at the level of consciousness of Google—an evolved organization. Simply copying the structure and applying it to a traditional organization cannot possibly work since the management and employees need to operate from a more evolved consciousness.

SERVING PURPOSE

In an evolutionary organization, we see purpose emerge as a key construct to inspire and guide the behavior of people in the organization. The purpose is an active part of daily work life to orient and guide decisions and behaviors. Employees who are actively engaged and part of the creation of the organizational purpose will be inspired and motivated to work toward the common goal of the organization. Giving people purpose leads to the health and well-being of your team members and creates a positive and productive environment within your organization.

In traditional organizations, a clear organizational purpose may be absent. Even when there is a purpose, people usually do not feel connected to it or inspired by it. Success requires more than an organizational purpose being written down on a plaque on the wall or in the company slide deck for new employees.

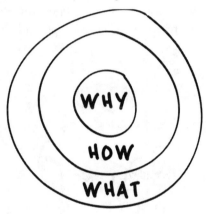

Why before *What*

Simon Sinek's book *Start with Why: How Great Leaders Inspire Everyone to Take Action* (2009) is very instructive for sparking shared motivation and desire. The powerful observation in the book is that *why* is much more important than *how* or *what* for inspiring people. Stated differently, the purpose is much more important than the plan or the goals.

> *Purpose is much more important than the*
> *plan or the goals.*

VISA is an incredible example of how an organization may evolve and emerge. The following quote captures the clear focus on the creation of an energized community of workers: "Since the strength and reality of every organization lies in the sense of community of the people who have been attracted to it, its success has enormously more to do with the clarity of a shared purpose, common principles, and strength of belief in them, than in money, material assets, or management practices, important as they may be" (Hock 2005, 94).

LEADERS SERVING PURPOSE

Every single use of power or authority can be measured by the level of alignment with the organization's purpose. Power that is used in ways that are not supportive of the organization's functioning lead to dissatisfaction with those interested in serving the organization. In contrast, power that is used to support the organization's ability to function is well received and gives people faith and trust in their leadership.

What does it take for leaders to serve a purpose? It requires that they put the needs of the organization and its people before personal preferences. This requires enough growth in consciousness to overcome the destructive tendencies of the ego to practice the openness and humility needed to truly serve the organization's purpose.

In the book *Good to Great* (2001), Jim Collins talks about leaders who operate very differently from "traditional leadership"—what he calls level 5 leadership—to unlock organizational performance: "Level 5 leaders channel their *ego* needs away from themselves into the larger goal of building a great company. It's not that Level 5 leaders have no ego or self-interest. Indeed, they are incredibly ambitious—but their ambition is for the institution, not themselves" (21). Here we see that the ability of leaders to evolve the organization is limited by their own personal evolution.

A shift in leadership to a more evolved consciousness, where the ego has been dissolved, is required to unlock an inspiring shared purpose. Consider this observation about the shift needed with leaders of Teal organizations: "Focus on higher purpose seems to be precluded when a leader is deeply rooted in ego because the currency of the ego is fear; how can a leader be available to lead others in a conscious way if they are busy defending a fractured ego?" (Sarah Morris quoted in Laloux 2014, 247).

Evolving one's consciousness and letting go of the ego is an essential shift leaders need to be able to lead the transition to high-performance organizations.

In Frederic Laloux's work studying Teal organizations, he found that the creation of a compelling purpose goes hand in hand with the cultivation of humility. "One way that leaders show humility is by reminding themselves and others that their work is in service of a purpose that transcends them individually" (Laloux 2014, 247).

When the people in an organization share a higher purpose—more important than any one individual—it creates a powerful dynamic for evolution. From a psychological perspective, it has been experimentally verified that helping others leads to the highest levels of human fulfillment or happiness (Santi 2017).

PRINCIPLE: LEADERSHIP EMERGES FROM THE RESPONSIBLE USE OF POWER

The best and only use of power by leaders in organizations is in service of the organization and its people—to serve the purpose. When power is used in a way that supports the shared desire and in a way that supports the people, then we may say power is being used for the good of the organization. Of course, this possibility is fully dependent on the evolution of leaders. An easy test to see if power is being used for good is to see if people agree with the decisions.

When executives and managers fall into the trap of serving goals, the sight of the purpose and the motivation that comes with it is lost. In such a context, any use of power will be unlikely to effectively serve the organization or its people, and leadership will inadvertently fall into the trap of breaking the trust and confidence of those they hope to lead.

YOUR TURN

- How motivated and connected are people in your organization to the purpose?
- Where do leaders' egos or personalities get in the way of serving the organization's purpose?
- Do the majority of people believe decisions and goals best serve the purpose of the organization?
- Are people inspired by management's level of humility and their service to the organization?
- Where does self-interest and fear impact decisions?

We don't need more command and control; we need better means to engage everyone's intelligence in solving challenges and crises as they arise.

—Margaret Wheatley

PATTERN 11.3: FROM COMMAND AND CONTROL TO LETTING GO OF CONTROL

KEY POINTS

- Most organizations are trapped in the poor performance of the command-and-control paradigm.

- Executives and managers are not in control, as organizations are complex systems—they shape outcomes through decisions and actions.
- Sharing power and letting go of control is a shared journey of evolution between leaders and workers.
- Embracing emergence and letting go of control creates the freedom needed to create great outcomes.
- An integrated shift in consciousness (identity, values, beliefs, behaviors, and actions) is required for leaders to embody letting go of control.

COMMAND AND CONTROL

An overreliance on command and control for governance is the hallmark of a low-performance traditional organization. The existence and function of the hierarchy is based on the prevailing and usually tacit belief that people need to be told what to do for anything to get done.

Connected with this is the assumption that people are more like Theory X—unmotivated, unambitious, and needing to be governed. This in turn creates a vicious loop where people become disengaged and unmotivated, and organizational effectiveness is far from the potential. Why on earth would any reasonable, well-intentioned manager continue such a devastating system?

Even worse, those at the top of the organization become busier and busier. While this may fuel the self-importance that the ego feeds on, most managers realize that they have become a bottleneck for decision making. They realize that they are trapped between the dilemma of taking a vacation or impacting the rate of progress with work. Across the organization, there are harmful delays introduced by getting approvals and working through steering committees. Then there is the gnawing awareness and concern that a surprisingly high number of decisions and plans just don't work out. Even though there is an unstated collusion to sweep the dirt under the carpet, the mounting challenges take away from work satisfaction.

IT'S ABOUT FEAR

Let's face it: the words "let go of control" confuse and frighten most leaders. Common objections are: How will we be able to get anything done? How will we make sure people are working on the right things. Even more frightening, what will my role be?

The real challenge here is fear. Fear of the unknown. Fear of loss of status. Fear of not achieving results. Even though it has been proven again and again that sharing power with employees leads to higher performance, managers just can't do it. While overcoming fear is the ultimate solution, an important starting place is for leaders to have a clear understanding of how letting go of control is a key element of high performance.

LETTING GO OF CONTROL

Various new forms of leadership have been proposed to move beyond command and control. All of these point to one key shift: letting go of control.

FACT: EXECS AND MANAGERS ARE NOT IN CONTROL

The truth of the matter is that managers do not actually have control over the people who report to them. For sure, power and authority can be used to achieve compliance. Yet at each moment, a worker is fully in control of what effort and energy they bring to an activity. High-performance leaders are simply recognizing the underlying reality and flowing with it.

PRINCIPLE: CONTROL IS AN ILLUSION

People are complex systems. It's hard to predict how people will react. Then we have organization systems that are a collection of people—that's complexity squared! Organizations are very complex systems. It's hard or impossible to predict what might happen when we take action. How can any leader be certain that a particular decision, choice, or use of power will actually have the intended consequences? This fact is, of course, readily apparent when leaders are open to unlearning and discovering reality.

If leaders do not have control, what do they have? High-performance leaders understand the importance of leading through influence as well as the effective use of power.

SHARING POWER

One key aspect of the shift from low-performance culture to high-performance culture is the sharing of power. A transitional pattern seen in organizations that seek to move beyond command and control is the focus on the empowerment of workers. With evolutionary organizations, there is an extensive dismantling of the typical power infrastructures. This is manifested either by eliminating a fixed power hierarchy entirely or by evolving leadership to such a point that the hierarchy is fully in service of the workers and the organization.

In the remarkable case study documented in *Turn the Ship Around*, a whole new way of working came out of one simple choice by the captain of the submarine: "I vow to never give another order" (Marquet 2012). In that moment, the captain chose to give up control out of necessity. As a new captain, without the usual yearlong training program, there was no way he could make intelligent orders with his low level of knowledge. There was simply no other workable solution to his situation. On Marquet's submarine, they unwittingly stumbled upon one of the key characteristics of high-performance leadership: giving up control.

Ricardo Semler explains the motivating philosophy at Semco—an Evolutionary case study: "I wanted to know if it was possible to liberate people and free them from the elements of life that make it a drag by creating an entirely new kind of organization. The answer lay in relinquishing control. It was a deceptively simple principle because it would mean instituting a true democracy at Semco" (Semler 2004, 9). An *entire chapter* is dedicated to the importance and details of how Semco handled this change: "Order of the Day: Give up Control, Sir!" (111).

For further descriptions of how evolutionary organizations around the world and in different industries have handled sharing power, we refer readers to *Reinventing Organizations* (Laloux 2016).

Keep the Hierarchy—It's a Journey

A popular myth around the future of work is that you need to get rid of the hierarchy to create high performance. It's simply not true. A key source of misunderstanding is the book *Reinventing Organizations* (Laloux 2016), where the existence of a hierarchy in the largest case study, AES, was simply overlooked. Other high-performance organizations such as Semco and *Turn the Ship Around* also retained the hierarchy. It's not about having a hierarchy or not—it's about the behavior and mindset of the people in positions of power.

If you are in a position of power, don't worry, it will take time before anything like full self-organization can function well. Everyone at the organization will likely need to evolve to operate effectively with higher levels of autonomy. You will more likely have your hands full working to develop people.

The ability to give up control and share power is a leadership capability. Depending on the situation, a leader will decide to what degree to exercise this capability—how much power to share, whom to share it with, what constraints to provide, and so on. In *no way* are we advocating a complete abdication of power. That has worked in unique situations but probably won't work in your environment. Instead, we are suggesting sharing power and control in an iterative and incremental way as people are developed.

EMBRACE EMERGENCE

High-performance people and organizations learn to embrace emergence. As every organization is a complex system, there is no possible way any leader can directly control the organization or its evolution. Hock speaks to this invitation of a broader and deeper understanding of leadership: "To be precise, one cannot speak of leaders who cause organizations to achieve superlative performance, for no one can cause it to happen. Leaders can only recognize and modify conditions that prevent it; perceive and articulate a sense of community, a vision of the future, a body of principle to which people are passionately committed, then encourage and enable them to discover and bring forth the extraordinary capabilities that lie trapped in everyone" (Hock 2005, 55).

As the leaders in an organization start giving up control, an organization will naturally move to distributed decision making. The low-performance model of top leadership making decisions shifts to become a web of decision making based on who has the best information and wisdom to serve the purpose of the organization. In this situation, everyone is coleading and cocreating the future. As a result, the path taken by the organization will evolve as a function of many independent decisions. This is emergence: the future of the organization emerges from the whole. There is no one person or group in control.

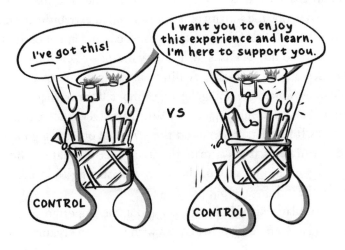

Emergence is actually a direct result of complexity. The future will emerge regardless of whether leadership chooses to acknowledge the underlying reality.

CULTIVATE SURRENDER

As leaders learn to let go of control, they will evolve to understand and practice surrender—fully letting go. In fact, creating great outcomes is fully dependent on releasing into the unknown.

In *Artful Making* (2003), Robert Austin and Lee Devin explore lessons of high performance from the perspective of the theater. They investigate the patterns of highly successful productions. High performance requires letting go and moving beyond plans: "The things you are able to plan are those things that you see as being possible. Impossibilities never make it to the planning stage. Whereas envisioning involves faith in a maybe and a belief in the chance that the 'maybe' can become a 'yes'" (Austin and Devin 2003, 173).

The same pattern is observed by John Paul Getty when speaking of how to create extraordinary outcomes (Getty 1986). One example of his achievements is the commercialization of oil in the Middle East in an area that was an undeveloped desert. He turned a "maybe" into what has become one of the largest industries in the world, yet at the time people thought he was crazy.

Austin and Devin continue to describe the key way that the director of an ensemble is able to lead to success. They use the team "release" to describe the activity of letting go so that extraordinary results can emerge. The role for leaders is to use focus and attention to influence the outcome: "Focus is the primary means by which the director influences efforts at release. A director/manager cannot necessarily know what workers are doing; he/she cannot tell them what to do. But often, he/she can influence focus" (Austin and Devin 2003, 89).

Successful leaders understand the principle of letting go and release. It can be used to cocreate the emergence of what is unfolding in an organizational system. It's more like surfing the waves than moving the strings in a puppet show.

In a similar vein, Semler speaks about the importance of emergence and the serendipity that comes with it: "In an organization, the road taken can also permit ambling and rambling—and unexpected learning. It just requires losing control. As I've said, most business leaders find that difficult, if not painful. But it is also profoundly rewarding" (Semler 2004, 236).

Letting go of control is a natural practice with the evolution of consciousness of the leader. At the start of the journey, it's not about enjoying letting go of control, it's about realizing the necessity of it.

THE EVOLUTION OF LEADERS

Let's face it. Although essential, it's not an easy journey for a leader to make the shift to let go of control. Marquet, as captain of the submarine, gave up control when he had no other choice. Laloux notes the challenge shared among leaders: "Fighting the inner urge to control is probably the hardest challenge for founders and CEOs of self-managing organizations" (Laloux 2014, 245).

High-performance leaders exhibit a shift from controlling and planning to cocreating and flowing with emergent creation. Embracing emergence and letting go of control is not a technique or a piece of information. *It requires a shift in consciousness:*

- *Identity*—from directing to a supporting leader
- *Values*—from importance of their expertise to the contribution and wisdom of others
- *Beliefs*—from "I am in control" to "The future is an emergent"
- *Behaviors*—from talking to listening
- *Actions*—from telling and deciding to growing, guiding, and enabling

It's one thing to know that letting go of control is a good idea, it's a completely different thing to put it into effective practice. This pattern, like many, is an invitation to your leadership journey.

YOUR TURN

- How well do you think command-and-control behavior is working in your organizational system?

- What amazing outcomes might happen if there was a shared desire to embrace emergence?
- How much growth is needed for leaders in your organization to surrender outcomes?

Freedom is the oxygen of the soul.
—Moshe Dayan

PATTERN 11.4: FROM ELIMINATING HIERARCHY TO INCREASING FREEDOM

KEY POINTS

- Hierarchy is a tool that can be used to oppress people or to improve conditions.
- The core challenge of hierarchies is the low-consciousness and egoic behaviors of leaders.
- Dropping the hierarchy is a very special case intervention that will not reliably work well in most situations.
- Flat organizations and self-management is a destination on the journey to high performance, not the starting place.
- Increase freedom through the effective use of power.
- Increasing freedom depends entirely on the evolution of leaders.

ELIMINATING HIERARCHY

Another famous trap is that of abolishing the hierarchy to create a flat organization with self-management. There are many change advocates who promote eliminating the hierarchy (Pflaeging 2014, Laloux 2016, and Gill 2018). It sounds promising, since many of the problems of low performance seem to stem from the hierarchy and the oppression that accompanies it. We have a different view to increase the performance of an organization and create a smoother transition for organizational change.

DISSOLVING THE HIERARCHY IS NOT THE GOAL

Dropping the hierarchy is not the ultimate goal or objective. Rather, it is a means that one might hope to create an outcome. A useful goal is to create a high-performance organization through people who are able to contribute at their best. With this in mind, we might be curious: What is the impact of dropping the hierarchy? How might this help? How might this be harmful? What are the preconditions for it to work? How can we increase the chances of a successful transition?

We have no objection to the elimination of the hierarchy as an emergent outcome that best serves the evolutionary path of an organizational system. What we see as harmful is the treatment of dissolving the hierarchy as a universal prescription for success. Attempting to shift culture by changing structures will not work unless it is led or accompanied by a shift in consciousness.

DISSOLVING THE HIERARCHY = HOW TO CREATE FEAR

In most organizations, even the merest discussion of dropping the hierarchy will trigger intense fear for execs, managers, and workers. Their sense of order and stability goes out the window. In the case of workers, they worry about what new demands may be placed on them and how they will be able to do their jobs. In the case of execs and managers, they wonder if they have a future at all and may be baffled as to what role they may have and how they might contribute what in the future. The impact of dissolving the hierarchy is illustrated in figure 11.1.

The fear triggers the fight-or-flight system and the resulting loss of intelligence due to reduced blood flow to the brain. Fear has numerous biochemical reactions that create physical limitations. There are numerous studies on the effects of fear and how it can make people sick. Symptoms of fear in the physical body are rapid heart rate, nausea, digestive disorders, immune deficiency, lack of sleep, and so on— all creating a long-term taxation of imbalance and disease in the physical body.

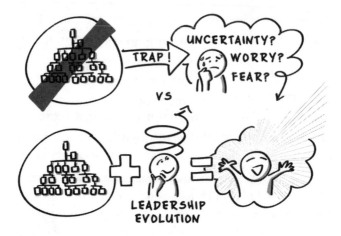

Figure 11.1: Trap of Eliminating Hierarchy

Without psychological safety, people's abilities to navigate through the confusion of a lack of hierarchy is severely limited. Just at the moment when maximum brain function and learning is needed, the very opposite is created. In most situations, even exploring the concept of dropping the hierarchy is unhelpful, as it throws leaders and people into the deep end of organizational change without adequate preparation. Maintaining a sense of order in a hierarchy provides the safety needed for people to evolve.

In terms of evolutionary sequence, dropping the hierarchy is a late-stage game that demands a high level of leadership evolution. For most organizations, there is a substantial amount of growth and evolution before people are ready and interested in such a dramatic change.

Don't discard the hierarchy until people no longer need it. Effective leaders use power for the greater good of the organization. Discarding all power is an abdication of leadership, and while well-intentioned is unlikely to be successful in most situations.

 INCREASING FREEDOM

How can you make people free? It's impossible, since they are already free—we can't make someone something that they already are. On the one hand, when we recognize people's freedom and we respect it, we will not tell people what to do. On the other hand, we may only function effectively when we have agreements about how we will cooperate and work together. Herein lies the essence of the paradox of power. Ultimately, we need leadership to resolve this challenge—someone who leads in such a way that people willingly follow. Hock captures this leadership challenge eloquently: "There is no way to give people purposes and principles, yet there can be no self-organizing self-governance without them. The only possibility is to evoke a gift of self-governance from the people themselves. It is there that a true leader may be useful, perhaps even essential" (Hock 2005, 67).

PRINCIPLE: ELIMINATE OPPRESSION
Oppression and misuse of power is the real challenge to overcome. The challenge experienced with low-performance culture systems is the existence of a power hierarchy where the supposed leaders—the executives and managers—do not actually lead with wisdom and fail to serve the organization. It's a misuse of hierarchy that limits performance.

Hierarchy is neither inherently good nor bad. It is just a tool. Everything revolves around how the tool is used. In healthy organizations, hierarchy is used to create sufficient order and structure to support the psychological safety needed for people to function.

Hierarchy is a naturally occurring structure in nature and in organizations. Regardless of whether or not there is a formal hierarchy, there will always be an awareness of who is more knowledgeable, wise, skilled, and so on. That creates an informal network or ad hoc hierarchy. Some high-performance organizations have a *natural hierarchy* of *leaders who lead with responsibility*.

IT'S ABOUT LEADERSHIP CONSCIOUSNESS
When digging deeper into case studies in literature and our own consulting work, there is a shift toward the more conscious leadership characteristic of evolutionary organizations. There appears to be a certain level of evolution in the consciousness of a leader needed to begin the journey to self-organization or self-

management—a willingness to learn and grow, to let go of control, and to learn to develop others. We define this set of characteristics as Evolutionary Leadership and dedicate a series of patterns to clarify the essence of it.

The choice and commitment of a leader to create self-organization appears to be the essential pivot in the evolution of the organization. For some leaders, the choice comes from a deep inner yearning for equality and fair treatment of human beings (e.g., AES or Morningstar). For other leaders, the change is born out of necessity or simple practicality (e.g., *Turn the Ship Around* or Favro from *Reinventing Organizations*). A final source of motivation may come from the awareness that they as a leader are not functioning in a way that will yield the success of the organization that they hope to create. Ray Dalio of Bridgewater is a good example of this type of leader (Dalio 2017).

The choice to change begins two parallel journeys. One emergent journey is the evolution and discovery of the organization of how it will function and what it will be. The other is that of the leader: the journey to self-organization is a profound teacher that supports leaders in the evolution of their consciousness. Every time they hit a Leadership Edge, they have no alternative but to evolve or to give up on their goal. An illustrative example of these shifts is shared as a business novel that highlights the principles of S3 (Cumps 2019).

TOOL: BOUNDARIES
Boundaries support people's psychological safety. Every organization has and needs a set of boundaries to indicate what is allowed and what isn't. Human systems dynamics identifies the concept of a container as a mechanism for organizational coherence. The book *Good to Great* (2001) by Jim Collins describes it as follows: "Build a culture around freedom and responsibility, within a framework" (124). Human Systems Dynamics uses the term *exchanges* to represent the boundary between different containers (Eoyang and Holladay 2011).

The culture of the organization can be understood as a very complex organizational boundary. While the structures (processes, roles, etc.) are explicit and usually clear, the informal style aspects are often much more tacit but equally important.

There have been numerous attempts to codify rules for human interaction to generate high performance, such as core protocols (Kasperowski 2015) and Holacracy (Roberston 2015). These attempt to use structures to govern human beings to shape behavior. Some people really like rules because it gives them a feeling of safety, yet for most people they are too unnatural and block the fluidity of natural human interaction. The consensus from actual Teal organizations seems to be that a compact, minimal set of rules works well when people have a high level of personal responsibility. Further, the patterns seem to be that evolving the practices that suit the people and the organizational system is essential.

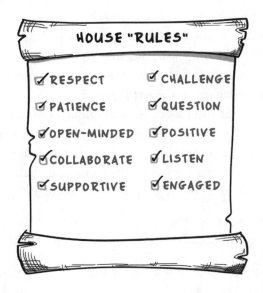

House Rules

An example tool from a training context is to create house rules that describe how we want to show up for ourselves and others. When the holder of power—the instructor—sets aside their authority and power, they can invite equality and responsibility. By inviting participants as equal adults to cocreate a set of rules for behavior, the basis for self-management can be established. See the illustration for an example agreement. The house rules can be understood as a behavior-oriented set of shared values. You can call them whatever you want—some people prefer the term *working agreement*.

TOOL: HOLD SPACE

Who can create a flat organization where people have equal decision-making rights? Only someone with power.

The real secret to shifting from a hierarchy to a flat organization is for the leader to hold space for the organization.

Harrison Owen created a powerful technology called Open Space. It was originally created as an unconference format where the participants would cocreate the agenda themselves. There is a special role called the convener that only has the power to set the ground rules for collaboration and to hold space for participants (Owen 1997). On the outside, holding space doesn't require any specific activity. Holding space is about not using power as a convener and holding a positive intention about the participants.

The secret of holding space is for the holder of the power to not use that power. This is the secret of self-organization and self-management—the holder of the power must choose not to use it. Looking closer to examples of organizations that have successfully gone down this path, we see that this is an essential ingredient.

The key to supporting self-organization is for the leader to hold space for others by not using their power.

The example of Captain David Marquet in *Turn the Ship Around* captures the essence of holding space: "I vow never to give another order." The constraint to willingly choose to limit one's power acts as a forcing function to guide a leader's development to overcome their ego to move into a new way of working and, more importantly, a new way of being.

YOUR TURN

- What percentage of the people in your organization would feel excited and safe with a move to eliminate the hierarchy?
- How clear are the boundaries in your environment?
- How much freedom do people in your environment have to make independent decisions?

There's an interdependence between flowers and bees. Where there are no flowers there are no bees, and where there are no bees, there are no flowers. They are really one organism. And so in the same way, everything in nature depends on everything else.

—Alan Watts

PATTERN 11.5: FROM AUTONOMOUS TO INTERDEPENDENT

KEY POINTS

- Autonomy is the effect, not the cause, of high performance in organizations.
- The creation of autonomous teams in most situations impairs collaboration to suboptimize performance.
- A mindset of interdependence is a necessary precondition for higher levels of autonomy to yield high performance.
- Creating shared purpose and goals supports a sense of interdependence among people and teams.
- The key shift in consciousness is from *me* to *we*.

AUTONOMOUS

There are many compelling advocates for creating high levels of autonomy in the workplace, such as Dan Pink's book and video: *Drive: The Surprising Truth about What Motivates Us* (2011). Agile is relentless in its focus on autonomous self-organizing teams as a key structure for creating high performance. The move toward flat organizations and self-management all seem to share the message around increasing autonomy.

Autonomous is defined as "independent and having the power to make your own decisions" (Cambridge Dictionary, n.d.). The questions we explore are:

- Is it helpful to create people, teams, and groups that are autonomous?
- Is focusing on autonomy helpful or harmful?
- What is the maturity level needed to have autonomy?

The Autonomous Team Trap

Many organizations that have tried to go Agile have encountered the enormous damage caused by setting up autonomous teams. When management tells teams that they are autonomous, people on teams may believe it. If they believe management, then the teams will start to make decisions as if they are autonomous. Invariably, what happens is twofold. It may be that management has not fully revealed or has not been fully transparent in what decisions the team can actually make. Another is that management realizes that the team is not capable of such a high level of autonomy and then overrules a decision. We call both of these examples hitting the "invisible electric fence." It's shocking to team members and undermines the psychological safety they need to function. At that moment, the team realizes that they are not really autonomous, and faith in leadership drops. As illustrated in figure 11.2, this can cause a great deal of disappointment, resentment, and resistance within any organization.

Autonomous Impairs Collaboration

Imagine your organization has multiple teams or groups. What happens when we tell them that they are autonomous and tell them to

Figure 11.2: Autonomous Team Trap

focus only on their goals? They will! Then the organization is typically introducing significant multiteam challenges that can be avoided. The results are typically a lack of collaboration, dependency challenges, and conflicting goals. It's ironic that the introduction of autonomous teams to break down silos are actually inadvertently creating new silos.

Autonomous Impairs Global Optimization

The lesson from Lean is that when we optimize locally, the global optimum falls. So creating high levels of autonomy is often actually counterproductive for organizational performance. Instead, what we may seek are healthy levels of autonomy that serve our organizational purpose.

There is no value for seeking autonomy for its own sake.

The way forward is then straightforward: to work together to improve the global outcome.

Autonomy, Not Autonomous

In truth, no team in an organization is truly autonomous. A fully autonomous team would make all decisions independently of others (managers, other teams, etc.). The requirements needed are to have all the context and capabilities to make decisions effectively on their own or know when to involve others. While this is theoretically possible in cases of peak performers in a high-functioning ecosystem, in practice it's not an optimal system for regular organizations.

AUTONOMY IS AN EFFECT, NOT THE CAUSE

Despite many efforts in the agile community and those seeking to create Teal or flat organizations, a focus on autonomy does not itself create high performance. Depending on the people involved, a shift to higher levels of autonomy may be beneficial for some while worse for others. Why is that? The reason is that autonomy is not the cause of high performance. Instead, it is an effect or reflection of an underlying shift in the whole system—not just practices but more importantly consciousness.

AUTONOMY IS A SPECTRUM

When we consider the shift to evolve from Traditional to Evolutionary, more evolved cultures have greater levels of autonomy. We agree wholeheartedly that higher levels of functioning are correlated with higher levels of autonomy. The question is not so much whether autonomy is good or bad, it is more effective to ask: What level of autonomy will serve this group at this time based on their level of evolution?

REQUIREMENTS FOR GREATER AUTONOMY

The key requirements for increasing effectiveness through higher levels of autonomy are that people are able to independently make decisions that reflect the greater organizational purpose and that they use their power responsibly. In turn, these requirements can only be satisfied to the degree that people show up as Theory Y (motivated, engaged, and responsible), have a growth mindset, and have the skills and context needed to function at the higher level of autonomy. The organization shows a high level of maturity in their functioning.

INTERDEPENDENT

The alternative principle of focus, to create a shift to high performance, is the development of a sense of *interdependence* among people, teams, and groups. Interdependence recognizes the dependency on one another. It turns out that everyone works for the same company and that success is shared. Evolutionary organizations even move beyond internal optimization to understand that success is shared with business partners and the larger ecosystem.

PRINCIPLE: AUTONOMY FOLLOWS INTERDEPENDENCE
Creating higher levels of autonomy without a sense of interdependence will lead to local suboptimations that are harmful to the organization. People will focus on their silo rather than the whole. The only way to support greater independence in decision making is for those making the decision to integrate the good of the whole organization.

A sense of interdependence is not a skill, process, or practice. It is a shift in how we see ourselves at an individual and team level as well as how we view the importance of our relationships with the other groups we interact with.

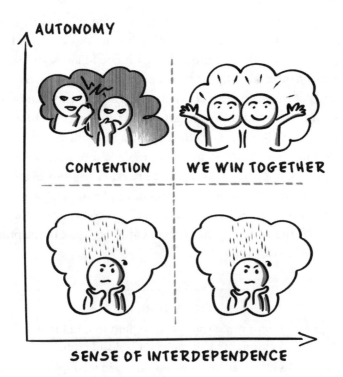

Figure 11.3: Autonomy Follows Interdependence

Win-Win

It is possible to invite the development of interdependence through shared purpose, shared goals, shared metrics, and so on. As the sense of interdependence grows, people will become aware of not just how a decision impacts their local activity but they will also be able to take a broader perspective that incorporates the larger organizational system. Figure 11.3 illustrates that higher levels of autonomy will only produce the desired outcomes with an evolved sense of interdependence.

The principle of win-win is that of mutual success. When people realize that their success is based on shared success and shared purpose, they begin to operate from the perspective of interdependence. In this way, the pure self-interest and desire to succeed can motivate this important shift in perspective.

We Not Me

Ultimately, a sense of interdependence is a shift in consciousness. The phrase: from "me to we" captures the essence of the shift from the ego and self-interest to a sense of interdependence. Individuals balance the needs of themselves with the needs of the team. Teams balance their needs with that of other teams and the rest of the organization. In this situation an increase in autonomy will not create challenges and may be beneficial.

One important place to put this principle into practice is when discussing what is going wrong with a project. The protocol is simple: drop all names—*I* and *you*—in favor of *we*. Example: "We noticed there was a problem early on, but we did not communicate it effectively." "We did not complete component X until late in the project, and this led to cascading delays."

YOUR TURN

- Where is your organization struggling to find the balance between autonomy and more centralized authority?
- Are individuals and groups encouraged through metrics, goals, and behaviors to optimize locally or globally?

- What would your organization feel like if there was a strong sense of interdependence among groups? What changes in behavior would you see?

Liberty means responsibility. That is why most men dread it.
—George Bernard Shaw

PATTERN 11.6: FROM SELF-ORGANIZATION TO RESPONSIBILITY

KEY POINTS

- Self-organization is the outcome, not the starting place.
- The introduction of self-organization introduces conflict in hierarchical organizations.
- Responsibility is the key factor that will lead to successful self-organization and self-management.

SELF-ORGANIZATION

One of the debacles of the past decade is the addiction to and overemphasis of self-organization and accompanying autonomy for agile teams. In most cases, the essential prerequisites within and outside of teams are not present. While there are certainly great successes, there is more than often confusion, tension, and a failure to improve performance.

Self-organization is a process where independently functioning people are able to organize themselves effectively without external support. These concepts can be considered at the team, group, and organizational levels. The basic premise of introducing self-organization is that it prevents micromanaging behaviors that reinforce the use of power and authority typical of a traditional organization.

SELF-MANAGEMENT

Very closely related is self-management, which extends self-organization to include the responsibility to govern and manage itself. Self-management implies getting rid of the hierarchy to create a flat organization. As such, the introduction of self-organization as a goal is a first step toward self-management and eliminating the hierarchy.

IT'S AN EMERGENT OUTCOME

The concept of setting up self-organizing teams doesn't even make sense. As per the definition, self-organization is a process: it's an emergent outcome. The managers of a system or transformation program can't create self-organization. All that can be done is to create the *conditions* for effective self-organization. So if self-organization is the outcome, what is the cause?

ORGANIZATIONAL CONFLICT

Most organizations that explore the use of self-organization do not understand that the very notion and concept is designed to disrupt the hierarchy and act as a forcing function to move the system toward increased worker freedom and a weakening of the grip of the oppressive hierarchy. There is some thin hope that the whole system will then evolve to a more mature way of working. In practice, this seldom happens. Instead, there is usually a clash of cultures that results in conflict, confusion, resistance, and disillusionment.

ALL ABOUT AUTONOMY

At the core, self-organization appears to be the justification for creating higher levels of autonomy. It is possible to increase levels of autonomy in hopes that effective self-organization may happen. A far better question to ask is: What level of autonomy will serve this person or team? From the earlier pattern, we see that autonomy only makes sense to the extent that there is a sense of interdependence, various levels of maturity, context, capability, and so on.

RESPONSIBILITY

Responsibility is the single largest factor to determine whether self-organization or self-management will produce the desired outcome of high performance. Self-organization is the outcome, and by focusing on responsibility, we might enable it.

MODEL: RESPONSIBILITY SPECTRUM

Responsibility is a spectrum. The concept of responsibility is very closely related to Theory X and Theory Y, with X at the low end of the spectrum and Y at the high end. On the low end, we have people who do not take any responsibility for their actions and choices. At the high end, there are Evolutionary or Teal organizations where we see that people act like adults and take full responsibility for their behaviors, choices, and actions. Here, people move beyond fear, guilt, and shame to honestly look at what is happening and seek to grow.

One must overcome denial, blame, and justification to take full responsibility. For an in-depth exploration on responsibility—one aspect of Theory Y—we refer you to the work of Christopher Avery and the Responsibility Process (Avery 2001, 2015).

PRINCIPLE: SELF-ORGANIZATION FOLLOWS RESPONSIBILITY

In high-responsibility environments, it is not only possible to have self-organization but also self-management and a flat organization. One excellent example of an evolutionary organization that operates this way is Valve. At Valve, they only hire responsible people. Telling people what to do would only destroy their ability to contribute. Instead, every desk has wheels that can be unlocked so workers can move their desks to wherever they need to be in order to serve the organization. No one tells workers what to do, each person is seen as a responsible adult and is the best person to figure out how to contribute to the organization's success (Valve Corporation 2012).

As shown in figure 11.4, the appropriate level of self-organization depends on the level of responsibility of the individuals. It is only with the high levels of responsibility that come with people who show up as Theory Y that self-organization adds value instead of creating challenges.

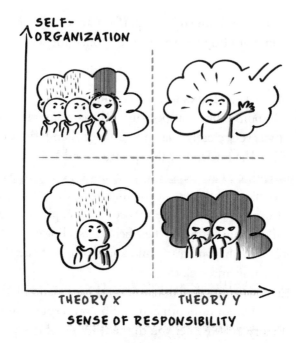

Figure 11.4: Self-Organization Follows Responsibility

Developing Responsibility

Responsibility is not a skill. It is not knowledge. It is a shift in our inner being—our identity, values, beliefs, and behaviors. While knowledge, skills, and training can support increasing a sense of responsibility, it is ultimately a choice and represents an evolutionary shift in consciousness.

The good news is that if you have been keeping a journal and completing the Your Turn exercises, you are on your way to taking responsibility for how you show up. In part three, there are more activities to support taking responsibility for how you lead yourself and others. To go deeper on the topic of personal responsibility, we refer readers to Christopher Avery's book, *The Responsibility Process: Unlocking Your Natural Ability to Live and Lead with Power* (2015).

YOUR TURN

- How well are your organization's attempts to support self-organization of self-management working?

- How ready are people in your organization to take full responsibility for their behaviors and for serving the organizational purpose?
- Do your people, teams, and organization have the maturity for self-organization?
- Would your part of the organization benefit from more or less opportunity for self-organization?

Nearly all men can stand adversity, but if you want to test a man's character, give him power.

—Robert Green Ingersoll

PATTERN 11.7: FROM EMPOWERMENT TO SHARING DECISIONS

KEY POINTS

- *Empowerment* is an unclear term, since sharing power is a spectrum.
- Sharing power through iteratively and incrementally sharing decisions supports the evolution of leaders and staff.
- The Decision Cards technology supports the clarification of decision-making authority to support better decisions and more effective collaboration.

EMPOWERMENT

Merriam-Webster (n.d.) defines *empowerment* as "the act or action of empowering someone or something: the granting of the power, right, or authority to perform various acts or duties."

The term implies that there is someone giving power and someone receiving power. It is often used as a term for progressive management where power is shared with the lower ranks. The chief problem with the term is that it seems to imply that empowerment is a characteristic or trait for a progressive organization, and as such it is misleading and confusing.

PRINCIPLE: POWER SHARING IS A SPECTRUM

The core concept is about the level of power sharing in an organization. As organizational culture evolves from Traditional to Evolutionary, there is progressively greater and greater sharing of power. From very little sharing of power with Traditional to the key characteristic of shared power with Evolutionary/Teal, there is no point on the spectrum where one can declare, "We support empowerment" as if to proclaim victory.

THE TRAP OF RAPID POWER SHARING

A large problem with well-intentioned change programs is to share too much power too quickly when people are not ready for it. For example, with the shift to autonomous self-organizing teams, there is a large shift of power from managers to teams. With the move to a flat organization, there is a big bang shift of power from managers to individuals. In virtually all organizational contexts, this leads to conflict, since leaders are not prepared to give up power, and individuals on teams are not prepared to effectively use the power. As such, we can see this approach as well-intentioned, but it in fact creates significant psychological suffering for all involved.

SHARING DECISIONS

Sharing power is really about sharing decisions. Decisions are the manifestation of power in the organization. Every time someone makes a decision or takes an action, they are signaling: I have the authority and power to make this decision.

An effective way to understand and shift the use of power and authority is to focus on decision making. It is a key dimension to move from command-and-control leadership styles prevalent in Traditional organizations.

The combined needs for fostering engagement and rapid decision making both call for sharing decision making. To avoid the bottleneck of centralized control, high-performance organizations keep decisions where they need to be made. In one Teal case study, AES, the responsibility of every manager was to move a decision to the lowest levels that could support and effect decisions.

PRINCIPLE: SHARE POWER ITERATIVELY
AND INCREMENTALLY

We advocate an iterative and incremental approach to sharing power through decision making. On a decision-by-decision basis, leaders may choose to relinquish power based on the specifics of the situation. The journey to high performance begins in earnest when leaders begin to ask themselves this question: Who is the best person to make this decision?

Decision making is the genetic code for control.

An iterative and incremental approach supports the evolution of the leaders and people in the organization. Leaders will only give up power as they grow in their ability to let go of control. People will be selected to make decisions as they take on more responsibility.

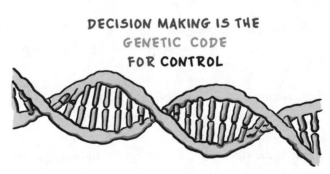

DECISION MAKING IS THE
GENETIC CODE
FOR CONTROL

LEADERSHIP EVOLUTION

For power to be shared, executives and managers need to develop both in their level of consciousness and learn the practicalities of sharing power. A key characteristic is that they are able to let go of control to embrace emergence and let solutions unfold over time instead of trying to control everything and everyone.

As such, an iterative and incremental approach provides a graceful way for leaders to share power in a way that makes sense based on the context. *Iterative* means that the leader will run experiments and adapt as they discover what is working and what needs to be changed. *Incremental* means that power is given away piece by piece rather than in a big shift.

EVOLVE PEOPLE AND LEADERS TOGETHER

It's a journey of coevolution for leaders and the people receiving the power. Just as leaders need to evolve to share power, people need to evolve to receive power and use it responsibly. Of primary interest is to invite the evolution of people from Theory X to Theory Y. As leaders create a healthier work environment and people's engagement levels increase, the people will be more able to receive power effectively.

As people receive power iteratively and incrementally, they can learn gradually how to take responsibility at a rate that is comfortable for them. We might understand sharing power in this way as safe-to-run experiments. The process is not just about making great decisions, it's about developing the people so they have the capabilities needed to be successful.

CHALLENGES WITH DECISIONS

If you have ever been to a meeting, you have probably experienced the business-as-usual challenges with making decisions:

- The most senior person deciding
- The loudest person in the room dominating
- The person who is the most stubborn gets their way
- People agreeing so they can go home and see their families
- Fake agreement with people saying yes but little follow-through
- Making compromises to avoid challenges so that the decision has little impact
- Endless meetings without decisions

- Committees that create solutions that avoid conflict but are poor for serving the purpose
- Decisions that get changed later by people higher up in the hierarchy

In short, the daily experience around decisions in traditional organizations is unpleasant for human beings and has very little relationship with high performance. In the upcoming sections, we share specific approaches that can be used to improve the effectiveness of organizational decision making.

THE HiPPO EFFECT

The key challenge to overcome with sharing decision making is to neutralize the damaging effects of a hierarchy. In particular, there is a well-known phenomenon called the HiPPO effect where authority distorts effective decision making. HiPPO stands for Highest Paid Person's Opinion. When a group of people are meeting, the most senior person's opinion will carry much more weight than others. As such, people with more junior status will be less likely to share their own perspectives, let alone challenge the more senior person.

As human beings in our society, we have a learned behavior to not question authority. In the famous Milgram experiments on obedience to authority in the 1960s, people were asked to take actions that they did not personally agree with. Most people follow orders even when they think they are wrong. For most of us, we learn at a very young age to comply with authority to avoid punishment or the withdrawal of love.

Ultimately, a shift in consciousness and clearing of emotional wounds from the past are needed to fully overcome our fears. However, we can finesse this challenge and make progress using the following practices.

LISTEN FIRST, SPEAK LAST

In pattern 10.3, "From Status and Domination to Equal Voice," we introduced the tool Listen First, Speak Last. As a leader, one of the very best ways to overcome the HiPPO effect is to stop talking and start listening. The practice of listening first will create the space for others to contribute. When a leader shares last, it elevates the status of others to support their psychological safety. We refer readers to the full explanation in the model Equal Voice.

TOOL: DECISION CARDS

We created the SHIFT314 Decision Cards technology to support iterative and incremental sharing of power.

Sharing too much power too soon may actually slow down or block the evolution of an organization. What we seek to do is to share the right amount of power based on what makes sense in the specific situation.

The cards represent an important evolution of Jurgen Appelo's delegation poker system (Appelo 2010). A key elevation is the removal of role and status from decision making. The Decision Cards technology is also designed to work hand in hand with the Advice Process (as described in pattern 11.8, "From Giving Orders to Using the Advice Process").

It turns out that in most meetings there is confusion and ambiguity not only around what decisions are being made but also around who has the power to make the decisions. The first challenge is that this may lead to poor decisions because of fear of speaking up. The more important challenge is that there can be excessive discussion and arguing about options or choices. The real conflict is usually about who has the power.

Decision Cards, shown in figure 11.5, are used to clarify one question: Who has the power? You can use them to increase awareness and options around who makes decisions and how those decisions are made. Note: you can use the concept without the cards.

- *I Decide*—I make this decision alone.
- *I Decide after Seeking Advice*—This decision is mine to make. I will make it after seeking advice from those impacted and those who have experience with this decision or domain.
- *We Decide Together*—This decision is mine to make as an equal with others.

Figure 11.5: Decision Cards

- *I Advise*—This is not my decision. I am impacted or have experience that I will share with the decision maker.
- *Please Let Me Know*—I have nothing to contribute to this decision.

Clarify Authority

With any group of people who are involved in making decisions together, the cards can be used to clarify who has decision-making authority. Or more importantly, how can the group work together to make the best decision for the organization?

1. Identify the decisions that need to be made, and explore one decision at a time.
2. Pick a decision that needs to be made. Explain it.
3. Everyone secretly picks a Decision Card, indicating their role in the decision.
4. When everyone is ready, reveal the cards.
5. If there is agreement about who the owners are, authority is clear.
6. If there is disagreement, have everyone share their thinking. Then repeat card selection.

There is agreement when there is just one decider or multiple people agree that they will make decisions as equals. If people do not agree on who has the power, then the most senior person will decide, or the various parties will escalate to their management. More progressive organizations will invite people to clear any emotional charges around the conflict and explore disagreement in a supportive way to discover what the underlying challenge really is.

Clarifying authority levels with direct reports is an essential practice to reduce confusion, increase alignment, and support staff development.

How to Clarify Boundaries

Decision Cards can also be used to clarify boundaries within teams, for teams, and between different groups to increase collaboration, responsibility, and psychological safety. For example, rather than telling a team that they are autonomous, a much healthier choice is to use Decision Cards to clarify:

- What decisions are they allowed to make?
- Where do they need to seek advice?
- Who do they need to seed advice from?

The tool creates a very natural way for a manager to start iteratively and incrementally sharing power with teams and help them grow in responsibility.

Getting Started with Decision Cards

The best way to start with this tool is to use it yourself without telling anyone. You can ask questions that cause self-reflection with the person or group:

- What decisions do we need to make?
- Whose decision is this?
- What level of involvement do you want with this decision?

For physical cards and online Decision Cards tools, please visit: https://shift314.com/decision-cards.

YOUR TURN

- Where is there confusion about who has decision-making authority?
- Where can intergroup decision-making boundaries be clarified to improve safety and collaboration?
- Where can you create a space for others to share before you?

I have long been aware of the value—both intrinsic and morale-building of consulting subordinates, asking their opinions and advice.

—John Paul Getty

PATTERN 11.8: FROM GIVING ORDERS TO USING THE ADVICE PROCESS

KEY POINTS

- Having only experts and senior people make decisions adversely impacts decision quality through information gaps and delay.
- Sharing decisions with junior staff is needed to develop the organizational decision-making capability required for high performance.
- The Advice Process supports better decisions, more engagement, and develops staff.

GIVING ORDERS

The default of hierarchical organizations is for the executives and managers to give orders and make decisions for what is to happen in the organization. As explored in other patterns around modern management, the entire structure and expectation is that top leadership sets goals and objectives, and everyone's job is to do what they are told. Even the CEO may not be fully in charge, as they need to do the bidding of the board of directors. As leaders direct and decide, they exercise their higher level of status to inadvertently dominate others and foster disengagement.

THE EXPERT TRAP

The default assumption is that the highest levels of performance will come if the most expert and possibly most senior person makes a decision. Even if the expert could make the seemingly best decision, having them make the decision is based on a bias toward short-term results. High-performance organizations balance short-term and long-term and thus invest in sharing decision making to develop the collective ability of an organization over time. The truth is that sometimes really amazing outcomes can only come from juniors because they are not constrained by previous experiences and assumptions. Even more interesting, moving decisions to senior people creates a bottleneck that increases delays (thus reducing the value of decisions) and poor decisions due to gaps in information.

THE RACI TRAP

Many organizations use the responsible, accountable, consult, inform (RACI) matrix to purportedly improve decision-making clarity (Wikipedia 2021b). Very few people have ever been able to use this reliably in most situations. The best description of RACI was shared by one of my leadership class participants: "It is what we use when we want to assign blame when things go wrong."

The artifact itself fosters neither motivation nor better decisions. In particular, the choice to separate responsibility from accountability leads to all sorts of challenges. In contrast, the Advice Process is designed to orient decisions and projects for success.

USING THE ADVICE PROCESS

In high-performance organizations, leaders give away decision-making power and limit themselves to the smallest set of decisions needed to support the organization.

The very best leaders learn to stop giving orders and start giving advice.

The Advice Process is a powerful structure invented by the organization AES to allow leaders and managers to move decisions to where the information is (Bakke 2005). The company grew to over 10,000 people running power plants worldwide. Extraordinary levels of performance were created through leaders asking one simple question: Who is the best person to make this decision?

TOOL: ADVICE PROCESS

The Advice Process is a way to approach decision making that tends to produce better decisions. It is a way to develop the leadership capability of people so that we may foster leaders at all levels. It fosters and encourages engagement and equal voice. The main benefits of the Advice Process are:

❑ Better decisions
❑ More engagements
❑ On-the-job education

Figure 11.6 summarizes the key points about the Advice Process. There is someone—the decider—who will make a decision to move the organization forward. With the Advice Process, the decider has ownership and accountability—they hold the full responsibility for the outcome of the decision. When people have ownership and accountability, their level of motivation for making a good decision increases dramatically.

Who is the best person to make a decision? Usually the best people to make a decision are:

1. Close to the issue
2. Know the day-to-day details
3. Understand the large context or big picture

With this criteria, it will be natural to move many decisions lower down in a hierarchy. It will also require a shift to higher levels of information sharing or transparency so that people lower in the hierarchy have access to the information needed for decisions.

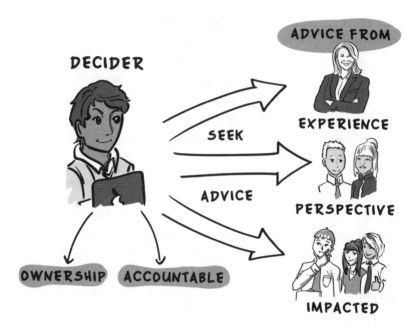

Figure 11.6: Advice Process

SEEKING ADVICE CREATES BETTER OUTCOMES

When someone is the decider, they ask for advice from the following groups of people:

1. People who have experience making this type of decision
2. People who have different perspectives (perhaps different departments or groups, different levels of the hierarchy, or from people outside the organization)
3. People who will be impacted by the decision

The Advice Process is a way to *listen to the voice of the system* to understand what decision will serve the purpose and the people in the organization. The Advice Process fosters *equal voice*. When we collectively pool our wisdom, we make better decisions. Better decisions mean higher performance. It's that simple.

SEEKING ADVICE CREATES BETTER RELATIONSHIPS

To follow the Advice Process is an act of humility: when we ask for advice we are really saying, "I can't make this decision without your help. Will you please help me?" When following the Advice Process, we strengthen relationships in the organization.

The Advice Process is a practice or structure that can be used to support a shift in people's consciousness and behaviors. The Advice Process will only work and be effective to the extent that one is operating in a more conscious environment where we value people learning and developing their leadership and where there is psychological safety.

GETTING STARTED WITH THE ADVICE PROCESS

The best way to get started with the Advice Process is to use it yourself. It's not about teaching or telling about it. All you have to do is start making clarifying statements and ask questions like:

- This is your decision. Would you like my advice?
- This is my decision, and I want to make the best choice for the organization. What's your advice?

If you are using it correctly, what you will observe is that over time people will start to copy your language and use it themselves.

On the other hand, if you are interested in sharing more directly with people as a practice on your team or group, there are some important prerequisites for it to be effective. Namely, there needs to be enough trust for more junior people to really be able to make decisions and enough safety so that they know if something goes wrong it will be seen as an opportunity for learning. Ultimately, success depends on a culture that values people learning and growing more than optimizing each specific decision.

YOUR TURN

- How motivated would you be to make a good decision when you have ownership and are accountable?
- How might your decision making improve if you followed the Advice Process?
- How much openness and support is there in your organization to develop people through sharing decisions?

---

12 ■ Organizational Evolution

Congratulations! You are now ready to move on from the outdated paradigm of organizational change to organizational evolution. In the pages that follow, we offer a fundamental rethink of everything you may have learned or practiced around organizational change. The evolution of high performance is open and accessible. It does, however, demand abandoning the usual tools of change and embracing something very different.

The preceding patterns have provided the necessary preparation so that the concepts contained in this chapter cannot be easily dismissed. It may be challenging to acknowledge the limitations and challenges of one's existing tools. If you encounter any frustration or resistance to the ideas shared, we invite you to reread chapter 7, "Unlearning Reality: Can You Handle the Truth?"

Organizational evolution is where the rubber hits the road, so to speak. It is only through changes to the organization that the results can materially change.

No problem can be solved from the same level of consciousness that created it.

—Albert Einstein

PATTERN 12.1: FROM BIG BANG TRANSFORMATION TO NAVIGATING COMPLEXITY

KEY POINTS

- Big bang transformations fail because they reduce people's psychological safety and do not adequately address the complexity of organizational systems.
- Traditional cultures are challenged with complexity, since they are only able to operate in slow-changing or static environments.
- Evolutionary cultures are able to operate effectively at higher levels of complexity.
- Using small, safe-to-run experiments is essential for evolving a complex organization.
- The ability to navigate complexity is essential to shift to a high-performance culture.
- Only an evolved leader can lead in an evolved way to effectively navigate complexity.

 BIG BANG TRANSFORMATION

Big bang transformations appear to be the current norm for introducing widespread change to organizations.

From a Traditional worldview, the organization is seen as a complicated machine that can be analyzed, predicted, and directly manipulated. The organization is in one state or way of function, and a transformation program is introduced to make the changes needed for it to conform to a new structure and way of functioning.

Believing in large-scale transformation programs is like believing that there is a silver bullet that will magically solve all the organizational challenges. While it is widely acknowledged that transformation programs generally fail to achieve their objectives, no alternate approach has taken hold. Our own estimates are that there is a 90 percent or higher failure rate for big bang transformations.

THE DANGER OF TRANSFORMATION PROGRAMS

Creating a transformation program will actually impede the development of high performance. Transformation programs are set up for failure before they start. When most people are told they have to transform, there is a threat response, and people experience fear about their roles, their jobs, and about change. As such, there is a drop in their levels of psychological safety and a reduction in the blood supply to their frontal cortex, impairing their ability to function at a high level of performance. Of course, there are a select few who enjoy transformation and are excited about it, yet this is not the norm.

FAILURE TO NAVIGATE COMPLEXITY

Another key challenge is that big bang transformation programs are by design ignoring the underlying complexity of the organization. There has not been a detailed "listen to the voice of the system" to discover and surface the real issues. As such, organizations are completely unable to navigate the actual on-the-ground realities of organizational change. A fundamental rethink in approach is required to navigate the complexity of an organizational system.

Before we embark on our journey of organizational evolution, it is helpful to pause and consider what we are really undertaking here. In particular, how complex is the task of undertaking the evolution of an organization and its culture? Organizations are complex systems. It is impossible to model the whole system at one time—there are too many parts and interconnections. The usual approach of copying another organization's solution or blueprint is a guaranteed recipe for disaster, or at best, mediocrity.

When we look even deeper, we see that each person in the organization is a complex system on their own—there is no way we can predict what will work with people. Reality is complex and messy. How can we approach organizational evolution effectively?

NAVIGATING COMPLEXITY

In a complex system, it is unlikely that there is a correct answer for how to shift the organizational system toward higher performance. Success comes when there is a shift from "We've got this" to "Let's discover how to move forward." We may replace the transformation program with a journey of organizational evolution.

OF SOCCER-PLAYING ROBOTS

What does Michael's academic career in artificial intelligence (AI) investigating soccer-playing robots have to do with navigating complexity? Soccer is a complex, dynamic domain with multiple competing and cooperating players, uncertain information, and unpredictable outcomes. Michael's published research advocates a novel path forward for robot architecture called Reactive Deliberation that combines responsiveness to the environment with intelligent decision making (Sahota 1993). A key contribution was integration of analysis and planning together with sensing and responding to the environment. This essential piece of understanding needed to navigate complex domains was presented in 1994 in front of thousands of leading AI researchers (Sahota 1994).

BEYOND CYNEFIN

Many years later, Michael encountered the Cynefin model and was fortunate to share time with David Snowden at a retreat sponsored by the Agile Alliance. The Cynefin model is widely understood as an effective framework to assess complexity and inform decision making (Snowden 2020). While it provides a key understanding of thinking around complexity, the Cynefin model is challenging to understand, explain, and apply.

What started out as a simplified way to explain the Cynefin model evolved into an alternative understanding of complexity that is easy to understand. It also reconnects to our foundational AI research for integrating planning with sensing to transcend the apparent paradox of competing needs. Most importantly, we provide an understanding that integrates with levels of culture and a shift in consciousness. As we explain our model, we will reference the related element of Cynefin for those familiar with it before sharing our unique contributions.

MODEL: COMPLEXITY SPECTRUM

Let's take a pause on understanding effective organizational evolution and instead focus on the question, How can we make effective decisions at a given level of complexity?

The way we make effective decisions in simple situations will be different from what we use in complex situations. It serves us to be adaptive and pick the right level of solution making for the level of complexity we are facing. We will be more effective when we pick the simplest tool for the job at hand and use more complex approaches when that is what the situation calls for.

Figure 12.1 introduces a model called the Complexity Spectrum. At the outset, we identify complexity as a continuous spectrum. Our model is about understanding how we perceive and interact with a situation. It's about the complexity "for us" rather than some external definition of absolute complexity. What might seem impossible for one person may have best practices or patterns for another person who has more domain knowledge.

Let's walk through the diagram from left (low complexity) to right (high complexity). We will visit four regions that help us understand effective decision making at different levels of complexity. Since it's a spectrum, these regions only form an abstraction to help wrap our minds around what is a continuous spectrum.

Low Complexity—Standards

At the lowest levels of complexity, we can make quick, efficient decisions. We create standards and best practices to guide our decision

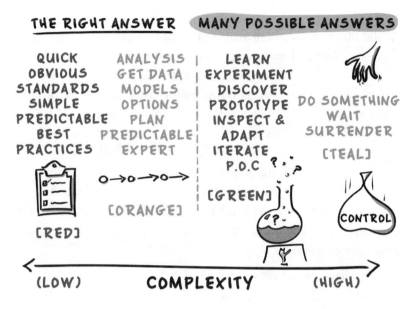

Figure 12.1: Complexity Spectrum

making. In simple situations, this leads to effective decision making. In our homes, an example of a standard would be the location of light switches on walls near doorways. In Cynefin terms, this would be similar to an obvious or clear domain where cause and effect are directly connected.

Moderate Complexity—Analysis
Once the complexity increases so that there is no longer a best practice or standard solution that will work reliably well in all situations, we now need to use our brains or frontal cortex to reason about what decision to make. We might hire an expert to collect the data, do the analysis, come up with options, and make a recommendation. In this context, we believe we are finding the right answer to solve our challenge. This is a very effective way of making decisions when we can discern the relationship between cause and effect so that we can understand the impact of our decisions. In the Cynefin model, this is parallel to the "complicated" domain.

High Complexity—Learning

As complexity increases further, and we can no longer accurately predict the impact and outcome of decisions and actions, a more evolved system of decision making is called for. When there is no defined answer, effective decision making requires that we explore possible solutions to see what will actually work in our context. With high complexity, we have entered the world of learning and discovery. We create hypotheses, run experiments, and test how well they work. We may do this through prototypes, proof-of-concepts, or iterating on a product or solution. This is the world of "inspect and adapt." We begin to see a shift from the belief that the world is controllable to the belief that solutions are emergent. In the Cynefin model, this is called a complex domain.

Very High Complexity—Surrender

What do you do when the complexity gets so high you don't even know what experiment to run? Imagine you have no idea how to tell if a particular idea or action might be useful. The usual trap is to pretend you know what you are doing and create a disaster. There are some more effective options. The first is to do something random and see if you can learn something. Another is to wait to see if new information emerges that might inform an experiment. The final one is to surrender to the situation. This is an act of honesty and humility—to accept that you do not know what to do. It is only when we surrender, to completely let go, that the spark of cosmic intelligence or intuition can inspire insight and action.

In contrast, the Cynefin model uses the terms *chaos* and *disorder* to characterize high levels of complexity. Here, we depart from alignment with the Cynefin model, since no intelligent action is possible in a truly chaotic system. Our view is that we have the capacity to use the full capabilities of a human being to guide decision-making choices at all times.

COMPLEXITY AND ORGANIZATIONAL EVOLUTION

Take a moment to consider: What parts of the Complexity Spectrum are useful? On the evolutionary journey of an organization, will it be valuable to use:

- Best practices and standards?
- Models and analysis?
- Learning and experiments?
- Surrender and/or taking random actions?

Our answer is: all of the above.

❑ *Best practices*—It is helpful to use best practices such as leaders to model behavior and listen before talking. The patterns in this book identify many best practices in the form of principles.

❑ *Analysis*—Models that may be used to guide analysis and understanding of the organizational context. We offer both models and maps.

❑ *Learning*—Most of the time in organizational evolution, one will be learning what works and what doesn't by running experiments to shift our system. By using best practices and performing analysis, we will be able to identify more successful experiments.

❑ *Surrender*—Some of the time, we will not know what to do. Having the humility to admit it is the first step toward making effective progress. A shift in consciousness is important, as surrender is a comfortable and productive known state.

The greatest levels of success will come from experiments that are guided by best practices and analysis. And when it is no longer possible to identify a feasible experiment, then surrender is the only and most effective option. Like our original artificial intelligence, we need planning and responding to the environment. It's not "either or"— it's "yes, and . . ."

GET COMFORTABLE WITH THE UNKNOWN

In traditional organizations we live in the myth of control and predictability. Even when making decisions where there is no clear answer, we pretend as if things are certain and create an unending series of poor decisions. Here we live under the illusion that there is a right answer. As there is a shift in consciousness, we open up to a broader worldview where there are many possible answers and we cannot know for sure what will work best.

There are two traps that block our evolution—one inside ourselves and one in our organization systems.

The block inside each of us is that we crave predictability and certainty. The Buddhist view is that uncertainty is the root of human suffering. To avoid this fear we will sabotage ourselves by operating in the lower parts of the Complexity Spectrum under the illusion of control. To operate at higher levels of complexity, we need to shift our consciousness so we are comfortable with the uncomfortable.

The external challenge is that our organizational systems will ask us for predictability. We will be asked for the cost, budget, timelines, and detailed plan. This is a trap for most organizational change undertakings. Forget about organizational evolution—most projects or product deliveries operate at the high-complexity part of the spectrum.

COMPLEXITY IS IN THE EYE OF THE BEHOLDER

Effective organizational evolution depends on the moment-by-moment decisions as to what parts of the spectrum can guide effective action. It is essential to keep in mind that we are speaking of a level of complexity as it appears to us with our current consciousness and understanding. As we grow in our levels of consciousness, we gain a deeper understanding of both organizational evolution and the organizational state. As a result, the apparent complexity of the situation will reduce, and we will be able to unlock more effective solutions.

For example, many people may see shifting culture as very high complexity with no idea how to effect change. After attending our courses or reading this book, people discover principles and maps to guide them, use models to collect data, and analyze situations to create reasonable experiments.

TOOL: SAFE-TO-RUN EXPERIMENTS

We shift from the Snowden term of *safe-to-fail* to *safe-to-run* experiments. When people have enough psychological safety to acknowledge that they don't have all the answers, this kind of awareness provides access and an opening for their intelligence to choose an experiment that will be successful. This requires a radical shift in honesty and transparency from most organizations today.

As we are in a learning or exploration mode for discovering our evolutionary path, we will be running experiments to navigate the road forward. An essential concept to support successful execution of this approach is to only use safe experiments wherever possible to reduce the cost of learning. The net result will be an increase in the rate of learning. We also like the S3 formulation: "Good enough, and safe to try" (Cumps 2019).

Of course, a prerequisite for running experiments is that we can tell good from bad. A goal or star on the horizon guides the creation and evaluation of experiments.

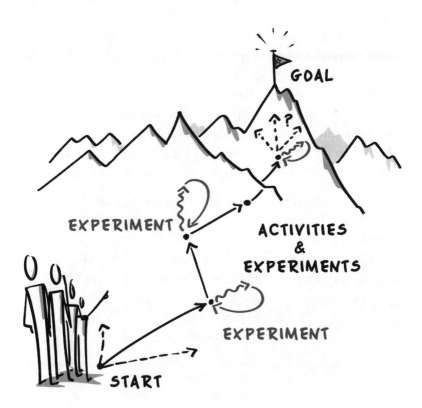

Figure 12.2: Safe-to-Run Experiments

The field of Lean start-up is about how to run experiments to find a product that fits the market (Ries 2011). In a similar vein, we are speaking of running experiments to find an evolutionary path that fits the organizational system. As shown in figure 12.2, we may test assumptions or hypotheses by running experiments, and the whole exercise is then about discovering what to do. There is no cookbook solution for your organization—it's up to you to discover and learn a path that will work.

 PRINCIPLE: ABILITY TO NAVIGATE COMPLEXITY DEPENDS ON CONSCIOUSNESS

A cognitive understanding of the Complexity Spectrum is of no particular use by itself. What is needed to unlock this model is a shift in consciousness (worldview and related behaviors—in particular, an evolution to higher states of consciousness) to internalize the meaning of it. Knowledge that one needs to run experiments does not create change. What creates change is the actual running of experiments in one's environment. A shift in consciousness is needed for people to change their behavior and have the inner psychological safety to actually run experiments.

The culture of your organization determines its ability to navigate complexity. Please refer to the Complexity Spectrum model as we link it to the SELF Evolutionary Culture Model from pattern 8.3, "From Business as Usual to High-Performance Organizations."

1. Red organizations (power and hierarchy) can use the Red part of the Complexity Spectrum to operate best practices and standards.
2. Orange organizations (achievement) are more evolved and can access the Red and Orange parts of the Complexity Spectrum to use best practices as well as to conduct analysis to determine action. In Orange organizations, people can run any experiment that they want as long as it is guaranteed to succeed. At this point, of course, it is really a plan and not an experiment at all.
3. Green organizations (people and empowerment) can access Red, Orange, and Green parts of the Complexity

Spectrum. In Green organizations there is enough support for learning and psychological safety so that people are actually able to run experiments. Here, failures are seen as a way to learn. This is a perception where there is really no such thing as a failure. Learning equals success.

4. Teal organizations (adult and emergence) can access all parts of the Complexity Spectrum. The organizational environment and the operating characteristics create a level of psychological safety that cultivates a powerful level of inner stillness and peace within each individual. There is an understanding that the consciousness/mindset and perceptions of people are very different in a Teal organization. Therefore, they function in a high-performing way regardless of the level of complexity.

Organizations that operate from a more evolved consciousness can use innovations and approaches of less evolved organizations. Evolutionary organizations may use the same structures and approaches as traditional organizations. However, they will adapt their approaches from their level of consciousness to enable more effective results.

PRINCIPLE: THE CONSCIOUSNESS OF THE CHANGE APPROACH LIMITS THE CONSCIOUSNESS OF THE OUTCOME
We return to the opening quote from Albert Einstein: "No problem can be solved from the same level of consciousness that created it." To shift the culture of an organization to a higher level of evolution, the solution has to come from that higher level. The consequence is that:

The consciousness of the change approach limits the consciousness of the outcome.

The use of the Traditional paradigm of predictable big bang transformation based on design templates of "industry best practices" cannot possibly lead to a shift in the culture or consciousness of an organization. A new approach reflecting a different consciousness is required.

Only a high-complexity approach compatible with an Evolutionary paradigm can lead to the shift to a more evolved culture. How can an organization operate a change approach from a different consciousness from that which it currently functions from?

The answer is that there must be some individuals that function in a higher level of consciousness and are capable enough to guide the evolutionary journey of an organization. The corollary is that lasting change will only be possible to the extent that this new awareness and understanding spreads through the organization. Ultimately, the only possible path for evolution is a person-by-person shift in consciousness.

YOUR TURN

- What parts of the Complexity Spectrum are people in your organization comfortable operating in?
- Where is your organization applying a lower consciousness approach in an area that requires a more evolved approach?
- Do leaders in your environment run and report on their experiments?

Culture eats strategy for breakfast.
—Peter Drucker

PATTERN 12.2: FROM STRATEGIC PLANS TO EVOLVING CULTURE

KEY POINTS

- Strategic plans are insufficient to significantly evolve the production capabilities of an organization.

- Culture is the essential element to unlock high performance.
- Tactics and strategy depend on culture.
- As organizations are complex systems, culture is a dynamic emergent cocreation of all the people.

STRATEGIC PLANS

In most traditional organizations, strategic plans form the backbone for making progress. Wikipedia defines *strategic planning* as "an organization's process of defining its strategy, or direction, and making decisions on allocating its resources to pursue this strategy. It is here that priorities are set" (Wikipedia 2020c).

The overall metaphor is that of perceiving the organization as a predictable machine. Goals are defined and plans are drawn up that will allow it to be achieved in a step-by-step fashion. The mechanism allows those at the top to direct those at the bottom.

While the act of planning and the creation of plans is valuable for certain activities, there is a very strong limit to what can be achieved through this level of thinking or consciousness. Organizational systems are complex, and people even more so. Creating a shift in the people and ways of behaving in an organization requires a level of thinking far greater than treating the organization and people like a machine. Even more importantly, the focus on strategic elements misses out on a key dimension: the people and the culture.

EVOLVING CULTURE

"Culture eats strategy for breakfast" is a well-known business maxim by Peter Drucker. Although the phrase is widely believed to be true by almost all organizational leaders, the main challenge is that no one has really known what to do about it. As a result, culture gets ignored or there are misguided culture initiatives that fail to achieve results.

Our assertion is that prior to this book, culture change has been an unsolved or at best a partially solved problem. Our extended version of the quote is:

Culture eats strategy for breakfast,
and strategy eats tactics for afternoon tea.

Breakthrough results only come from culture—not tactical or strategic approaches. There is no strategy or tactic that can shift your organization toward ongoing sustainable shifts in performance. There is no strategic plan to shift culture—this is a contradiction in terms.

Before diving into evolving culture, it's important to understand why it's so essential to organizations.

 PRINCIPLE: PRODUCTION CAPABILITY = YOUR FUTURE
In an organizational system, time, money, attention, and energy is divided between two competing interests: Production and Production Capability (Covey 2004). Figure 12.3 illustrates the tension between Production and Production Capability.

1. *Production (now)*—The focus here is on serving the organizational purpose: delivering products, serving customers, earning revenue, etc.
2. *Production capability (future)*—The focus here is on growing the ability of the organization to deliver in the future: developing people, capabilities, research, improvements to how the organization functions, etc.

In any particular day, week, month, or quarter, managers divide attention between these competing interests.

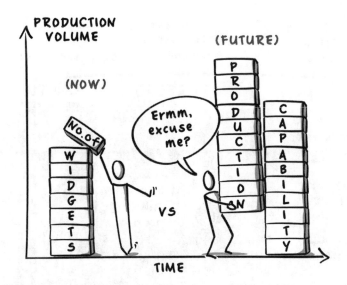

Figure 12.3: Production vs. Production Capability

In business as usual, production gets most of the attention even though the job of a manager is to improve operational efficiency. Without an investment in production capability, organizations will not improve. In fact, due to organizational entropy, capability tends to degrade naturally over time.

Investment in production capability is required to increase organizational performance.

High-performance organizations are those that find a way to deliver production and develop production capability. An evolutionary organization understands the importance of production capability. The capability of organizational functioning is just as or even more important than the current state of production. Production capability increases the rate of navigating complexity and rapid response to change, which enables an organization to deliver under any circumstance.

MODEL: TACTICS, STRATEGY, CULTURE
A key question to explore is where an organizational system is investing to increase production capability. We use the SELF model, Tactics, Strategy, Culture, for understanding and clarifying various investment options. Any particular effort to

Figure 12.4: Tactics, Strategy, Culture

improve an organization may fall into one of three theme areas: tactics, strategy, or culture. This model may be used to explore these themes.

Figures 12.4 and 12.5 illustrate theme areas for investment in production capability:

- *Tactics*—"How do we work?" is about day-to-day practices and process elements. These are processes a team or organization can adopt.
- *Strategy*—"What do we want to achieve?" is about aligning the company around key goals and initiatives.
- *Culture*—"Who do we want to be?" is about clarifying the organization's reason for existing as well as its values and vision—how we want to function internally and relate as human beings.

Figure 12.5: Map: Culture Is the Foundation

MAP: CULTURE IS THE FOUNDATION
Most organizations want to be able to rapidly evolve products to meet changing market needs. The confusion is on how to get there.

What is needed to create a fundamental shift in results?

- Results depend on tactics.
- Tactics depend on strategy.
- Strategy depends on culture.

PRINCIPLE: STRATEGY FOLLOWS CULTURE
The only possible way to evolve a high-performance organization is through culture. In Silicon Valley, it is well understood that hiring people for culture is one of the most important of all organizational activities. At Netflix, hiring meetings were given precedence over meeting with the board of directors.

When Lou Gerstner as chairman of IBM was reinventing the organization, he primarily focused on developing the culture:

"Culture isn't just one aspect of the game, it is the game" (Gerstner 2002). Gerstner was a hard-nosed businessman playing to win the game and was very successful through his focus on culture.

Strategy depends on culture. The success of any strategic change or plan is entirely dependent on the culture of your organizational system. The way to get a good strategic plan is to upgrade your culture so new possibilities can emerge.

 PRINCIPLE: CULTURE IS A DYNAMIC, EMERGENT PHENOMENON

As described in the pattern "Understanding Culture," culture is the dynamic emergent cocreation of the unifying fabric of organizational reality.

Each individual is a complex system. We have conflicting identity, values, and beliefs with others and within our own self-identities. Actions and behaviors are governed by many variables and are inherently unpredictable at an individual level. People's behaviors are governed by the subconscious mind, family patterning, and perceptions based on an individual's view of reality. As an organization is a collection of individuals, it is also (an even more) complex system (Pflaeging 2014). In any complex system, outcomes can be influenced, not directly controlled.

Schein explains it as: "Culture is both a 'here and now' dynamic phenomenon and a coercive background structure that influences us in multiple ways. Culture is constantly reenacted and created by our interactions with others and shaped by our own behavior" (Schein 2010, 3).

The evolution in thinking that we offer is to understand that people's behaviors collectively define the culture and that it is a process of constant cocreation.

CULTURE SHIFT IS A MOMENT-TO-MOMENT CHOICE

Jack Welch, former Chairman and CEO of General Electric, differentiates vision from culture. He holds that vision is where we want to go and culture is how we get there.

Our view is that there is a paradox in culture change. We may hold a shared vision of how we would like our organization to function in the future—however, the approach we take to get there is based on our existing culture.

Paradoxically, the change in approach taken moment by moment by moment is setting the pattern for the vision of the future. When we as leaders exhibit the behaviors of the future vision, we immediately begin to manifest it here and now. As such, there is no journey to go on. It is always now, and the culture is a moment-by-moment cocreation of all of the people.

Culture shifts person by person. The only way to shift culture is to shift behaviors. This is the definition of *shifting consciousness*, an awareness of how thought, behavior, and conditioning is impacting our actions.

As such, our approach to culture change is less of a journey and more of a choice in the here and now, a conscious awareness of impact. Out of each individual's choice to grow and evolve, there will be an evolution of culture. It's a daily ebb and flow between Traditional ways and Evolutionary ones. Each choice, each moment, counts.

YOUR TURN

- How much attention is paid in your organization to production versus production capability?
- Use the model (tactics-strategy-culture) to assess where the focus of investment is in your organization. What percentage of time and energy is invested in each area: tactics, strategy, and culture?
- What would happen if more leaders in your organization focused on evolving a healthier culture?

You can make buffalo go anywhere as long as they want to go there.
—Gerry Weinberg

PATTERN 12.3: FROM URGENCY TO DESIRE

KEY POINTS

- Creating urgency is a trap.
- Focus on fostering the desire and passion to make change.
- Most change programs create confusion between means and ends.
- Agile/Digital/etc. are a means, not the end. The key is to focus on organizational goals.
- Clarify organizational goals by asking, "Why?"

URGENCY—IT'S A TRAP!

One of the most famous and popular approaches to organizational change is promoted by John Kotter. In his study of successful transformation programs, he discovered that people operate with a high level of urgency (Kotter 1996). This, unfortunately, got translated into a disastrous formula with step #1: Create a sense of urgency.

The usual way of creating urgency is to tell people that business as usual is unacceptable and that change is required for survival. Leaders extol the necessity for change to survive in the new business landscape. These actions increase the level of fear and reduce the level of psychological safety. As a result, the blood supply to their frontal cortex is reduced, leading to an impairment of one's abilities to reason and perform. Key symptoms include stress and mixed sentiments about change.

In the ensuing organizational chaos, large change programs that typically do not have the willing support of management and staff are foisted upon the organization in the name of survival. People comply out of obligation, and another failing transformation unfolds.

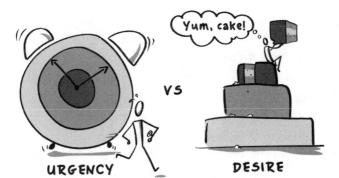

*It is time to retire urgency as a key ingredient for change
and replace it with desire and passion.*

DESIRE

The key, then, for effective organizational growth is to spark the desire of people to create a shift in the organization. When people desire change, they will be passionate and put in the energy required to unlock progress. It takes a unique leader who can lead an organization and create desire to influence high performance through inspired leadership or Evolutionary Leadership.

CHANGING URGENCY TO DESIRE

When an organization has evolutionary leaders who are capable of functioning in higher states of consciousness, their mindsets, perceptions, and behaviors are aligned in a deep state of inner psychological safety, and they are committed to the organizational purpose through growth and evolution. There would never be a sense of urgency. The behavior and actions modeled from Evolutionary Leadership is through inspiration, a natural ability to motivate and influence the organizational purpose that creates desire for the organization to perform and deliver.

STOP DEMOTIVATING PEOPLE

The single biggest challenge to fostering desire is the myriad ways that leaders and organizations unwittingly kill desire. Before seeking to spark desire, the first step is to diagnose and remove the ways that people's motivation is being harmed. The antipatterns in this book are the fast path to identifying the ways your organization may be killing motivation. You've got to take your foot off the brake before hitting the gas.

Operating like a traditional organization is a very powerful brake on people's natural desire to contribute. A holistic shift in all aspects of organizational functioning is needed to remove the organizational constructs that keep people from pulling other people toward a lower state of functioning. Removing the blocks is 90 percent of the work. What follows is the positive 10 percent of new activities to undertake. This will create an immediate shift in functioning that you can begin immediately, yet there is more needed to solve the full challenge.

PRINCIPLE: ALIGN ON THE GOAL

For several years, we have witnessed our students gain the biggest breakthrough results and success by working on organizational alignment. Alignment is often overlooked when there is no technique to effectively address it. The "Why Workshop" below is one tool to quickly bring any organization into alignment.

Most change programs are conflicted and confused. The actions taken often do not align with the high-level goals. Another common problem is that there are no clear high-level goals that everyone agrees with. One key challenge is that the ends and means are confused.

Perfection of means and confusion of ends seems to characterize our age.

—Albert Einstein

Often people believe that Agile, Digital, Lean, innovation, and so on are the goals because that is what they are being asked to do. They are not the goals—they are the means used to achieve organizational goals, but they are not in themselves the goal. Ultimately, organizational goals are around high performance or whatever the definition of *organizational success* is. Once an organization (or your part of the organization) has a shared understanding of success, forward movement is much more likely.

Agile/digital/etc. are a means, not the end. The key is
to focus on organizational goals.

The solution is to ask, "Why?" This is the insight referenced earlier from Simon Sinek's book *Start with Why: How Great Leaders Inspire Everyone to Take Action* (2009).

Our insight to ask why is to break through the veneer of false alignment. By asking why, we may increase organizational alignment and focus. The question provides a pause for those to reflect on the actual goals of the organization. The question brings the organization back into alignment of the shared goal, creating a sense of organizational purpose.

In the SELF approach to high performance, we use the question to transcend tactical and strategic approaches and get to the real ambitions of leadership. We use Why as a tool to reveal the misalignment in the system and to surface important conversations that foster alignment. If you are just starting or are already in a transformation program, the questions are: Why are we doing this? Why do we want Agile/Digital/innovation/etc.?

TOOL: WHY WORKSHOP

We created the Why Workshop as a tool within the framework of SELF. The workshop is a facilitated meeting to increase organizational alignment. It is held when there appears to be misunderstanding or conflicting ideas of what is important and how to proceed. The workshop is primarily intended to create alignment for a leadership team. The facilitation steps will work for groups of eight or less.

Why Workshop facilitation steps:

1. Give each participant a sticky notepad and a marker. Have them write down their reasons for the initiative.
2. Have participants share their sticky notes in reverse seniority order.

3. Have the group cluster the sticky notes on the wall to see what patterns emerge.
4. Label the clusters.
5. Identify the most important clusters, using dot voting or an alternate approach. (Gibbons 2019)

Detailed instructions are provided in "'WHY Agile?' Workshop" (Sahota 2014): This workshop will likely increase the alignment among the participants. As can be seen, the workshop structure itself leverages key practices such as listening, equal voice, and elevating the status of juniors.

YOUR TURN

- How motivated are people in your organization to improve the ways things are working?
- What demotivates people in your organization?
- To what extent is there a compelling shared goal that binds conversations and activity?

In preparing for battle I have always found that plans are useless, but planning is indispensable.
—Dwight D. Eisenhower

PATTERN 12.4: FROM ROLLOUT PLANS TO LOCAL EVOLUTION

KEY POINTS

- Organizations vary in terms of the level of cultural coherence in different groups and locations.

- Ultimately culture is a local phenomena, since it is a reflection of leadership consciousness and behaviors.
- The way to create a global shift in culture is to support the evolution of Culture Bubbles.
- Build adapters around Culture Bubbles to keep healthy relationships.

ROLLOUT PLANS

There are two significant problems that arise when there is a rollout plan for any nontrivial effort to improve an organization. The first is the word *rollout*, and the second is the word *plan*.

Using the term *rollout plan* reveals an underlying belief that leaders can manipulate and control the organizational system and the people in it like a piece of machinery. This traditional and simplistic approach assumes that all parts of the organization operate the same and that the exact same prescription is needed for all parts. That's like a doctor visiting a remote community and prescribing the same medication to everyone without taking the time to understand their state of health.

> *Much of what passes for transformation programs is, in our view, organizational malpractice.*

Using a rollout plan is a traditional business model and a mindset contrary to more evolved cultures. You can't use business as usual to go beyond business as usual. When we do new things, we always learn more about how and what we should do as we go along. While planning is helpful, believing that there is a plan that can be followed is disastrous.

"Responding to change over following a plan" is a guiding principle of the Agile movement (Cunningham 2001).

LOCAL EVOLUTION

Evolutionary organizations understand that globally coherent change emerges from many independent local shifts in a coherent direction. The additional principle needed to effectively navigate complexity is to focus on local change. Successful organizational evolution utilizes the principle that people in different parts of the organization will evolve at their own rates.

Consequently, almost all changes to organizational functioning—tactical, strategic, and cultural—are best approached from the integration of local perspectives.

In this pattern, we explore the specific understanding needed for cultural evolution as this underpins strategic and tactical efforts. It is important to note that the principle of local change also applies to tactical and strategic changes that are independent of culture change.

The principle of local change applies equally to tactical, strategic, and cultural changes.

DIFFERENT PARTS OF THE ORGANIZATION EVOLVE AT DIFFERENT RATES

Culture change can be made by anyone at any level of an organization. We will explain in detail the SELF technology called Culture Bubbles that supports this phenomenon. The purpose of this pattern is to explain the mechanics of creating healthy Culture Bubbles to support local shifts in culture. This is the most rapid and effective means to scale an organizational transformation.

CULTURE COHERENCE VARIES

Consider the level uniformity of a culture within an organization. The level of culture coherence is a spectrum from high to low:

- *High*—High level of uniformity in the organizational culture between groups, levels, and locations
- *Medium*—Local variations within a more homogenous overall culture
- *Low*—Very little coherence with different ways of operating across the organization

High-performance organizations have a high level of coherence around a more evolved culture. For a detailed exploration of the above phenomena, we refer you to *Cultures in Organizations: Three Perspectives* (1992) by Joanne Martin.

PRINCIPLE: CULTURE IS A LOCAL PHENOMENON

Culture is ultimately a local phenomenon, since it is a reflection of the consciousness and behaviors of the people.

Some organizations have a more coherent culture with small local variations, while others are more diverse with very different ways of functioning throughout the organization.

Traditional organizations have diverse cultures or ways of working in different parts of the organization. A simple example to illustrate this is that a product development department typically may have a culture focused on innovation and creating change, while operations may have a culture focused on stability, limiting change, and risk avoidance. This particular tension has birthed the field of DevOps to increase alignment and create a shared alliance between development and operations. It's normal in organizations to have these differences in culture, and resolving them can only be undertaken through overall culture change.

Culture Is a Reflection of the Leader

Culture is a reflection of the consciousness and the structures organization. The culture will vary locally as the consciousness varies from person to person and from group to group. When there is a global set of procedures and policies, this may act as an attractor for a uniform way of working. However, consciousness dominates structures, so ultimately what we experience as organizational culture is a reflection of the people—their identity, values, beliefs, and behaviors.

The leader of a group, due to the power they hold, is the one who has by far the greatest influence on the culture. A key lesson from the research from Gallup is that the biggest determiner of performance is the behavior of the immediate manager (Buckingham and Coffman 1999).

PRINCIPLE: FOCUS ON LOCAL EVOLUTION

Culture shift is by its nature a local phenomenon. As a shift in culture depends on a shift in the consciousness and behaviors of people and ultimately the leaders, it cannot be otherwise. The fact that culture is a local phenomenon is very good news for creating high performance within an organization. It is possible to create local shifts in culture to create higher levels of performance. It is possible for everyone in the organization to influence culture.

Think Global, Act Local

For those interested in a broad program of evolution across an organization, the path becomes very clear. Provide broad support and encouragement for those who are ready to evolve, and provide patience to increase psychological safety for the rest. We say, "Go where the interest is." Then there will be many local acts of evolution that will contribute to a rising tide of global change across the organization.

 MODEL: CULTURE BUBBLE
Let's explore the SELF technology to support Culture Bubbles. A Culture Bubble is a part of an organization that operates with different cultural norms than the rest of the organizational system. The most common way that Culture Bubbles form is due to a more evolved leadership on the part of a manager or executive that supports a very different culture. The other way it may form is through progressive ways of working such as Agile, Digital, innovation, Lean, and so on. Most of the time, the formation of a Culture Bubble happens without people even realizing it.

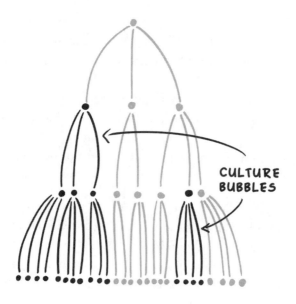

It starts with a leader who has a progressive consciousness that introduces a new way of working. What happens is that a new culture is introduced or evolves within this part of the organization. Inside the bubble there are new ways of working that are often quite different from the rest of the organization. This pattern applies at multiple levels of the organization: teams, groups, departments, and so on.

Unhealthy Culture Bubbles

There are common actions people take that inadvertently reduce the health of a Culture Bubble. Here are the common traps to avoid:

- Refusing to follow processes or refusing to create artifacts needed by the rest of the organization.
- Failure to respect other groups' and managers' decisions to use their own ways of working.
- Expecting, demanding, or encouraging other parts of the organization to change.
- Thinking that our group is cool or progressive and other people are not.
- Announcing to the rest of the organization how great your group is (and indirectly how poor everyone else is).
- Evangelizing or promoting the group's new way of working.

All these activities harm the relationship this group has with the rest of the organization. The harm to relationships makes change outside the group much less likely. Also, it usually creates challenges for the cooperation needed for the bubble to be successful.

Healthy Culture Bubbles

Culture Bubbles are the most rapid and effective means to scale organizational transformation.

Over time, we have collected a set of tactics that support a healthy sustainable Culture Bubble, as illustrated in figure 12.6. They are as follows:

1. Create healthy relations with the rest of the organization. A sign that we are in a healthy place is that we act from

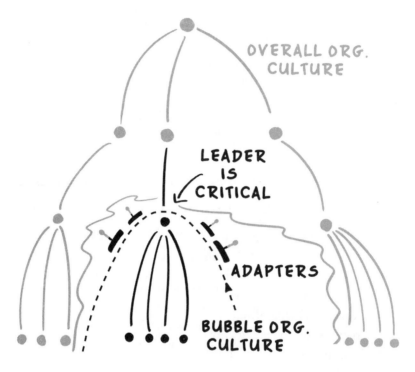

Figure 12.6: Culture Bubbles

this place: "We're ok, you're ok." Another word to describe this is *respect*.

2. Build *adapters* around your bubble so you provide the artifacts that are needed to support the rest of the organization. This let's your group fit in, so there are no ripples or problems with external groups.

3. Focus on growth inside the bubble. Develop people and their abilities to deliver on organizational results.

4. Celebrate success in a quiet way that is inclusive of all the people and groups you collaborate with.

The real secret here is to focus only on what you control within your bubble and have a healthy relationship with the rest of the organization. Yes, there will be constraints from outside that slow things down and limit success. The reality is that you don't have control over it.

 TOOL: CULTURE ADAPTERS
SELF Culture Adapters are a mechanism, process, or person that adapts from the way of working inside the bubble to the way of working outside the bubble. It's a way to bridge the difference in cultures and the worldviews of what success looks like and how to get there.

For example, inside an Agile Culture Bubble, people may use very lightweight planning and forecasting. In contrast, the rest of the organization may require the creation of very detailed plans based on the assumption that this will support success. The adapter in this situation would be the bubble (or group) and would do the work and produce the required plans at the required level of detail to support the needs of the rest of the organization.

An adapter bridges the two worlds and is there purely to support the integration of the Culture Bubble with the rest of the organization.

Pay Taxes to Keep Good Relations with Other Groups

A helpful metaphor is to think of all the nonvalue-added work for the rest of the organization as taxes. We all pay taxes. It's just part of life. In organizations, we need to pay organizational taxes for the privilege of working in the organization.

What happens when you do not pay taxes? What happens if you do not have good relations with the rest of the organization?

The organizational antibodies will attack and collapse the Culture Bubble. The attack may come in the form of extra taxes or bureaucratic red tape created to punish this group. Alternatively, a common pattern is for the leader of this group to be replaced with a new leader that matches the host organizational culture, thus collapsing the bubble. If there is a transformation program in place, then the group may be excused for a time, but the taxes still keep piling up, so there is an enormous bill or backlash when the transformation program ends or loses steam. This usually takes about 18 months to three years.

Expanding Culture Bubbles

Of course people are often very interested in changing things outside of their bubble. There are common reasons for this:

1. They are so excited about their way of working, they want others to follow suit.
2. The culture of the rest of the organization is so different that it is a burden to operate all the adapters.
3. The bubbles are so successful that the organization has asked to scale this way of working throughout the entire organization (this is the most common ask of our graduates and the most common trap).

Let's look at what you have influence over:

• People outside the bubble: No.
• People inside the bubble: Yes!

Focus on Creating a Thriving Bubble

The secret is to focus on being successful within your bubble. Build passion. Ship products. Delight customers. Be amazing. This is 100 percent within your control. Here's what will happen over time:

1. Other parts of the organization may want to emulate you. Wait for people to come to you and ask for help. Then help them.
2. The leader of the bubble will get promoted. Then the bubble can grow since this leader now has the power to influence a larger group.

Focus on quiet success and good relations. Any attempts to showcase or celebrate this group will typically backfire and revert your group back to the unhealthy bubble situation.

Woody's Trick to Expand Faster

Woody Zuill—the thought leader introducing mob programming and #NoEstimates—shared a trick to make the culture within a bubble spread faster: help other people. Here is how it works. The usual thing we do is to focus on our own success even while others around us are having challenges (that's actually the default Scrum process). Zuill's idea is this: Hey, other people and departments are struggling. Why don't we help them? Instead of asking others to change their ways of working, you just help them be successful. Well, guess what usually happens? The relationships with other groups improve. They notice that people in the bubble are happy and engaged. They become curious about what's happening in the bubble. Then they want it, too.

YOUR TURN

- Where have you seen a part of the organization that had a different kind of culture or way of operating?
- How can you start the creation of a Culture Bubble or increase the health of one?
- What adapters can you create to improve relations with other parts of your organization?

A common belief is that a change in the structure is a means for changing culture or behaviour. Changing structure alone is never enough.

—Peter Block

PATTERN 12.5: FROM CHANGING STRUCTURES TO EVOLVING PEOPLE

KEY POINTS

- Changing structures can only yield full benefits when it has been preceded by a shift in consciousness.
- A shift in consciousness is needed to enable an effective shift in structures.

- Evolving the culture of an organization requires a shift in the consciousness and behaviors of all the people.
- The rate of evolution of an organization is limited by the rate of evolution of the people in the organization.
- The creation of a healthy environment will foster the evolution of people.

CHANGING STRUCTURES

Changing structures is the principal means through which traditional organizational transformation is undertaken.

And it's a horrible trap. Within the Traditional worldview, the organization is seen as a machine that can be understood and manipulated by making structural changes. How else can one change an organization except through structures? There isn't even space to consider other alternatives.

All too often, organizations fall into a prescription or copycat mentality. The prescription is to introduce Agile, Lean, Digital, open offices, and so on. You can fill in the blank with the latest buzzword that will solve your organization's challenges. Or even worse, there is copycat thinking where one believes it is possible to replicate another organization's way of working. The thinking is that organization ABC (e.g., Google or Spotify) applied the XYX model (e.g., OKRs), and all we need to do is copy their solution. Even though the organizations differ in many important ways, there is still a belief in a universal solution.

There is a hope that somehow changing structures will lead to a shift in the mindset and consciousness needed to shift culture. Despite decades of pervasive industry experience that changing structures does not change culture, it has persisted for lack of a better alternative. The main challenge with changing structures is that we can only interpret and make changes from our current level of consciousness or the current way of operating.

When the operating behaviors (consciousness) of the organization has not shifted, we will attempt to copy other people's solutions and changes in a way that matches our consciousness. *It's not possible to effectively introduce an Evolutionary pattern with a Traditional mind-set.* As a result, while there might be minor benefits, the main part of the value will be missed.

THE CENTRALIZATION–DECENTRALIZATION DANCE

One symptom of the failure of intelligence associated with low-consciousness organizations is the incessant number of reorganizations that occur. Each may on the surface seem to address some challenges; however, nothing of any real consequence changes. Noticing a challenge with lack of alignment and incoherence between groups, the assessment is made that decisions are too decentralized and the fix is to centralize decisions. Several years later, people notice that the organization is too slow to respond, and the assessment is made that decisions are too centralized and the fix is to decentralize. Of course, the underlying problem is how the organization is sensing and responding to challenges.

EVOLVING PEOPLE

Instead of changing all the structures and creating chaos, evolving people is a more effective strategy to maximize ROI of change efforts. Organizational results are a reflection of the people. The secret to creating lasting change is to focus on the evolution of the people *before* the structures.

PRINCIPLE: STRUCTURES FOLLOW CONSCIOUSNESS

In the pattern "Understanding Culture," we explored how culture consists of the interplay of consciousness and structure through the SHIFT314 Culture Model (see figure 12.7). The consciousness or mindset represents the people and energetic properties of a system—behavior. The structures represent the 3D world material tangible constructs that ground the culture into our world—structure.

To create a permanent and lasting shift would require us to co-evolve all the elements of culture. Yet, where to start? Are all elements of equal suitability and value? Or are some starting places more effective?

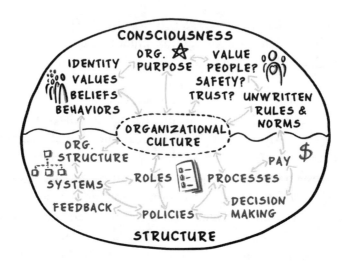

Figure 12.7: SHIFT314 Culture Model

Ultimately, we can think of the culture as a reflection of the collective behaviors of all the people in the organization. Once a group of people have evolved their consciousness—their mindset, worldviews, and behaviors, then it is possible for them to introduce structural changes or ways of working that support their new ways of being.

*A shift in consciousness is needed to enable
an effective shift in structures.*

There are multiple patterns in this book that illustrate how the intention of a specific change in structure can only be realized by evolving people and a shift in consciousness. For example, this theme is explored in pattern 11.4, "From Eliminating Hierarchy to Increasing Freedom," where the shift in consciousness required to increase freedom is the key success factor rather than making a structural change, such as removing the hierarchy.

PRINCIPLE: A NEW WAY OF BEING ENABLES A NEW
WAY OF WORKING

The most effective starting place for organizational evolution of culture is with the consciousness of the people. As people evolve, they can undertake changes to the organizational system in more conscious ways to fully realize the possible benefits of Evolutionary ways of working.

Ninety percent of what happens with people is a function of the system. However, it is important to note that the system is not just the structures—it's the culture too! In fact, the organizational culture will dominate what happens with people. And culture is a dynamic, moment-to-moment creation of everyone—especially influenced by leadership.

 PRINCIPLE: ORGANIZATIONAL EVOLUTION FOLLOWS PERSONAL EVOLUTION

The rate of evolution of an organization is limited by the rate of evolution of the people in the organization. We will have an adaptable, learning organization to the extent that the people in the organization are adaptable and learning.

Consider figure 12.8. The operating characteristics of our current organizational system are shown as a straight triangle. The way our organization functions is a reflection of all the behaviors of the people, which is shown as smaller triangle people.

We are exploring the notion of evolving to an organizational system that has fundamentally different operating characteristics, which is shown as a wavy line triangle. For our organization to function in a completely new way, we will need to have new behaviors from people at all levels of the organization, which is shown as wavy triangle people (Sahota 2016).

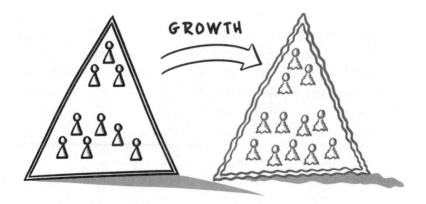

Figure 12.8: Organizational Evolution Follows Personal Evolution

Q: Who needs to evolve and grow for our organization to develop a high-performance culture?

A: Everyone.

Your people are your most important assets. Leaders need to grow. Managers need to grow. Staff need to grow. A similar observation linking the evolution of people to organizational evolution is reported in *Peak:* "Corporate transformation follows personal transformation" (Conley 2007, 85). Schein also identifies the necessity of personal evolution as a key element of organizational evolution: "Culture change inevitably involves unlearning as well as relearning and is, therefore, by definition, transformative" (Schein 2010, 315).

EVOLVE PEOPLE TO EVOLVE THE ORGANIZATION

What is the shift that people need to undertake for there to be an evolution in the culture of the organization? It's a shift in consciousness and practices touching on the mindset, identity, values, beliefs, and behaviors of each person. As people evolve, so will the organization.

Traditional	Evolutionary
Theory X (unmotivated, unambitious, and avoiding responsibility)	Theory Y (interested, ambitious, motivated, and seeking responsibility)
Fixed mindset	Growth/Evolutionary mindset
Lower consciousness	Higher consciousness

What determines how a person shows up? Is it the environment that rules over them, or is it their individual nature? Is it nature or nurture? This is an age-old philosophical debate that has led to generations of debate. Some understanding of the answer to this conundrum is needed to enact evolution of our organizational system.

Here we share our practical resolution in two parts:

1. The impact of the environment on the individual
2. The ability of the individual's intrinsic behaviors to overcome the environment

Figure 12.9: SELF Evolutionary Culture Model

IMPACT OF THE ENVIRONMENT ON PEOPLE

Take a moment to consider the impact of the cultural environment on how people act. As a reminder, we include the model showing the various stages of evolution. A Traditional environment will encourage Traditional behaviors. In contrast, an Evolutionary environment will foster Evolutionary behaviors.

Here we can see the following relationships:

- Traditional cultures foster and encourage Theory X behavior.
- Evolutionary cultures foster and encourage Theory Y behavior.

So the way to foster and encourage people to show up more as Theory Y is to shift the organization toward a healthier organizational culture. As the whole environment improves, it will support and foster the evolution of the people in the organization.

Most people want to be successful. Most people want to achieve and create. Most people want to grow. The challenge is that most people have been deeply conditioned since birth to show up with aspects of Theory X—unmotivated, unambitious, and avoiding responsibility. The work for leaders is to reduce environmental elements that suppress people and model healthier behaviors.

LEADERS OR BYSTANDERS?

As we have seen above, the environment may foster and support the development of a certain behavior. What about the individual? May their intrinsic characteristics dominate and enable them to overcome the environment? We will examine this in two ways.

First, have you ever seen someone who was able to show up as Theory Y (motivated, ambitious, etc.) even in a Traditional culture system? Many people reading the book will say, "Yes, me!" We all know someone who was able to act in inspiring ways despite the overall challenge of business-as-usual environments. This is what we call leadership.

Now consider the converse: Have you ever seen someone show up as Theory X (unmotivated, unambitious, etc.) even in a very healthy supportive environment? Perhaps an Evolutionary environment? Perhaps where they were given the freedom to be on a self-organizing team?

Consider the challenge faced by long-term prisoners in jail. When they are finally released, they do not know how to function in the world. They have been so deeply conditioned that they are unable to handle freedom and responsibility.

In our organizational systems, we face the same challenge: people who have been so deeply conditioned that they continue to show up as Theory X even when the environmental context becomes more supportive of a new way of functioning. The work of evolving culture is to evolve the people.

The core of the work of evolving the culture and ultimately the performance of an organization entirely rests with the development of people.

Evolution can and must follow those who have evolved first. Those who can rise above the downward pull of the organizational culture. As they evolve, they can then guide others on the journey. This is Evolutionary Leadership.

- What success have you seen with structural changes to the organization?
- How ready are people in your organization to evolve?
- How possible do you think it is for people to evolve under the right conditions?

You can't change anyone else, you can only change yourself.

—Anonymous

PATTERN 12.6: FROM LEADERSHIP SUPPORT TO LEADERSHIP LEADERSHIP

KEY POINTS

- Leadership support is useful for tactical and strategic change, but it is of little value with culture change.
- Culture change is not delegatable.
- Organizational evolution follows leadership evolution.
- The rate of evolution of an organization is limited by the rate of evolution of the leadership.
- Leaders either evolve, exit, or block growth.
- Leaders that model new behaviors act as powerful attractors for others.
- Values are best used for leadership growth, not for telling others how to behave.

LEADERSHIP SUPPORT

In traditional organizations, a key factor for a successful change program is leadership support or leadership buy-in.

It's true: leadership support is necessary and sufficient for making tactical and strategic changes to an organizational system.

Support is, however, completely insufficient for shifting the culture of an organizational system. Shifting culture involves the evolution of the people in the organization, including the leaders themselves. This kind of shift requires much more than support: it requires an internal choice to evolve.

In the pattern "Culture Follows Leadership," the connection between the leader's behavior and the culture of an organization was clearly established. The consequence is that a change in culture can only come through a change in leadership behaviors.

At the same time, culture is a local phenomenon, so there is an important exception to this rule. When a leader grants part of an organization full or high autonomy, then support may be sufficient for local evolution.

LEADERS LEFT BEHIND

One of the great tragedies of the modern business age is that leaders are either neglected or they receive inadequate support for their evolution. Most organizational transformation programs often target the work and workers. For example, Digital, Agile, and Lean are all very much focused on the value stream of creating working products. Leaders are at best a secondary consideration and do not usually get the support they need to evolve their consciousness and model new behaviors.

The 2019 Deloitte Global Human Capital Trends Survey reports that 80 percent of organizations see leadership as a top issue. Even more interesting is the report that "research shows that while organizations expect new leadership capabilities, they are still largely promoting traditional models and mindsets" (Deloitte 2019).

 LEADERSHIP LEADERSHIP

To create the culture shift required for high performance, what is required is *leadership leadership*—leaders who model and lead to a new way of being and working. As

leaders grow to model the characteristics of high-performance leaders, then they will be better able to support the evolution of people
around them and the organizational environment. Thus, a shift in
organizational culture requires a shift in leadership behaviors that
require much more effort than just "support" or "buy-in."

CULTURE CHANGE INVOLVES EVERYONE

The pattern "Evolving People" introduced the principle: organizational evolution follows personal evolution. What does this mean
in practice?

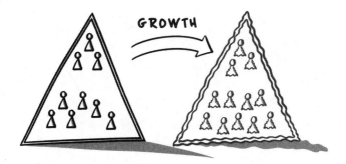

Imagine your organization is in some initial state where performance is not as desirable as one might prefer. The operational performance is not desirable: too slow, not responsive, disengaged
workers, and so on. The operational characteristics are a reflection
of all the people in the organization—including the leadership. This
is shown in the diagram as a triangle with dark straight lines.

Imagine for a moment that the leadership wishes to move to a
higher-performing culture where the organization has very different
operating characteristics: more responsive, effective, faster, and so on.
In this case, there are new behaviors throughout the organization—
including the leadership. This is illustrated by the triangle on the right
with wavy lines. The lines are wavy to show the movement from a
rigid organization to an adaptable and fluid one.

MODEL: THE LEADERSHIP CHOICE

It is helpful to use scenario analysis to see what is possible for a given organizational system. Because change

Figure 12.10: The Leadership Choice to Evolve

is local in nature, the example could be for a team, a group, a division, or the entire organization.

There are only three possible scenarios when considering the role of leaders in culture change in an organization. These are depicted in figure 12.10.

- *Scenario 1: The leaders evolve*—The leaders evolve to model an evolved organization (grow).
- *Scenario 2: The leaders exit*—The leaders leave the organization, and new leaders come in who have the desired consciousness to model the future organization (go).
- *Scenario 3: The leaders say "no"*—The leaders realize that culture change requires significant effort on their part and say *no* to cultural evolution and thereby decide that the status quo is acceptable (no).

It is 100 percent up to the leadership of an organization to decide what path they choose for themselves and the organization.

Scenario 1: The leaders evolve—This book is written to give leaders who want to grow, the tools and techniques to model an evolved organizational mindset or consciousness. The SELF is the key that unlocks successful outcomes.

Scenario 2: The leaders exit—It is common for founders of start-ups to step aside as CEO and give the role to someone more capable of growing the organization at a larger scale.

A famous case study from Lean for replacing leadership is that of NUMMI, where Toyota helped GM turn around the worst GM plant in the world. The Fremont, California, plant had alcoholism, wildcat strikes, absenteeism, and drug abuse. In the change program, they kept all the workers but brought in management who had the right mindset from GM, Toyota, and general industry. It took less than one year to become the best GM plant in the world. This illustrates the profound impact leadership has on organizational culture and performance.

Scenario 3: The leaders say "no"—Leadership has the full authority and power to decide what they want to do with the organizational system. It is common for normal people to want the benefits but not be willing to put in the needed effort. It all depends on how strong the desire for growth is. We will explore this in the next chapter.

PRINCIPLE: ORGANIZATIONAL EVOLUTION FOLLOWS LEADERSHIP EVOLUTION

As can be understood by the Leadership Choice model, a shift in the culture of the organization depends entirely on a shift in the leadership. The only way for all the people in an organization to evolve is for leaders to evolve first. Leadership evolution is not only necessary, it is the key to the evolution of the people and hence the whole system. To map it out:

Leadership evolution → people evolution →
organizational evolution

Leaders who evolve themselves can in turn evolve the organization. Organizational culture is a reflection of leadership. As such, we can now see the essential role played by leadership in organizational evolution: organizational evolution follows leadership evolution.

Leadership Leadership

Success comes from leaders who lead. Organizations are best served by leadership teams that demonstrate leadership: leadership leadership. It seems a bit silly to have to use a term like *leadership leadership*. However, the norm in business is leadership teams that do not exhibit leadership.

Leaders Act as Attractors

Our insight is that a leader's behavior can act as an attractor or detractor.

When a leader goes first to model the desired behavior, they act as an attractor for everyone they are in contact with. The default conditioning we have as human beings is to conform to the behavior of others.

When people see leaders modeling new behaviors, automatic conditioning kicks in, and people unconsciously start copying the behavior. This is how to use a hierarchy to safely accelerate culture change—through the indirect use of power.

From a complex system dynamics view, it is helpful to create attractors that invite the future shape of an organization (Snowden 2020).

Evolving Leadership Teams

The fastest way to evolve an organizational system is when an entire leadership team goes on the journey of evolution together. In this situation, they are able to uplift and support one another as they grow. Peer support and peer pressure are accelerators for growth.

When an entire leadership team goes together on a journey to shift their consciousness to model a new way of being and working, there is a massive impact on the evolution rate of the organization.

Figure 12.11: Leaders Go First

 MODEL: LEADERS GO FIRST

Imagine for a moment the scenario where a leadership team chooses to evolve themselves so they can model the future culture of the organization. This evolution of leaders and the organization is illustrated in figure 12.11. Such leaders show people very directly that they are committed to their own personal growth and evolution. They not only show that change is possible, they also inspire people to evolve themselves. Further, when the leaders evolve, they create an environment that supports the evolution of the rest of the people in the organization so that over time the whole organization moves to a new way of being and working.

Culture Change Is Not Delegatable

It is quite common in a traditional organization or from a business-as-usual strategy that culture change is delegated by leadership to a transformation team or to human resources. This of course does not work, since the culture is a reflection of the behaviors of leadership, and they are the only ones capable of regulating their own behavior. A similar observation is made by Connors and Smith in *Change the Culture, Change the Game* (2011): "Culture change must be led. It cannot be delegated to . . . anyone else" (155).

The insight that culture change requires leaders who lead stands in stark contrast with the billions of dollars spent each year by organizations on transformation programs where there is leadership support.

Our quote "leaders go first" has taken on a life of its own, and the term *leadership leadership* can be misinterpreted as advocating a top-down change in the organization. It is actually quite the opposite. Change is possible at all levels of the organization. Every manager and every individual has the capacity to influence their part of the organization. Leaders at all levels will evolve the culture quickly to create the high performance organizations seek and desire. There is no excuse or need to wait just for top leadership to change. Each of us may take action. Specific guidance on application of local culture evolution will be explored more in the Local Evolution pattern.

> *Leadership is possible at all levels of an organization.*
> *It does not require authority, permission, or a budget.*

The Rate of Organizational Evolution Is Limited by the Rate of Leadership Evolution

Ultimately, the rate of organizational evolution is limited by the rate of leadership evolution. Faster growth of leaders means faster growth of the organization. The best way to accelerate the evolution of the organization is to accelerate the evolution of those who hold leadership positions.

Little or no growth of leadership means little or no growth of the culture. Of course, there may be tactical and strategic changes that yield benefit; however, this is not an evolution of the very fabric of the organization—its culture.

Train and Mentor Leaders First

Leaders need much more support than typical leadership programs or isolated executive coaching. While these are helpful, it is important for leaders to have a real shift in consciousness. Leaders require the capability to not only operate in line with high-performance culture, they require the capability to evolve an organizational system.

A small example of this is the need to have an evolved understanding of the integrated relationship of culture, leadership, and organizational evolution. Without a shift in their mindset and behaviors to align with healthy ways of working, a change in culture is simply not possible.

In our own work with organizations, leaders receive both evolutionary training and on-the-job integration support. Leadership development needs a new paradigm to support an evolution within an organization, a way of being to evolve self, others, and systems. An evolution at an organizational level is experienced through a powerful shift in consciousness that is applicable and grounded in a new worldview, practices, and behaviors. To overcome muscle memory and conditioned behavior, practical guidance, coaching, and mentoring is needed to fully integrate a shift in consciousness.

YOUR TURN

- In what ways does your leadership team function like a true team (trust, safety, collaboration, connection, respect, etc.) to model evolved behavior?
- For each of the three scenarios (evolve, exit, no change), what percentage of leaders are in each of the categories?
- Where do you see leadership acting like leaders? Where do they not?
- What is the rate of evolution of consciousness of the leaders in your organization?

People don't resist change; they resist being changed.
—Peter Senge

PATTERN 12.7: FROM RESISTANCE TO INVITATION

KEY POINTS

- If you are encountering resistance, you are trying to change people.
- Red-list words and behaviors (*make, drive, tell*, etc.) demotivate people.

- Due to our conditioned behaviors, people unconsciously become agents of oppression.
- Green-list words and behaviors (*pull, inspire, invite*, etc.) foster desire and motivation by treating people with respect.
- The work of leadership is to shift our being and behaviors to operate from a more evolved state.

RESISTANCE

Have you ever experienced people who resisted change? Perhaps people who did not support making changes for the better? People who were not onboard with organizational decisions?

The challenge with traditional organizations is that they make decisions without consulting with the people impacted by those decisions. Then they create communication and rollout plans in hopes of convincing and making people do things that they may not see as valuable or are at odds with other goals. This is a guaranteed killer of the desire needed to create real change.

MODEL: RED LIST = HOW TO CREATE RESISTANCE

It turns out that most normal people are experts at creating resistance. The Red List, illustrated in figure 12.12, is a list of behaviors that leaders use to foster resistance. It is a key part of the business-as-usual lexicon.

- push
- make
- drive
- tell
- sell
- convince
- mandate

Take a moment to read through the list. Consider for a moment the impact on people when a leader uses a Red List word. What happens is that people start to shut down, feel unsafe, or feel like they are not valued. When people are made to do some-

Figure 12.12: Red List = How to Create Resistance

thing, their level of psychological safety falls, and along with it, their intelligence.

All use of the Red List develops resistance. Of course, the resistance is hidden—it wouldn't be safe for people to show objection. However, the damage is visible after the fact through low delivery and performance results, low engagement scores, workers showing up as Theory X, and failed change programs.

The Red List is illustrative—there are many other words that describe coercive behavior. The Red List helps one easily spot the damaging behaviors or traditional organizational systems: command and control, oppression, or excessive use of power to drive performance.

Red List = Normal

If you think that using the Red List is a normal part of work or your personal life, you are likely correct. Traditional business of command and control is prevalent all around you, and it is usually unseen. Most people are totally unaware of the damage that is causing you to show up as less than your fullest potential or the damage you are causing to others around you. The behavior and intentions behind the Red List are subtle—we are so conditioned, we do not know any other way to get people to perform. The way we relate to others or situations on a moment-to-moment basis is steeped in Red List behavior.

Please remember, it's not anyone's fault. Most people have had the Red List modeled for them since birth. Think of the first moment the Red List is modeled in people's lives. Most people have had the Red List modeled again and again by parents, by the education system, and by workplaces. People have been deeply conditioned to think the Red List is normal behavior or the normal way of management.

When leaders collectively act with normal Red List behavior, they create a traditional organizational culture. Leaders, collectively through behaviors, create the low levels of performance associated with business as usual. We attempt to change people and the organization and inadvertently create resistance.

THE OPPRESSED BECOME THE OPPRESSORS

Standard psychological responses and subconscious behavior patterns show us that those who have been oppressed are in turn oppressing others. Traditional business management structures, processes, and standard ways of conducting business are saturated in Red List behaviors. The challenge faced by leaders today is that they inadvertently use power in ways that suppress people.

> The oppressed, instead of striving for liberation, tend
> themselves to become oppressors.
>
> —Paulo Freire

As human beings, people are wounded through the environmental situations they have experienced since birth. There is a saying: "Hurt people, hurt people." When people are hurting, they hurt others. It's human nature. It's the fundamental nature of the egoic consciousness to be hurt and consequently create more hurt and damage. It is usually not intentional but rather an automatic conditioned behavior driven by buried emotional wounds.

THE DEATH OF DESIRE

Through counterproductive leadership behaviors, people are oppressed and thus Theory X (unmotivated and unambitious) behaviors are cultivated. This is how leadership suppresses the desire for personal and organizational evolution. Disengagement in staff can ultimately be traced back to leadership behaviors.

We find that most people struggle with unconscious patterns of resistance to authority. Even experiencing a normal childhood can bring up damaging subconscious patterning within all of us, regardless of the amount of personal growth work or focus on shifting behaviors. You may say that resistance to authority and subtle oppression is an inherent virus within our human psyche. And the damage this creates within any organizational system can be profound.

The true nature of humanity is to perfect itself, to be successful, to feel good about self and others. We unintentionally create subtle forms of damage that strip the human condition of all the desire it has to create, to have joy, and to have meaning in life.

INVITATION

We use the word *invitation* to capture the spirit of a more evolved way of working that builds desire, motivation, and passion. With an evolved mindset, it's not about eliminating resistance, it's all about how to avoid creating any. When leaders stop pushing and creating resistance, there will not be any resistance, and changes will happen very quickly. This type of leadership is how to create an adaptable organization that can surf the waves of change. Let's look at how to get there.

MODEL: GREEN LIST = LEADING THROUGH INFLUENCE

While the Red List words disengage people, the Green List words unlock people and foster motivation. The power of a leader to attract and inspire others through the Green List is illustrated in figure 12.13.

- pull
- inspire
- want to
- invite
- cocreate
- optional
- listen

Figure 12.13: Green List = Leading through Influence

When we use the Green List, we are operating from an evolved consciousness to lead through influence. We come from the understanding that people are sovereign beings with free will—not machine parts or chess pieces that are there to do our bidding.

As leaders truly begin to share power, the use of the Red List decreases. To lead through influence, it is important to treat people like volunteers. When leaders have this understanding integrated into their being, they automatically shift from the Red List to the Green List because it will create the outcome they desire. Leaders realize that power and authority expressed through the Red List has little or no effect on volunteers.

The good news is that with every step leaders take toward dropping the Red List words, they are on their way to creating a higher-performance culture. It is not, however, just about changing the words.

IT'S THE INTENTION, THE ENERGY, NOT JUST THE WORDS

A watermelon is a fruit that is green on the outside and red on the inside. You probably have heard someone use Green List words but in a Red List way. They may have said something was optional, yet you could tell it wasn't really optional. Inauthentic leaders use Green List words, but they have the intention of Red List on the inside. This dissolves the levels of trust and creates damage in relationships.

It's not about the words—it's about the intention, the mindset, and the level of consciousness that it comes from. We all have built-in detectors for sensing threat in our environments that can tell us what kind of energy is coming at us.

You can't fake it.

The simple advice is to be honest and authentic about your inner state. Do not tell people something is optional if it really isn't. It's better to say it like it is. Then comes the real work of how to shift your inner state as a leader—a leader who is authentic, influential, and inspires others to show up high performing at their fullest potential. There is no way to candy-coat the way to more evolved leadership.

 PRINCIPLE: ALL RESISTANCE IS CREATED BY YOU
Most readers at this point will realize that they are the problem and not someone else. We are the ones operating in a Red List way—pushing, killing motivation, and blocking the evolution of the organization. As this information can be challenging, now might be a good time to review the patterns in chapter 7, "Unlearning Reality," and especially how to keep two opposed ideas in mind at the same time.

If you are encountering resistance, it means that you are trying to change people.

The bad news is that you are the problem. The good news is that you are the problem. And even better news is that once you realize you are the problem, you can be the solution.

You Are the Problem and You Are the Solution

If you hope to lead and evolve organizations toward high performance, an early and essential step is to reduce or eliminate the diet of Red List language. Every time a leader uses the Red List words or has the subtle intention of Red List behavior, they are fostering a traditional organization with limited performance.

Invitation is a code word for the set of words and behaviors that fully value and respect people. Here we explore the words and related behaviors that invite the emergence of Theory Y behaviors (*motivated* and *ambitious*) and other characteristics of high performance. Invitation is a key practice for leaders to learn to navigate the patterns shared in chapter 11, "The Paradox of Power."

Focus on Eliminating Red List Behaviors

To be very clear, we are not inviting leaders to cultivate Green List words and start using them. This is a trap. Instead, we are inviting leaders to do the hard critical work of leadership: being aware of damaging behavior to accelerate their own personal evolution.

We are inviting leaders to reduce or eliminate their diet of Red List words. From psychology, we know that one negative activity requires five to ten positive activities to balance it out. So the greatest impact leaders can have right now on their performance is not to sprinkle in some Green List but to eliminate the Red List thinking, intentions, and behaviors from their way of being. This will greatly improve relationships and have an extraordinary impact on their ability to effect change with the people around them.

Experience Report

"My biggest disappointment, aha moment, was the Red List and Green List, where I saw these things and I said, 'Why am I the red person? Why would I do all these red things? Why didn't anyone tell me that these things are bad?' And then I think the biggest aha moment in a good way was that I am the solution to the problems that I'm causing. I am causing the problems, but I can also solve them. And that's helped me see things also from a different perspective. When a challenge comes, when a conflict comes, or when I start seeing that, why did that leader say that or why is he responding to me like that? Okay, let's revisit. Why did this happen? What was my approach on that? Maybe I should go now and say, 'Hey, sorry, Mr. X, can we please talk about that? I think we might have a different perception about what we just discussed. Can you please share again your thoughts and maybe I can share mine?'" (C. Tsonis, personal interview, December 2020).

YOUR TURN

- Where are the places where you are encountering resistance? Would you characterize the situations as defined by more Red List or Green List words?
- Review each Red List word and notice how you feel when your boss or someone with authority over you uses each word.
- Close your eyes and notice the physical sensations when you think about someone using Red List words. Now do the same for the Green List words.
- Where are the places in your life (work, home, etc.) where you tend to use the Red List words?

If you want to go quickly, go alone. If you want to go far, go together.
—African Proverb

PATTERN 12.8: FROM MANDATE TO INSPIRATION

KEY POINTS

- Mandating change kills motivation and desire, which is a key to creating a successful change program.
- Go with the energy: focus effort on those who desire growth.
- Set up the environment so there is time for growth and learning.
- Have patience with those who are not ready yet. Support their choice and safety, and over time they will join when they are ready.

- To support the energy for change, authority and power may be used to energize the system to get it cooking.

- Create attractors to encourage helpful behaviors, and remove unhelpful attractors that foster regressive behaviors.

- People who repeatedly choose not to participate must be exited to prevent the evolution of the system from stalling.

MANDATE

The typical approach to change is to mandate a transformation program. Typically a small transformation team will create a program, and top leadership then mandates that everyone must follow it. It is not optional. People are not asked if they agree with the program. Nor are they asked how the program can be changed to make it more effective for their group or for the organization.

There is usually resistance to the change program before it is officially launched. Good managers do their best to comply while protecting their people so real work can be done. Everyone knows that the program will fail (like all the preceding programs) and that things will go more or less back to a new normal until the next change program is announced.

Mandating a change is usually very well intentioned. However, it falls into the trap of thinking of the organization as a machine. People's best interests, and ultimately the best interests of the organization, are ignored. Mandate is the birthplace of disengagement when engagement and desire are the very things needed to create a successful change.

From a traditional organization mindset perspective, it seems baffling: How can any change be achieved without using power?

INSPIRATION

The alternative is to create an inspired change program through a deep understanding of the paradox of power. Can you imagine how effective and successful a change program would be if people were excited and interested? How might an inspired change program be created?

The purpose of this pattern is to explain step by step what it means to operate from a more evolved leadership perspective where we lead through influence. The starting place is to treat people in our organization as adults that can and will make up their own minds. By assuming an Evolutionary mindset, we can achieve Evolutionary results.

MODEL: ORGANIZATIONAL READINESS MODEL

Imagine for a moment that you want to cocreate a high-performance organization with others who share a similar passion and desire. When you consider the readiness of other people in the organization, you will notice that they fall into roughly three distinct groups. These are illustrated in figure 12.14.

1. *Early Adopters*—Some percentage are interested in growing and making change now.
2. *Wait and See*—Some percentage will come on the journey once they are ready, have validated results, and the way is clear.
3. *The Challenged*—These are the resistors. Some percentage are really not sure if this is the right thing for them. Maybe not now and perhaps never.

We can understand this model as an analog of the technology adoption curve (Moore 2002). While this model is very well known

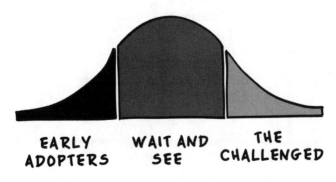

EARLY
ADOPTERS

WAIT AND
SEE

THE
CHALLENGED

Figure 12.14: Organizational Readiness Model

for product adoption, it has not until now been fully defined and explained for organizational change. What we offer here is an evolved perspective—one that places human freedom and desire at the center of lasting change.

The main difference from a theoretical model is that what percentage of the people with the organization are at different stages will depend on *your unique situation*—it likely won't follow nice statistical boundaries. In one context, the early adopters could number 50 percent, while in another context this might be as few as 10 percent. In either case, progress is possible since there are some who are willing.

A simple way to use this model is to consider the people involved: Where are they in terms of their readiness?

 PRINCIPLE: GO WITH THE ENERGY
Invariably, change initiatives have limited staff, budget, attention of senior management, and so on. The results from investing in each of the different groups will have very different outcomes.

Table 12.1 is a simple way to help understand the outcome with each group. It is best to invest that capacity into those who want to make change now. The return on investment of the early adopters far exceeds the other groups. It's a smart investment strategy to create the most rapid change possible.

START WITH EARLY ADOPTERS

What will happen if we "go with the energy"? All of our effort and attention will be on helping the Early Adopters become successful.

Table 12.1: ROI for Investing in People

Group	Outcome of Investment
Early Adopters	Positive
Wait and See	Neutral
The Challenged (Resistors)	Negative

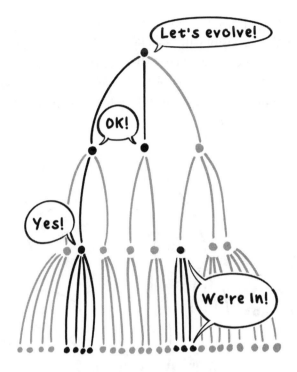

Figure 12.15: Start with Early Adopters

We will spend minimal time and energy on people who are not yet ready to change. Figure 12.15 depicts how we may listen for where the energy is and focus attention on evolving those parts of the organization.

Imagine this: The early adopters will become more successful. They will get better results. They will enjoy coming to work more. They will be happier.

The agents of change who are responsible for evolving the organization will also be more effective and happier. They will now only spend their time with people who want help instead of pushing and creating resistance.

Wait for the Wait-and-See Group

When people in the Wait-and-See group see that they have a voice in the change, they will feel respected. Their level of psychological safety will go up because no one is forcing them to change. Their openness and curiosity will grow little by little, and their resistance will become more quiet. They will notice the achievements and satisfaction of the early adopters and will likely start to have envy. They will ask, "What about us?" This is the pull signal indicating that they are ready to start the journey.

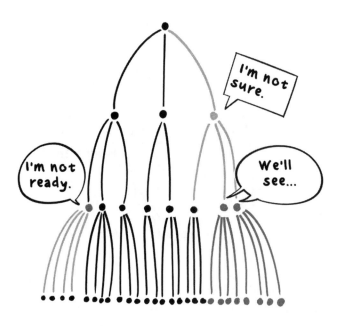

The secret is to wait for the pull signal that indicates the spark of their desire to grow.

Among the chief traps are making this group feel like they are less important than the early adopters. This is usually done by highlighting the "great work" done by the others. Anything that smells of a communication strategy or evangelism of the change will lead to increased resistance.

Give people time to choose, to have validation of real change happening. Spend this time with the upgrade to the environment so that saying yes to changes becomes easier. Below we explain in practical detail how to give people time to shift their perspectives and ways of working. We will also explain how to work on the environment and how to increase the rate of evolution to what people can handle.

MODEL: ORGANIZATIONAL TEMPERATURE

Our job as organization evolution chefs is to get the system "cooking" (Pelrine 2009). This means applying the right amount of heat (power/direction). Too little heat and the soup will be cold. Too much heat and the soup will burn. It takes time in a cooking state to make good soup.

Here we highlight the tension within the paradox of power and provide guidance for sensing how to adjust power usage.

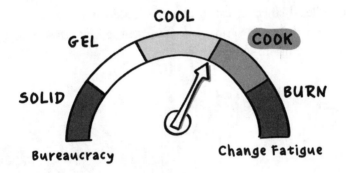

Principle: Get the System Cooking

Many change programs suffer from too much heat. There is too much change all at once. The result is burning, not cooking. In this situation, to get things cooking one will have to drop the temperature. For example, have people decide what changes are most important and focus on those. Drop the rest. It's better to do three things well than ten things badly.

Some systems are in a solid state. Often people have been in their jobs for 10 or more years, and personal growth (evolving their behaviors) has never been a job requirement. It's a delicate situation. People may genuinely believe that they can continue working as they are today and everything will be totally OK. For these people, they are not cooking—they are at the level of solid or gel. What is required to get to cooking is more heat. This might come in the form of new performance requirements, so people become aware that what was OK before is not OK any longer.

It's important to turn up the heat slowly. If too much heat is applied too early, the system will start burning. Most traditional organizations have the worst of both worlds. On the one hand, they are solid and, at the same time, there is so much heat that they are burning, too! No wonder people are so disengaged.

Tool: Amplify Helpful Attractors
There is a powerful understanding of the new way of working to deal with a complex organization system that Michael learned firsthand from David Snowden at a private Agile Alliance retreat in 2014. As leaders in a system, our work is to shape the organizational environment so that it is supportive of people's evolution.

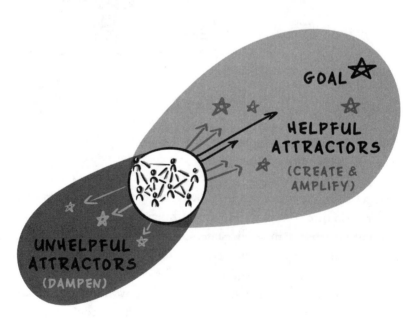

Figure 12.16: Amplify Helpful Attractors

As shown in figure 12.16, one way to energize people is to create helpful attractors that encourage people to shift toward our star on the horizon. As such, we may create intermediate goals to encourage the journey and foster helpful behaviors. This would be an example of how to add heat to a system to get it cooking.

An attractor can be anything. For example, the most powerful attractors that we have seen in our training and consulting work are through behaviors of the leaders. While leader behavior pretty much trumps everything else, it is helpful to have models and principles that remind people of what they have chosen to create. Keeping reminders of some SELF principles such as "employees first" or "listen first, speak last" visible or in mind during the day support the awareness needed to make different choices.

Tool: Dampen Unhelpful Attractors
The other key activity is to reduce, dampen, or eliminate unhelpful attractors—the organizational structures that keep people stuck in the status quo. These might be existing systems that demotivate people or encourage unhelpful behaviors. Attractors that create damage are very important to remove outright, or use the SELF adapter tool from Culture Bubbles to mitigate.

In most traditional organizations, employee performance management is a very damaging attractor that typically introduces all sorts of distortions to a system that limits healthy growth. Other unhelpful attractors include status reports that focus on outcome and timeline but do not include the health of the teams and people involved.

We advocate an approach to apply listening to the system to investigate what can be removed and modified to what is appropriate within the organization. A rule of thumb is that each organization is a complex system and has its own unique DNA. To create and remove attractors is done with care and respect to the people and the organization. We promote a conscious way of doing, where impact is taken into account and all points are considered.

PRINCIPLE: MAKE TIME FOR GROWTH

Most people are open to learning and growth—at their own pace. In evolutionary organizations, improving how things work is part of everyone's job.

Create a work environment where people have space and time to improve how the organization is functioning. Long-term gains in performance come from many small improvements, not big dramatic changes. It's not rocket science: making things better requires some investment of time. This was highlighted with the principle Invest in Production Capability from pattern 12.2, "From Strategic Plans to Evolving Culture." For there to be learning and growth, there needs to be time for learning and growth.

On-site with a client, when talking about time for learning and connecting as a team, someone realized the organization did not have a timecode for learning. It was not recognized as a valid activity, nor was it valued or budgeted. Once they added in the timecode and people realized that learning was encouraged, the whole system started to shift.

COMPASSION FOR THE "CHALLENGED/RESISTORS"

Often those who are not ready or interested are labeled "resistors" or "laggards." It is normal and natural that some people will not be interested in or will be hesitant to change. They are best treated with empathy, compassion, and patience. These individuals are either usually challenged for one of three reasons. They are:

1. Deeply conditioned so that they are only comfortable with a slow rate of growth.
2. Unable to see any personal gain out of growth or change.
3. Unable or less able to change—some might not know it's possible or how to change.

It's not that there's anything wrong with the resistors, it's just that they are experiencing organizational reality from their unique perspectives. They might just want to see results or validation that change will really happen.

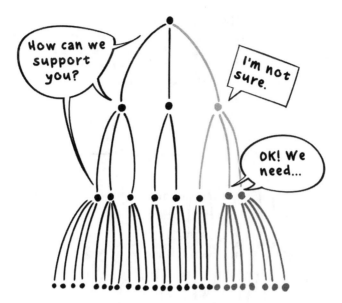

The main focus early on is to make it safe for such people to re-duce the chances they will block or undermine those who want to grow and evolve.

The best advice has already been shared—leave the challenged few until later on. Focus energy on those who want to create a shift, start-ing with the early adopters and then shifting to the wait-and-see group. Once a large group of people makes a shift, it will become increasingly easier for the remainder to do so. No one gets left behind. Also, as the majority begins to shift, it will be possible to make the environment much more supportive of those who are in this group to grow. This will address all three potential reasons keeping people stuck.

PRINCIPLE: EXIT STAFF TO SUPPORT A HEALTHY ENVIRONMENT

As an Evolutionary Leader, we understand both the human and financial costs of people who over time re-main part of the challenged few. The needs of the many outweigh the needs of the few. To create a healthy environment for everyone else, it is sometimes necessary to exit someone.

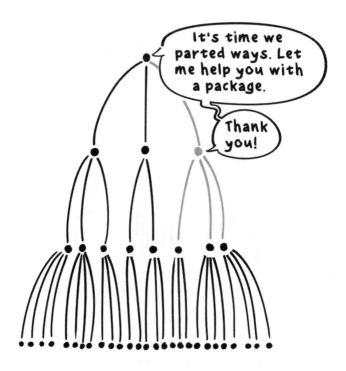

Where there is hope of change, we work through the first three karmas: Peace, Enrich, and Energize (from the tool the Four Karmas). Over time people will discover if they want to come on the journey or not. Out of kindness for them and for all others they work with, we may exit them outright or use a performance improvement program to give them a final chance to wake up to what they really want for themselves.

As indicated in our principle "organizational evolution follows personal evolution," a choice must be made between the health and evolution of the organization or to exit an individual. In our experience, this is one of the hardest decisions faced by managers.

Effective leaders create a high level of clarity of where the organization is going. In the book *Good to Great*, a key characteristic for successful evolution is to "get the right people on the bus" (Collins 2001, 13). Another powerful quote from this book is, "The first clean kill awakens the herd." Total clarity of what is happening supports people's psychological safety.

It is essential to exit leaders who do not want to go on the journey. Richardo Semler shares his powerful experience, "Within days of taking over, I fired outright two-thirds of my father's most senior managers. I then spent the next two decades questioning, challenging, and dismantling the traditional business practices at Semco" (Semler 2004, 9). Semler demonstrated a very high level of patience. He took action not out of impatience but out of the understanding that those leaders really did not want to change and that no amount of waiting would change the situation. In his case, exiting those leaders was the most caring and compassionate move for them as well as the people who reported to them.

For some, the move to exit people may come from a concern for helping people find an environment where they are happy. For others, it may be made purely on financial reasons.

Let's look at some traditional organizations and get the perspective of a hard-nosed businessman, John Paul Getty. He explains a key element of his very successful strategy for turning around dozens of businesses: "In my own companies, we have instituted the policy of 'early retirement' to rid ourselves of personnel dead-wood that has accumulated over the years—and which, inevitably, collects in almost any business firm. . . . True, the cost of retiring these people and of paying them pensions years before they were due to receive them is very high. But we have found that the cost is significantly less than the cost of keeping them on our payrolls, where they not only draw full pay, but cause more harm than good, producing losses instead of profits" (Getty 1986).

The reasons to create a high-performing organization are unique to each individual and organizational purpose, yet the path is the same. In pattern 12.5, "From Changing Structures to Evolving People," we follow the principle: organizational evolution follows personal evolution—the "grow," "go," or "no" scenario. We can guide and lead those who want to go on the journey of creating an incredible evolutionary organization, fulfill a desire to lead, impact change, and grow leaders around us, or we can say "no" and walk away from the dream of high performance and the evolutionary journey. Sometimes it is the difficult choices and experiences where we have the most growth.

Patience Accelerates Evolution

Success with this approach requires a shift in consciousness to see organizational evolution as a journey and find the desire that will pull you through difficult times. It is an ongoing daily activity— more like a marathon than a sprint. Success requires a key leadership characteristic: patience.

When leaders do not have patience, they will usually fall into the trap of using the Red List and exercising power that is not in the best interests of the people or the organization. This will create short-term compliance and only a thin veneer of success. The laws of organizational dynamics dictate that success and growth will only come through desire and willingness to change. Without these, there is no hope of creating a shift to high performance.

When we have patience and focus our attention on those who want to grow, what will happen over time is that team by team, leader by leader, group by group, we will see the evolution we hope for spread over the organization.

A clear and powerful example of patience is illustrated in this case study of the changes that took place with Favi—the only surviving auto parts manufacturer in Europe: "For a few months after taking over, Zobrist tried to engage his executive team in discussions to break down some of these mechanisms but met strong resistance. Nine months after he had taken on the full CEO role, on the last working day of the year, just before the Christmas break, he decided to change tactics. He assembled the entire workforce in a corner of the factory. Standing on top of a few boxes, he shared that the way people were controlled in the company felt disgraceful to him. After the holidays, there would be no more time clocks at the factory entrance. The variable pay system would be replaced with a fixed salary—no more pay deductions to try to control people. The supply room would be unlocked and everybody would be trusted to take out the supplies they needed and to log what they took out for reordering purposes. Finally, the managers' canteen would be closed; everybody would have lunch together" (Laloux 2014, 273).

The case study points to how a dramatic change may be useful and feasible only when all other means are exhausted. This is an example of the conscious use of power to create an environment that will unlock growth. The greater the patience, the more rapidly a permanent, lasting shift will take place.

YOUR TURN

- In your organization, what percentage of people fall into each of the parts of the organizational readiness model?
- Use the organizational temperature model to evaluate your environment. Where is the system solid? Where is there burning?
- What would change in your environment if compassion and patience was the foundation of how change is approached?

---

13 ■ Evolutionary Leadership

Evolutionary Leadership is the lynchpin of any real material change in organizations. To put it simply: there is no evolution without evolutionary leaders. Of course there may be various tactical and strategic improvements, but no change in the culture or DNA of the organization.

In part one of the book. we introduced Evolutionary Leadership as a new paradigm for understanding ourselves and approaching change in organizations. In this chapter, we dive into the key elements that entail what it takes to be an Evolutionary Leader. Equally as important, we highlight the traps of more traditional forms of leadership.

It is all too easy to dismiss revolutionary ideas with excuses such as being impractical or new age. The challenge is to let it all in and be open to the possibility that effective leadership and real change stem from a different place than we may have considered.

We recommend rereading chapter 3, "LEADING: The Evolution of Leadership," after you have completed this chapter.

At the end of the day people won't remember what you said or did,
they will remember how you made them feel.

—Maya Angelou

PATTERN 13.1: FROM MANAGING PEOPLE
TO VALUING PEOPLE

KEY POINTS

- The concept of managing easily falls into antipatterns such as oppression, fear, domination, and disengagement.
- It's hard for people to feel cared for and motivated in the face of business-as-usual activities.
- When you treat people well, they will perform better.
- Create an environment where people are consistently valued as human beings.
- The best leaders and organizations seek to help people find their own passion in work.
- Employee self-interest is the highest form of corporate alignment.

MANAGING

Organizational systems need a form of governance that allows them to function well. The creation of managers who manage people and the organization is one approach for producing effective governance. Let's consider what management is really about. "Management is the administration of an organization. . . . Management includes the activities of setting the strategy of an organization and coordinating the efforts of its employees (or volunteers) to accomplish its objectives through the application of available resources, such as financial, natural, technological, and human resources" (Wikipedia 2021c).

As an approach to governance, management is severely challenged, as it easily falls into the antipatterns outlined in this book, such as:

oppression, fear, control, domination, and disengagement. People are viewed as "resources" to be manipulated. We have decades of evidence that management as an approach is sufficient for basic levels of functioning. However, something beyond it is required for sustainability and high performance.

It is time to retire Traditional management as a primary approach to understanding and governing organizations. The key challenge of the whole concept is that it is tied to the direct use and ongoing application of authority. The focus on leadership as the primary organizing concept for an organization supports more rapid evolution.

As a reminder, *we are at no point suggesting dropping the hierarchy* as is thoroughly explored in From Eliminating Hierarchy to Increasing Freedom. Instead, we are speaking of coevolving both managers and workers in tandem, so the damaging effects of hierarchy and the primacy of the concept of management are migrated gracefully out of the system.

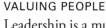 VALUING PEOPLE

Leadership is a much more effective governance principle than management. Our perspective is that what others might call "great management" are actually examples of effective leadership. In this book, the patterns outline how to iteratively and incrementally move from the paradigm of management to that of leadership. The focus of this pattern is the shift from seeing people as resources to fully valuing people.

 PRINCIPLE: WHEN YOU TREAT PEOPLE WELL, THEY WILL PERFORM BETTER

There appears to be a simplifying principle that summarizes the key insights from all leadership and culture models: when you treat people well, they perform better. Although, it's common sense, we find the opposite in traditional organizations. The reason is simple: we are so conditioned for command and control behavior, it's challenging to fully put this idea into practice.

Drucker's perspective is that "management is about Human Beings" (Drucker 2004, 47). In business as usual, we forget about the people and focus on projects, budgets, delivery, and due dates. To break this cycle, we treat people as knowledge workers: "Knowledge-worker productivity requires that the knowledge worker be both seen and treated as an *asset* rather than a cost" (157). Although Toyota pioneered this type of mindset within the manufacturing industry, it applies across all industries.

Perhaps we might think of our exploration in this book as a deep dive into "what the world's greatest managers do differently." We borrow this phrase from the subtitle of the book *First, Break All the Rules* that has world-class research on high-performance characteristics (Buckingham and Coffman 1999). In fact, the startling result from the research is that most performance is a function of the immediate manager, not the organization! The key lesson from this research and a major theme of this book is the simple truth that when you treat people well, they will perform better. Can it be that easy?

Value People as Human Beings

The essential leadership characteristic explored in this pattern is that of unconditionally valuing people as human beings. One can only create a caring supportive environment when one truly values people. Otherwise, other concerns will drive the agenda and inhibit the ability to create a supportive environment. Seeking to truly value people at all moments, in all decisions, is an evolutionary journey. The default and incorrect assumption due to cognitive bias is to assume one values people fully without taking the time to examine the totality of one's behavior.

Although it might seem obvious to value people as human beings, the truth of the matter is that most of us don't act this way 100 percent of the time. All of us have been deeply conditioned by the families we grew up in, society, and the educational system to operate, at times, in ways where we do not fully value people. For example, in those moments when we are annoyed, irritated, frustrated, afraid,

angry, or faced with deadlines and emergencies, we tend to lose all consideration for others, and the damage ensues.

John Paul Getty, a hard-nosed, no-nonsense businessman, observes, "In dealing with employees, it is essential that they be given recognition as human beings, as individuals" (Getty 1986, 82). He continues to explain, "If an executive is to achieve results through people, he must possess an element of compassion in his make-up, and must always bear in mind that every individual has his hopes, interests and fears" (83).

The Gallup 12 survey questions show what the world's greatest managers do differently. They create an environment where employees strongly agree with these statements:

- My supervisor, or someone at work, seems to care about me as a person.
- In the last seven days, I have received recognition or praise for doing good work.

From the perspective of the SELF Evolutionary Culture Model, we see that the highest levels of performance have people and wholeness as critical ingredients. To create an environment that operates at that level, leaders must demonstrate these behaviors. Not just some of the time. All the time.

PRINCIPLE: EMPLOYEE SELF-INTEREST IS THE HIGHEST
FORM OF CORPORATE ALIGNMENT

Imagine an environment filled with energized, motivated people. How readily will the mission of the organization move forward?

The biggest challenge here is the damage leaders do to reduce the passions and motivations of people. Many of the antipatterns in this book identify how managers inadvertently create havoc with people's motivations. So the most important activity is to stop causing damage. The concepts below are effective once the steady diet of demotivation ends. The rain needs to stop before you can start a campfire.

Deming speaks of the responsibility of a manager—what a manager's job actually is: "A manager of people understands that people are different from each other. He tries to create for everybody, interest and challenge, and joy in work" (Deming 1994, 125).

Semler (of Semco) takes a much deeper view of people in the workplace. He has a burning passion to create a workplace where people *actually want to come to work*. This mindset led to the extraordinary performance and growth at Semco. Semler explains his views: "I want people who are excited about their work. If they don't know how to create passion, I want to help" (Semler 2004, 48).

At Semco, the organization goes to extraordinary lengths to make sure people are doing what they want to do. This is similar to Valve, where people choose what projects they want to work on. To be clear, this concept goes well beyond business-as-usual concepts of motivating employees—we are speaking of something radically different.

Semler explains the Semco way to understand this concept: "Employees must be reassured that self-interest is their foremost priority, one they must take care not to replace with company or other interests. We advocate that out of corporate self-interest—an employee who puts himself first will be motivated to perform. At Semco, this is considered a form of corporate alignment" (Semler 2004, 48).

MODEL: EMPLOYEE MOTIVATION

High performance happens when people's individual self-interests are aligned with organizational self-interest (or goals). The usual approach of telling people what to do does not work as intended and instead creates oppression. As such, a different approach is needed.

Everyone has an ego. The secret is to leverage the ego for the benefit of everyone. There is a famous saying: "If you can't fix it, feature it." That's how to feature the ego.

Figure 13.1 illustrates the key elements of the Employee Motivation Model. For all people in an organization, leaders seek to help them discover the intersection of:

1. What they love
2. What they are reasonably good at
3. What adds value to the organization

The magic happens when we work together to find out how we can each spend the most time possible in our most productive and engaged place. Then we will be the most productive organization possible.

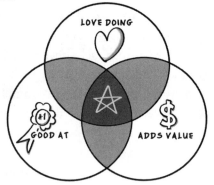

Figure 13.1: Employee Motivation Model

This concept can be understood as a simplified version of ikigai (García and Miralles 2017). The twist is that we shift perspective to that of employee-employer to create alignment. It's about creating a win for people and the organization. It's not a zero-sum game. Instead, winning is a game of mutual cooperation and collaboration.

Of course, there may be times we do what needs to be done to support the functioning of the organization. There may be essential work for an organization that does not fall within the ikigai of any worker. In these cases, the burden of working outside of people's passions is shared among the people in the organization. In the best organizations, people pitch in to do whatever needs to be done. This aligns with Theory Y workers, who show up inspired, engaged, and motivated no matter what.

YOUR TURN

- How much focus is there in your organization on what employees think is important for them?
- Where are the places and times that you may not be treating other people as well as you might like to?
- Use the Employee Motivation Model on yourself. Do you love what you are doing? Are you reasonably good at it? How much value do you add to your organization?

When you believe in people, they can believe in themselves.
—Audree Tara Sahota

PATTERN 13.2: FROM OUTCOMES TO DEVELOPING LEADERS

KEY POINTS

- Excessive focus on outcomes will actually inhibit those outcomes.
- Leaders in high-performance organizations focus on developing leaders and let the people focus on outcomes.
- Believing in people is required to support their development.
- Leaders can only help others to the extent that they first model the desired behaviors.
- Developing the capabilities of people is needed for them to contribute at their best.

OUTCOMES

The role of a manager is to make sure that the work gets done. In business-as-usual organizations, the primary focus is on delivery of projects, products, and programs to meet revenue or profit targets. The organization is often governed by cascading targets and metrics for success. All the attention and efforts are focused on the specific organizational outcomes.

Focusing solely on the outcomes themselves is a trap. In traditional organizations, managers focus on the outcomes over the elements that will actually lead to the outcomes. As a result, energy and attention are diverted away from the more effective organizational choices that will lead to the desired outcomes. The lesson from Lean is that seeking to cut costs will actually increase costs. It is far more productive to focus on improving effectiveness.

DEVELOPING LEADERS

Evolutionary leaders have a holistic understanding of the elements involved in creating successful outcomes. A manager can support outcomes by focusing on any of the following levels:

1. Work or production (outcomes)
2. System and work practices
3. Environment and culture
4. People
5. Themselves

Each successive level has a greater impact on the rate of evolution of the organization and a greater total impact on the delivery of outcomes or performance of the organization.

Stop Running Projects, Start Developing Leaders

Many organizations have discovered that the way to succeed with objectives is to focus attention away from objectives. For example, at NextJump, the co-CEOs decided that the best way to create high performance was to get out of directing projects and focus on coaching other leaders (Kegan and Lahey 2016, 22). We can summarize the guidance as: stop running projects, start developing leaders.

MODEL: LEADERS AT ALL LEVELS
High performance emerges as people at all levels of the organization think and act like leaders. A clear goal to unlock performance is to develop leaders at all levels. People will only act like leaders when they are fully engaged in a supportive environment. This in turn depends on the organization operating from an evolved mindset or consciousness. Figure 13.2 illustrates how developing leaders at all levels depends on supportive organizational elements.

Evolved org. mindset → supportive environment →
engaged people → leaders at all levels

 PRINCIPLE: DEVELOP LEADERS AT ALL LEVELS
High-performance organizations have leaders at all levels of the organization. The focus of effective leaders is to develop other leaders around them.

From a purely logical perspective, developing leaders makes total sense. Imagine an organization where the focus of everyone in

Figure 13.2: Leaders at All Levels

leadership is to develop leaders around them. Over time, the organization will have leaders at all levels of the organization. Everyone will be taking responsibility and energizing the company to move forward and to serve its mission. That's high performance!

The importance of developing people came up as a key factor in Gallup research into organizational performance (Buckingham and Coffman 1999). In a high-performance environment, people strongly agree with the following statements:

- There is someone at work who encourages my development.
- In the last six months, someone at work has talked to me about my progress.
- This last year, I had opportunities at work to learn and grow.

These are table stakes for high performance. These are not that hard to do. Yet, they are not common with traditional organizations.

Work on Preconditions

There are many preconditions that need to be satisfied before it is possible to develop leaders with any level of success. This book highlights the antipatterns that are inhibiting people from evolving and the patterns (preconditions) that will set up an environment supportive of growth. For example, psychological safety, equal voice, caring for people, and evolving people.

Lead by Example

In the pattern "Leadership Leadership," we explored how leaders act as attractors to inspire a new way forward. The most powerful means of developing others is when one leads by example. In this book we have used many various leaders, some who are known for Evolutionary Leadership, and in contrast we also explore leaders who may seem to some as Traditional or Red leaders. As in the "Unlearning Reality" chapter of this book, we want to explore possibilities, shake up your blue boxes, and be open to many different views to describe the principles of leadership.

In John Paul Getty's basic rules of leadership, he explains his core principles: "Example is the best means to instruct or inspire others. The man who shows them as well as tells them is the one who gets the most from his subordinates. The best leader never asks anyone under him to do anything he is unable—or unwilling—to do himself" (Getty 1986, 51). For further exploration of the role of the leader, please refer to pattern 13.13, "From Using Authority to Leading by Example."

Holding Space

In the pattern "Increasing Freedom," we explored principles such as "Create Boundaries" and "Hold Space." These are essential building blocks to support the development of leadership in others. An important aspect is to use power wisely to support the boundaries or context for people to exercise their freedom and their leadership. "There are two new and critical roles a CEO needs to play: creating and maintaining a space for Teal ways of operating and role-modeling of Teal behaviors" (Laloux 2014, 240). The role of the leader is to create a space where they retain power; however, they explicitly choose not to exercise it. They then create the freedom for people to develop their own leadership.

PRINCIPLE: BELIEVE IN PEOPLE
Before a leader can help someone develop, they need to believe in them. Although this may sound obvious, it is often missed, and its absence can undermine all possibility of growth. One of the most important things that leaders do to care for people is to believe in them. If you believe in someone, then they can learn to believe in themselves.

In pattern 9.2, "From Oppression (Theory X) to Enablement" (Theory Y), we explored the contrasting views that leaders may hold of people in the organization. Believing that people are capable of showing up as Theory Y (motivated, engaged, etc.) is an essential element of success. When leaders do not believe in people, then there is little or no hope of their development.

We are not speaking of blind faith—that is extremely destructive. Instead, it's about holding the possibility of greatness in the future while looking at the reality of how the person is currently showing up. This creates a tension that supports the evolution of the person.

Of course, there is an important prerequisite before a leader can believe in others: leaders must first believe in themselves. For most leaders, the typical egoic behaviors of command and control, agenda, and pushing and mandating come from primal survival mechanisms. The ego's menu of scarcity, envy, unworthiness, inadequacy, and so on must lose its grip before leaders can support the evolution of others. As such, investment in personal evolution is essential for developing the ability to develop others. More will be explained in the next pattern.

PRINCIPLE: DEVELOP PEOPLE'S CAPABILITIES

An essential area of focus to create high performance is to support people in developing their capabilities. To create the highest levels of performance, we do not just need motivated, energized people, we also need highly capable, competent ones with the tools and skills to be successful. High-performance leaders help people develop their capabilities. This has a dual benefit: people feel good because they are contributing more and the organization is more successful.

Kegan and Lahey argue for a deliberately developmental organization as a path to high performance. They illustrate this point through NextJump integration of development as a core part of the culture: "Better You is about the meaning people derive from work through helping others, inside and outside the company. NextJump's leaders are struck by the research suggesting human beings are wired to serve others" (Kegan and Lahey 2016, 20).

At Morningstar, the focus of leadership is on a coaching and mentoring culture (Kirkpatrick 2011, 92). That is seen as the job of leadership—to develop the people in the organization. We see this as an organization's best-kept resource, the experience and skill of leadership. Organizations have plentiful resources at hand to develop the skills and capabilities of the workers. Besides, what else do leaders have to do once people are showing up Theory Y, taking responsibility with the maturity and capability necessary to make effective decisions on their own?

Self-Evolution

As explored in pattern 10.5, "From Strengths Development to Self-Development," the focus of high-performance leaders goes well beyond focusing on strengths to helping people develop through their challenge areas. One key aspect of developing a leader is to support their inner evolution of consciousness. As they understand the workings of the ego and can come to peace with it, their abilities to be fully present and be the change will emerge.

The ability to directly help people on this journey is a very advanced skill and requires the advancement of one's own evolution and a shift of new ways of being, behaviors, and so on. As such, this topic is best handled by focusing on setting an example. If people are not demonstrating a behavior, then looking at one's own behavior first is the process to model and transmit the behavior desired in another.

The Coaching Trap

One of the big traps in industry is the shift of the manager to coach. Attempting to shift the identity of a manager to that of a coach results in overuse of a practice.

The development of the ability to coach others is valuable and important. The value is in using coaching practices where they will be effective among other approaches such as modeling and mentoring. It is helpful for leaders to have the ability to support people in finding their own solutions. However, in order of priority, this falls far below leading by example, creating a supportive environment, and the transmission of evolved ways of being. Once these are in place, using coaching practices may yield their full value.

YOUR TURN

- As a leader, where do you tend to focus more attention—on outcomes or developing people?
- Contrast the people or situations where you believe in others versus those where you do not have confidence in them.
- How much time and energy do you spend helping others develop their capabilities?

The only thing of real importance that leaders do is to create and manage culture.

—Edgar Schein

PATTERN 13.3: FROM USING AUTHORITY TO LEADING BY EXAMPLE

KEY POINTS

- Overreliance on authority leads to low-performance organizational cultures.
- Leading by example is the primary mechanism for shaping the culture of an organization.
- Leaders of high-performance organizations model high-performance behaviors.

- Exceptional self-management and ownership of one's behaviors is required to model excellence.
- Using authority is radically less effective and requires much less effort than developing oneself.
- Developing one's character to model high-performance leadership, while the only repeatable path to high-performance culture, is the road less traveled.

USING AUTHORITY

The default in most organizations is for leadership to use authority to make decisions to guide and shape the organization. "Management includes the activities of setting the strategy of an organization and coordinating the efforts of its employees to accomplish its objectives" (Wikipedia 2021c). The very definition of *management* locks leaders into a Tayloristic paradigm of telling workers what to do and diminishing their ability to contribute.

The damaging effects of Traditional use of authority was well reviewed through the antipatterns of modern management, oppression (Theory X), and business as usual. The ensuing impact on people includes psychological fear, domination, disengagement, and the lesser addressed physical well-being of an individual. These challenges lead to a variety of clearly visible problems, such as the inability to adapt to the changing marketplace or to attract and retain top talent.

In chapter 11, "The Paradox of Power," a clear path for the effective use of authority and power was illustrated. Authority is best used as a last resort and only for the good of the people and the organization. In this pattern, we outline an alternative to using authority to create change.

LEADING BY EXAMPLE

Leading by example is the single most powerful way to shape the culture of an organization: the people and the spirit of the organization. As detailed in the patterns "Culture Follows Leadership" and "Leadership Leadership," a shift in culture can only happen when leaders go first to model a new way of working and being.

The topic of leading by example is so critical that it has been referenced with a variety of terminology that have equivalent meaning:

- Walking the talk
- Modeling behaviors
- Mindset or shift in consciousness
- Role-modeling
- Living values

The opening quote by Edgar Schein is a powerful diagnosis of the impact leadership behaviors have on an organization: "The only thing of real importance that leaders do is to create and manage culture." For most leaders who are buried deep into the tactics and strategies

of operating an organization, this message may seem either baffling or impractical.

Now the meaning is clear: it is the character of the leaders that sets the tone for the organization, not their actions. It's more about *being* rather than *doing*. How things are done, rather than what is done.

In Laloux's observation of Teal organizations, he noted the importance of role-modeling more evolved behaviors: "CEOs that role-model virtues such as humility, trust, courage, candor, vulnerability, and authenticity invite colleagues to take the same risks" (Laloux 2014, 246).

It is worth highlighting that while high-performance environments share common characteristics, each evolutionary environment has a different focus and language to shape its unique path. In contrast with Laloux, we see modeling these behaviors as *choice* rather than risk. The only risk is a perceived psychological one, since the prescription is both a practical and reliable approach to foster high performance.

 PRINCIPLE: MODELING BEHAVIOR IS THE MOST RAPID WAY TO INSPIRE EVOLUTION IN OTHERS

The benefits of a high-performance culture are only accessible by leaders who model the behaviors of that culture system. People emulate leadership behaviors. Anyone who has kids knows that how we behave as parents has much more of an effect than anything we tell them. Often this discovery does not happen until they are teenagers. Everyone who has parents will recognize those disturbing moments when we react exactly like our parents did, even though we do not consciously choose to show up that way.

There is widespread agreement that modeling behaviors is essential for creating a high-performance organization. As culture is a reflection of leadership, a shift in leadership behaviors is necessary for any significant shift toward higher levels of performance. Modeling high-performance behavior effortlessly normalizes a culture of high performance.

Let's take a very practical example. Imagine a leader who uses Red List behaviors (telling, mandating, etc.). How can they influence people in their organization to shift to Green List behaviors (inviting, optional, choice)? There is no possible way. Nothing will really make any effective change in behaviors. On the other hand, imagine now that the same leader evolves themselves first to stop the damaging Red List behaviors. They no longer need to actively do anything to invite people to use the Green List. People will automatically start to emulate the leader and shift to the inclusive, people-oriented language of the Green List. It's a small, simple example of a shift in behaviors that leads to a shift in culture. It's not easy work, but the impact is enormous.

PRINCIPLE: YOU CAN ONLY LEAD OTHERS TO THE EXTENT THAT YOU CAN LEAD YOURSELF

The deeper understanding of leading by example that we will now explore is that of self-leadership. With modeling behaviors, there is a thought about the other. With self-leadership the focus is not on others but purely on ourselves: How can I show up more as a better example for others? With self-leadership, we seek our own growth and development for our own sake. Benefits to others and the organizational systems are simply a reflection of our own inner work.

We see the variety of terms related to this topic that can be understood as roughly equivalent:

- Self-leadership
- Self-management
- Lead yourself
- Leaders go first

If you cannot lead yourself, how can you lead others?

The SELF Evolutionary Culture Model shows a journey of organizational evolution with greater sharing of power as organizations evolve to later stages. In traditional organizations, leaders hold other people accountable for outcomes and decisions. As we shift to Evolutionary cultures with high levels of empowerment and autonomy, the focus of leaders is to hold themselves accountable for their choices. Drucker identifies the key: "The critical factor for success is accountability—holding *yourself* accountable" (Drucker 2004, 177). When leaders model self-accountability and self-responsibility, this forms the basis for the evolution of the people and the culture in the organization. The primary means to cultivate accountable, responsible staff is to improve your own accountability and responsibility.

The essential role of self-leadership is widely identified in both business books and case studies on high-performance organizations. The book *Culture Shock* identifies "leading yourself" as a key ingredient for success (McInnes 2012, 106). In *Change the Culture, Change the Game*, it is stated that "management teams must start with themselves" (Connors and Smith 2011, 106).

As described in the pattern "Leadership Leadership," a widespread change in the behaviors in an organization can only be achieved through the leaders modeling new behaviors. This in turn is only possible to the extent that leaders develop a high capability for self-leadership. One powerful and clear explanation of the importance of self-leadership is by Dee Hock, the creator of the VISA organization: "Without exceptional management of self, no one is fit for authority no matter how much they acquire. . . . The first and paramount responsibility of anyone who purports to manage is to manage self—one's own integrity, character, ethics, knowledge, wisdom, temperament, words and acts. It's a never-ending, difficult, oft-shunned task. The reason is not complicated. It is ignored because it is incredibly more difficult than prescribing and controlling the behavior of others" (Hock 2005, 48).

Anyone with authority can exercise it. Exercising authority requires no training, skills, capabilities, or personal growth. It's the easy path. The path of high-performance leadership and organizations is the road less traveled—that of developing character, capability, and personal growth. It is not an easy path—however, it is highly rewarding in both intrinsic and extrinsic benefits.

Put the Oxygen Mask on First

Leading by example is the first and single most important thing a leader can do. How can we help create a high-performance culture unless we ourselves as leaders model it?

As shown in figure 13.3, a powerful metaphor to illustrate leading by example can be found on an airplane trip. In the safety briefing, we are instructed to "put the oxygen mask on first before assisting others." It's just common sense. How can one help someone else if oneself is not taken care of? It is a deep transmission of showing up in a new way of being. You can only evolve another to the extent that you yourself have evolved.

Let's revisit the culture perspective where we are seeking an organization-wide shift in everyone's behaviors (to scale culture). The only possible chance this has of success is through individual people

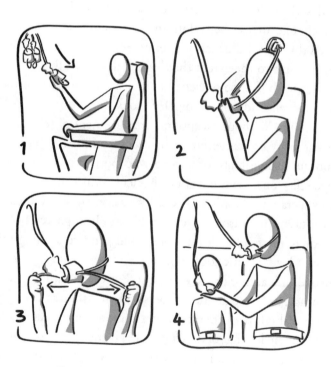

Figure 13.3: Put the Oxygen Mask on First

who chose to be leaders by shifting their own consciousness and behaviors first.

High performance comes from leading ourselves first and *then* helping others. As leaders evolve, they become a living transmission of an evolved way of being that will in turn impact the people around them, leading to a shift in the culture.

Tool: Oxygen Mask

The oxygen mask is a very powerful tool to support leading by example. It's not a physical mask, it's conceptual.

It's use is very simple. Every time you want to help someone else or help your organization, you pause and check your oxygen mask first. In practice, this means stopping what you are doing and using your self-awareness to examine how you are in this moment. Ask yourself these questions:

- Are you fully resourced right now?
- Are you clear of any destructive emotions?
- Are you connected with your highest vision for how you want to show up as a leader?
- Are your leadership edges about to cause damage?
- How well is your intended action going to support the people around you?
- What daily practices are you willing to use to become resourced in every moment?

YOUR TURN

- How accountable do you hold yourself for your behaviors?
- How much focus and investment do you have on how you show up as a leader?
- How often do you put the oxygen mask on yourself before helping others?

Eventually we come into an awareness that our consciousness determines the nature of our life.

—Joel S. Goldsmith, *Consciousness Transformed*

PATTERN 13.4: FROM UNAWARE TO CONSCIOUS

KEY POINTS

- Due to cognitive bias, people are unaware of the roles they play in the problems they face.
- Low awareness prevents leaders from improving and consequently leading by example.
- The term *mindset* is often used to describe a shift in consciousness.
- High-performance leaders and organizations operate from an evolved consciousness.
- An integrated shift in our identity, values, beliefs, and behaviors is required to operate at higher levels of consciousness.

UNAWARE

Low-performance organizations are filled with leaders who are largely unaware of their own behaviors and the impacts they have on their own success. In those places where the light of reality shines through, they may be discouraged since they have neither the means nor the support to make a shift.

When we are unaware of how our behaviors are creating problems, we are completely incapable of finding solutions. When there is a problem, we usually misidentify the source to other people and then apply countermeasures that are completely misdirected. As discussed in chapter 7, "Unlearning Reality," success comes from unlearning to discover the reality that you are the problem and that you are also the solution.

CONSCIOUS

The word *conscious* means to be aware of and respond to one's surroundings. We might understand that a conscious leader is aware of themselves, others, and the situations around them. Rather than reacting from low awareness and historical automatic conditioning, a conscious leader is able to sense the reality of the situation and respond with their full intelligence.

In the pattern "High-Performance Organizations," the connection between the consciousness or state of evolution of an organization and its performance was clarified. It's not just a new set of structures or practices, it's about evolving people, since the consciousness of an organization is a reflection of all the people and, most importantly, the consciousness of the leadership. An essential aspect of the leadership journey is moving from unaware to conscious. Self-awareness is key—however, this is only one dimension of a shift in consciousness.

PRINCIPLE: SELF-AWARENESS UNLOCKS CONSCIOUSNESS

Most leaders in organizations today have a low level of self-awareness of their own behaviors. They have a huge blind spot: themselves! It's totally normal for most leaders to have this challenge. One reason is that it is not customary in society to cultivate self-awareness. The second is that the default mode of operation of a human being blocks self-awareness.

The default mode of functioning for a human being's self-awareness is characterized by the term *illusory superiority*, which is an aspect of cognitive bias. Our default is to assume we are better, smarter, and more correct than we actually are. While this is the inherent nature of the ego, we may overcome through education and choice. "In the field of psychology, the Dunning-Kruger effect is a cognitive bias in which people with low ability at a task overestimate their ability. It is related to the cognitive bias of illusory superiority and comes from the inability of people to recognize their lack of ability. Without the self-awareness of metacognition, people cannot objectively evaluate their competence or incompetence" (Wikipedia 2020a).

OVERCOME SELF-DECEPTION

We now revisit McGregor's Theory X and Theory Y, shown in table 13.1, to provide a clear example of the damage that may be caused through low awareness and the importance of overcoming our own self-deception. Our comparison approach is inspired by Niels Pflaeging, who used it to create self-awareness.

Our purpose is to help you discover not only how you see workers but also how you see yourself and how becoming more conscious of your beliefs can support your evolution.

As leaders, we have an internal belief of how workers function. Every interaction and decision we make is based on our beliefs. The beliefs leaders have about workers will in part determine their effectiveness in leading organizational change and creating high-performance culture.

High-performance leaders have deeply held beliefs that workers are intrinsically Theory Y—that this is their natural state of being. They see that their role is to support workers in rehabilitating to their natural state—Theory Y.

To help workers show up as Theory Y, it's not just about believing in them. Leaders must also lead by example. Showing up as Theory Y is the minimum that is needed.

Due to the inability to navigate the tendency of illusory superiority, most leaders believe that they are Theory Y and that workers (others) are more a mix of theories X and Y. The discrepancy between

Table 13.1: Theory X and Theory Y

	Theory X	Theory Y
Attitude	Dislike work. Avoid it.	Take an interest in work. May like it.
Direction	Unambitious: prefer to be directed by others.	Ambitious: capable of directing own behavior.
Responsibility	Avoid responsibility.	Seek and accept responsibility.
Motivation	Unmotivated. Need to be motivated.	Are intrinsically motivated.
Supervision	Need supervision and control.	Self-direction and self-control.

our self-view and our view of others is a function of cognitive bias or a reality distortion field that is built into the ego structures of our brains.

As leaders, our work is to see the places where we operate like Theory X so that we can work through them to more effectively lead by example. It is also to see our habitual unconscious judgments about others to see people as Theory X. As we are able to resolve these limitations, our ability to cultivate leaders who operate like Theory Y will increase.

TOOL: SELF-AWARENESS

A key goal of this book is to pierce through the veils of denial and self-deception that form the basis for our self-views and interactions with others. The parallel goal is to show what good looks like so that leaders have a rubric to clearly evaluate where they stand. We offer a clear standard of performance that is vital to overcoming the self-deception and illusory superiority that block evolution.

Self-awareness is a built-in tool that every human being has access to. Self-awareness is simply the choice to pay attention to what is happening with one's self. One way to increase self-awareness is to use the oxygen mask tool described in the previous pattern to investigate various aspects of one's being. A deeper use of self-awareness is to really dig into the principles and tools in chapter 7, "Unlearning Reality: Can You Handle the Truth?" It's about paying attention to what is happening inside you by using tools such as Navigate Conflicting Ideas, Question Your Assumptions, Keep a Tension Journal, and Investigate Your Self. To accelerate the power of self-awareness to create a shift in behavior, we offer the 4A's Leadership tool that is part of the book resources shared in part three.

You Say Mindset, I Say Conscious

The term *mindset* is often used to capture the shift in internal perspectives and worldview needed to operate more effectively. In the business world, there are many words people use to describe the shift in consciousness to support new ways of working, such as:

- Agile mindset
- learning mindset
- growth mindset
- complexity mindset
- Lean mindset
- Design thinking
- innovation

While differences exist, all of these terms are pointing toward an integrated shift in people's worldviews: it's not just about knowledge, it's a shift in consciousness that forms an integrated view of what reality is. There is a realization that it's not just about work practices—something more is required to create success.

Evolution Is a Shift in Who We Are

We are speaking of seeing and experiencing the world in very different ways as well as responding and interacting with the world differently. Just having a cognitive or intellectual shift is not enough. Just being aware of a new model does not help. Success as a leader comes when a shift in perceptions and understandings are fully integrated with behaviors—when we model a new way of being and working.

A new way of being enables a new way of working.
Shifting mindset is key.

The sustained journey toward high performance requires an ongoing willingness to look internally to gain a deeper understanding of ourselves and the blocks of our inner world. We have adapted the neurolinguistic programming model of the logical levels of human behavior (Dilts, Hallbom, and Smith 2012):

- Identity
- Values
- Beliefs
- Behaviors

The shift in behaviors in the outer world that reflect our performance as leaders are a reflection of our beliefs, values, and even identities. Each level can be leveraged to support one's evolution. NextJump's "Better Me" speaks to evolving ourselves at the level of identity, not just behavioral change.

The journey toward high-performance leadership demands an integrated shift in our identities, values, beliefs, and behaviors. It's not just about what we do, it's who we are and how we see ourselves.

RESTORE BALANCE THROUGH INTEGRATION

In low-performance culture systems, there is little possibility for including the full talents and capabilities of a human being. The only part of a human being that is welcomed in these culture systems is the *logical, rational, left-brained, masculine* part of a person.

In contrast, higher-performance cultures welcome in the talents and capabilities of the whole person, such as:

- Logical and holistic
- Rational and intuition
- Structure and creation
- Masculine and feminine

When we invite people to use and develop their full set of talents at work, we not only achieve greater results but also fulfill and nourish the people.

For example, we all have masculine and feminine aspects of self within our beings. A shift in consciousness is required to integrate both the masculine and feminine aspects of ourselves. As the integration deepens, we find high performance and success through the effective use of both aspects of ourselves. There becomes a resolution of inner conflict resulting in a more balanced and unobstructed way of being. The egoic structures of the self begin to dissolve or resolve, and behaviors begin to match the peaceful inner state.

Laloux explains his understanding of Teal: "With this stage comes a deep yearning for wholeness—bringing together the ego and the deeper parts of the self; integrating mind, body, and soul; cultivating both the feminine and masculine parts within; being whole in relation to others; and repairing our broken relationship with life and nature" (Laloux 2014, 48).

Leaders who are able to integrate these seeming polarities are able to not only operate at the highest levels of capability but also to lead as a powerful example. High performance comes from transcending and integrating seeming opposites by observing from a different level of consciousness.

EXTERNAL INTEGRATION DEPENDS ON INTERNAL INTEGRATION

The usual state of affairs for people, for organizations, and for society is that of disintegration. Our society and organizations reflect thousands of years of dominance of patriarchy. The feminine aspects of our being that represent holistic, intuition, and creation have been repressed at individual and societal levels.

As human beings, organizations, and societies, we have not been operating in a balanced way. It impacts not only our ability to function at our full potential but impairs our ability to fully enjoy life and truly thrive. A journey of shifting consciousness creates the ability to have compassion, patience, unconditional love (or high regard), collaboration, the ability to listen, nonjudgment, and so on.

The higher states of conscious evolution are not about having matriarchal supremacy, they are about resolving the conflict and returning to balance. As individuals return to balance within their own beings, we will see a return to balance as organizations and societies. Without a shift in consciousness and reintegration of our beings, it is unlikely humanity's greatest challenges will be overcome.

 MODEL: JOURNEY TO CONSCIOUS COMPETENCE
When we are unaware or unconscious of our shortcomings or challenges, we have no hope of improvement. We offer a modified version of Martin Broadwell's four stages of competence to understand and orient oneself on the journey from unconscious to conscious.

Figure 13.4 shows the evolutionary path of becoming more conscious of one's capabilities. For each skill, behavior, or way of being, one can consider what stage one is operating at:

1. **Unconscious incompetence:** This is about low awareness. One holds a low level of capability, and one is not aware of one's level of competence.

2. **Conscious incompetence:** At this stage, one becomes conscious of one's incompetence. There is a realization that there is a gap in skills or behaviors needed to create an outcome. This is an essential and productive stage, since it is the foundation for growth.

3. **Unconscious competence:** We diverge from Broadwell's model. Our observation is that one can have unconscious competence *without conscious competence*. At this stage, one is competent but is unconscious of what one is doing or being. The challenge with the places where we have unconscious competence is that it is very difficult to help others develop, since we are unaware of what we are doing that leads to success. Many top leaders are successfully able to create amazing outcomes. However, they are not able to help others develop the same abilities because it comes

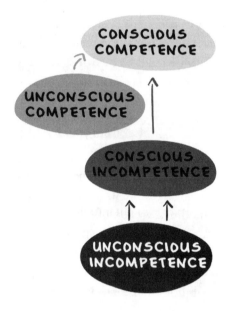

Figure 13.4: Journey to Conscious Competence

naturally to them. As such, this stage is insufficient for developing others.

4. **Conscious competence:** One is not only competent but aware of what one is doing or being. It is from this state of doing and being that one can fully develop people and systems. Conscious competence is needed to develop the evolutionary capabilities of others.

The absolute best thing you can discover as an Evolutionary Leader is how you are making mistakes and failing. While it may be psychologically confronting and uncomfortable, it allows you to move from unconscious incompetence to conscious incompetence. For someone committed to growth, this is a moment of celebration! The discovery of every leadership edge is great news. You have discovered a behavior that was causing damage and now have the opportunity to grow out of it to be more of the leader you want to be to create the outcomes you want to create. Taiichi Ohno, one of the founders of the Toyota Production System and Lean, advises people to appreciate the discovery of problems, since each problem holds the promise of greater performance and success.

YOUR TURN

- With regard to Theory X and Theory Y, in what ways does your self-image differ from your view of workers?
- How aware are you of your behaviors and the impact they have on others?
- How much effort do you put into discovering your leadership edges?
- Reflect on where you have conflict in your life and where and how you are conflicted in your inner state.

Be the change you want to see in the world.
—Mahatma Gandhi

PATTERN 13.5: FROM DOING TO BEING

KEY POINTS

- Most important is not what one does but how one does it.
- All doing rests on our inner state of being.
- It is our state of being that gives our words and deeds impact.
- As one shifts to more evolved levels of consciousness, there is a shift in one's being.
- Emotional awareness is essential in evolving one's state of being.

DOING

There is often a belief that all one needs to do as a leader is to learn the right model, concept, skill, or technique. The basic premise is that we are fine and that new information or training will help create the success and impact that we want.

When we are focused on doing, we see people (including ourselves) as black boxes where we don't need to concern ourselves with what is inside the box. We can create success by focusing on the boundary of the box—the actions or doing. When we examine the ways of business as usual, they are almost entirely about external measurable actions and behaviors. The whole of the human experience is relegated to the rational, logical, and measurable.

The trap of traditional organizations and leadership is to focus on the external aspects of action and doing. It's a waste of time since we are trying to fix the external effects rather than the inner causes. For example, the surface-level external problem of responding angrily to an email is ultimately caused by the internal challenges with emotional regulation and conditioned behavior patterns. Addressing challenges at the surface level will only lead to temporary superficial change.

BEING

Evolutionary Leadership is a state of being that comes from the choice to evolve. Being is about who you are and how you show up for others—your inner state. It's about one's identity, values, and beliefs that ultimately shape behaviors. Our state of being has a profound impact on others that goes beyond words and actions. There are people who feel good to be around. There are other people who give off a bad vibe. A leader walking into a meeting room can uplift and support people or take out the whole room. They don't even need to say a word.

PRINCIPLE: BEING IS THE FOUNDATION OF DOING

The doing is about the "what," while being is about the "how." Any given action can be taken with a different way of being.

Consider the act of giving feedback about a critical matter to someone else in your organization. There is a doing: the sharing of information that is potentially uncomfortable for the other person. Then there is the being: the manner in which you undertake the sharing of the feedback. The beingness can be supportive, caring, and focused on that person's growth and success. Conversely, the beingness can be about the error, the person's performance level, and correcting them to get the job done.

There is no way to fake caring or other positive ways of being. As human beings, we are equipped with mirror neurons that allow us to sense the emotional states of others around us. Consequently, there is no strategy or tactic to overcome challenging emotional states and judgments about others.

Of course, success requires both the doing and the being. The key point is that being is the foundation of all doing. While skills and accurate models to understand the world are important, what is even more important is how one shows up. As was shared in an earlier pattern, a new way of being unlocks a new way of doing.

GANDHI'S STORY

There is a story about Mahatma Gandhi that is instructive in understanding the principle on which this key leadership practice is based. The consciousness of Gandhi was so great that people from all over India would come to him to seek his advice for unsolvable problems. Consider what insights come from this story:

> A woman came to see Gandhi, waiting in line for more than half a day with her son at her side in order to have an audience with him. When at last it was their turn to speak to him, the woman said, "Mahatma, please. Tell my son he must stop eating sugar. It is ruining his health, his teeth, it affects his mood. Every time he has it, I see the change in him and there is nothing I can do to stop him from eating it, and then eating more. He's a good boy, but when it comes to sugar, he becomes a liar and a thief and a cheat and I'm afraid it will ruin his life. Please, Gandhiji, tell him to stop."

Gandhi looked at the boy for the longest time as he cowered there, trying to hide in his mother's sari. Finally, Gandhi broke the silence and said, "Come back to me in two week's time."

Two weeks later the woman returned with her child and once again waited in line for hours before finally it was their turn to see the master. "Mahatma," said the mother. "We have returned. We come to you for help with this boy and eating sugar and you asked us to come back after two weeks."

"Yes, of course I remember," said the master. "Come here, child." He motioned the boy forward.

The boy, at the urging and prodding of his mother, disentangled himself from her sari and stepped up to the Mahatma who reached out, putting his hands on the boy's shoulders and pulling him in close. He looked at the boy squarely in the eye and said, firmly, "Don't eat sugar," then released him.

"That's it?" said the mother. "That's all you're going to say?" She was flabbergasted. "Why didn't you just tell him that two weeks ago?"

"Because," replied Gandhi, "two weeks ago I was still eating sugar myself." (Reilly 2008)

BE THE CHANGE YOU WANT TO SEE IN THE WORLD
The following quote speaks to the key insight into the reality of leadership: "Be the change you want to see in the world."

For many this might be understood as an inspirational message. But it is more, much more. It is very specific guidance into how to unlock your leadership, the leadership of others, and high performance in organizations.

The first level of understanding of this story is at the level of behavior. The only way Gandhi could authentically instruct the boy was from a place of integrity where he also did not eat sugar. Here, we could say that Gandhi was leading by example.

The deeper level of understanding is at the level of being. Consider for a moment the power of Gandhi's words. They had such an impact that the boy did indeed stop eating sugar. From this, we can understand that *leading by example is a basic requirement for leading*

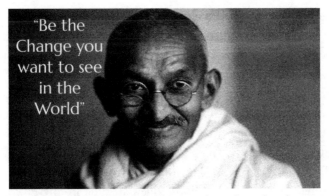

"Be the Change you want to see in the World"

Image source: Wikipedia, labeled for reuse: https://en.wikipedia.org
/wiki/Mahatma_Gandhi#/media/File:Mahatma-Gandhi,_studio,
_1931.jpg

at a more evolved level of consciousness. The impact of our words and deeds becoming a transmission depends entirely on our being.

Daily Operational Guidance

The above quote from Gandhi is not just motivational, it is daily operational guidance for high performance. The essence of great leadership is about being, not doing. Focus on your being. Focus on how you can show up as the future you want to create in your organization.

Gandhi's activities allowed India to be liberated from the British through nonviolence. This is an incredible accomplishment. It is our inner state of being that transmits and has an immediate and direct impact on those around us.

CONSCIOUSNESS IS A TRANSMISSION

Our inner state of being or level of consciousness is a transmission. Unlike knowledge or skills that can be taught, one's state of being is a result of personal evolution. Focus where it counts.

Creating an evolutionary organization requires a leader who holds an Evolutionary consciousness. They have gone on a journey or transformational process to evolve into a higher state of consciousness. They hold a transmission of evolution. Only from that state of being can doing lead to the desired outcome. High performance is ultimately about our state of being, not our doing.

The Power of Being

There are many examples of conscious leaders that have been able to achieve extraordinary results. Through their evolved consciousness they were able to have great impact.

For example, Victor Frankl was able to inspire people all around the world. He was able to model powerful human behavior while in Nazi death camps. In *Man's Search for Meaning,* he describes all human beings as having a choice about how they choose to show up: "Everything can be taken from a man but one thing: the last of the human freedoms—to choose one's attitude in any given set of circumstances, to choose one's own way" (Frankl 1959).

Nelson Mandela liberated South Africa from apartheid—a system of segregation and oppression of black people by caucasians. When imprisoned for leading change efforts, he saw himself as more free than his jailors, as he was able to shift his perception of his own personal reality. This seemingly radical shift in perception unlocked his extraordinary achievement (Mandela 1994).

Ultimately the successes of Frankl and Mandela are more about who they are as people—the transmission of evolved consciousness that they hold, their inner state that enables an enlightened state of perception—rather than specific choices or actions.

EMOTIONAL REGULATION IS CRITICAL

More evolved leaders are conscious of their inner states of being and focus not only on effective emotional self-regulation, they also focus on growing through repetitive patterns that limit personal effectiveness. They are mostly or entirely in resourced emotional states throughout the day: calm, peaceful, energized, happy, or excited. Although challenges still arise, evolved leaders have the means to regain a resourced state. They are conscious of their impacts and understand the importance of a calm, stable presence in the face of the unknown and uncertainty.

Our view is that people have been misinformed, or to speak frankly, lied to about how their emotional systems work. We are not faulting anyone's efforts. Instead, what we have observed is that people do not fully understand how their emotional system actually works. To develop your ability to navigate emotions, we refer you to our book *Emotional Science: The Key to Unlocking High Performance* (Sahota and Sahota 2018).

Less evolved leaders are often not conscious of their inner states of being and may experience emotional states that cause damage around them. Less resourceful states of being are worry, concern, fear, anxiety, apathy, frustration, judgment, anger, jealousy—the list of less resourced human emotions is long.

As leaders, every time we are in a less resourced emotional state, we take out the people around us. Most traditional leaders are not even aware of the impacts their state of being has on the people around them.

Example: Psychological Safety

To illustrate this point, consider the relationship between the level of psychological safety and one's being. Evolved leaders hold a very high internal level of psychological safety that allows them to be that calm stable presence amid the chaos. It is embodied in their being. From this place they are able to support the safety of others.

YOUR TURN
- How do people's internal states of being impact their abilities to work effectively with others?
- How much of your attention is focused on doing versus your inner state of being?
- Where have you noticed people having challenged reactions to your inner state of being?

Knowing others is intelligence;
knowing yourself is true wisdom.
Mastering others is strength;
mastering yourself is true power.

—Lao Tzu

PATTERN 13.6: FROM LEADERSHIP DEVELOPMENT TO SELF-EVOLUTION

KEY POINTS
- Traditional training and coaching are insufficient for creating the shift in consciousness seen in high-performance organizations.
- Evolutionary capability is the ability to evolve.
- Evolutionary learning extends the growth or learning mindset to include self-learning and self-evolution.
- The prerequisite for self-evolution is desire and a willingness to grow.

- The keys to self-evolution are the awareness of oneself and the means for self-evolution.
- The practice "working through leadership edges" is an effective means for self-evolution.

LEADERSHIP DEVELOPMENT

As clarified in other patterns such as Culture Follows Leadership and Leadership Leadership, the crux of the shift to high levels of performance depends entirely on the leadership capabilities within an organization. This is not surprising information, and it's not a new topic. Eighty percent of organizational leaders report that leadership is an important or very important issue for their organization (Deloitte 2019).

While there is a $366 billion investment globally in leadership development, most organizations are not getting results (Westfall 2019). The key challenge is that organizations are using Traditional approaches and are getting traditional results: "Research shows that while organizations expect new leadership capabilities, they are still largely promoting traditional models and mindsets" (Deloitte 2019).

Traditional training and coaching approaches are generally targeted to support the existing cultural paradigm rather than shifting to a new one with a more evolved consciousness.

The top organizational challenges of the last decade—employee engagement, leadership, and culture—have not been resolved. The truth is that organizations are severely challenged in solving the most pressing problems. A fundamental rethink of leadership development is needed to create high-performance organizations.

SELF-EVOLUTION

The key requirement of evolution is the ability to grow. We make the following definition:

Evolutionary capability is the ability to evolve.

In this pattern, we deepen the understanding that leadership evolution depends on leaders who embody evolutionary capabilities. It's not about attending a training program or certification. It's not about having an executive coach. It's about developing the ability and choice to explore your assumptions about who you are and how you show up. Leaders that evolve themselves first can then support the organization's evolutionary journey.

Model: Evolutionary Mindset

To understand the concept of evolutionary learning and evolutionary mindset, we extend the notion of growth mindset. "In a growth mindset, people believe that their most basic abilities can be developed through dedication and hard work—brains and talent are just the starting point. This view creates a love of learning and a resilience that is essential for great accomplishment" (Dweck 2006). A growth mindset can equivalently be understood as a learning mindset, since people are open to new ideas.

To create a learning organization, we require individuals who learn. "Organizations learn only through individuals who learn" (Senge 2006, 129). Self-development or personal evolution is essential, since the organizational behavior and functioning is a reflection of individual behaviors. As such, a growth mindset is a requirement for creating a learning organization that can adapt to changing circumstances. In contrast, a fixed mindset blocks the learning needed for growth and adaptation.

It is one thing to learn about processes and work practices. It is entirely another thing to learn about who we are and how we might behave more effectively. Kegan and Lahey (2016) identify the powerful concept of a deliberately developmental organization. We highlight and extend the focus and importance on personal evolution.

As shown in figure 13.5, the Evolutionary mindset is about self-learning that leads to self-evolution. It involves understanding the nature of ourselves and how we play a role in all relationships and interactions. It involves moving from unaware of our internal state of being, to becoming conscious of how we are showing up and the impact it has on everything we do. Moving beyond skills and knowledge, it's about evolving *your self: who you are—*

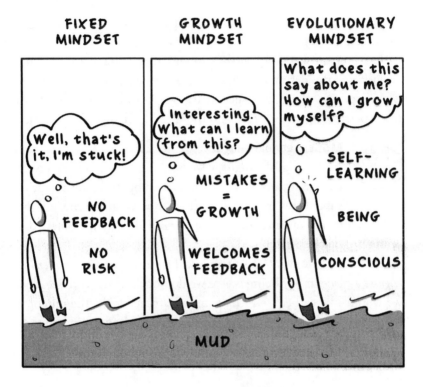

Figure 13.5: Evolutionary Mindset

your sense of identity, your values, your beliefs, your behavior, that shifts your inner state of being. Ultimately this takes us to understanding and exploring our egos.

Evolutionary mindset is a powerful evolutionary capability. It is an essential requirement for Evolutionary Leadership.

LEADERSHIP EVOLUTION IS THE GAME

Leadership evolution is the way to win the game of creating a high-performance organizational culture. We call this Evolutionary Leadership: leaders who are committed to grow and evolve as human beings. They have an understanding that their inner state of being has a greater impact than what they actually do. A leader's impact is ultimately a reflection of their level of consciousness—it's a transmission of how they show up. As such, the organization as a whole will ultimately reflect the consciousness of the top leadership. This concept was explored in the Self-Development pattern through NextJump's Better Me concept.

The prerequisite of leadership evolution and for organizational evolution is the desire to evolve. In *Creating a Lean Culture* (2010), Mann speaks of two key success factors: "Leaders' willingness to make personal changes" (141), and the "need to change habits" (18).

MODEL: LEADERSHIP EDGE

In the English language we might understand a leadership edge as a place where we have a competitive advantage or superiority over others. That's not what we are talking about. Quite the reverse. We use the term to identify the outer edge or limit of our leadership.

We extend the work of Austin and Devin to define a *leadership edge* as a place in our being where we do not show up as the leaders we would like to be. It's a challenge area that blocks the outcome we desire. We use the term analogously to poor leadership habits or our shadow self. The concept provides clearer focus over Bridgewater's "pain + reflection = progress" phrase that was explored in the pattern "Self-Development."

EMBRACE LEADERSHIP EDGES

Here we present an evolutionary capability called embracing leadership edges. When we embrace our leadership edges and work through them, we may see the shift in our being and behaviors that unlock the people around us. Figure 13.6 shows that attention to the leadership edge will help us move from where we are now to where we hope to be.

Austin and Devin identify the importance of working through limitations: "Learning to work on the edge is part of learning to achieve reliable innovation, and it's the manager's job to help with this task" (Austin and Devin 2003, 123). There is an understanding that an edge can take many forms, and that going into the pain is required for growth: "A physical, social, or emotional edge requires the same kind of careful but insistent exercise as a physical edge: learning to be okay with the discomfort of the edge; learning to move the edge outward by releasing into the discomfort for controlled

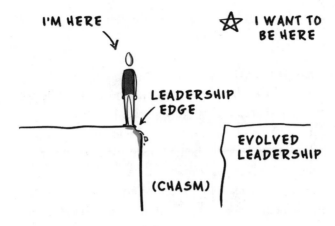

Figure 13.6: Leadership Edge

periods" (125). The key to the practice is to lean into our leadership edges instead of avoiding them.

Anderson and Adams argue that the development of the leadership "inner game" is the essence of high performance leadership. Their understanding that "the inner game runs the outer game" aligns with the patterns in this book. Success as a leader is primarily dependent on inner growth. They list a dozen additional references that articulate the need for personal growth (Anderson and Adams 2015, 33–35). They see deep awareness of one's inner being as a key step: "Engaging and harvesting the shadow is the second leg of the Hero's/Heroine's journey" (282).

Your Organization Is a Reflection of You

Imagine for a moment a leader who wants to create an evolutionary organization. This is very straightforward. It is not about the structures but rather the consciousness of the leader that matters most. It simply requires the leader to work through all their leadership edges that are preventing them from modeling the behaviors and consciousness of an Evolutionary Leader. Easy to understand—the challenge is in getting there.

If you want an evolutionary organization, be an Evolutionary Leader first. Then it will happen automatically around you. If you aren't seeing an evolutionary organization forming around you, the prescription is simple: just keep on working through your leadership edges.

SELF-EVOLUTION IS A JOURNEY

At the end of the day, it is how we show up as leaders—our behavior—that determines what we create in the world. Simply becoming more aware of something is not enough. A permanent shift in our behaviors and state of being is required to create greatness.

The highest levels of performance are accessible to each of us. For those who want to create high-performance organizations, there is now a clearly demarcated path. Each of us, as a sovereign being, has a choice about whether to pursue this path or not.

For those who chose the path of evolving to high-performance leadership, the task ahead may seem overwhelming. For most of us, there is a significant gap between our current state of being and how we hope to show up in the world. It is important to remind ourselves that there is no destination. While words such as *Evolutionary* and *Teal* might inspire us, they best serve us as a star on the horizon.

PRINCIPLE: YOUR OWN EVOLUTION IS THE MOST DIRECT AND RAPID MEANS TO CREATE HIGH PERFORMANCE
To the degree that you focus on your own evolution, the people around you will also evolve. As people see changes in you, they will be inspired to change themselves. We move from telling and selling to embodying the possibility of a better future.

The good news is that each step we take along the journey toward high-performance leadership will yield results. Each time we speak less and listen more, we have an impact on those around us. Every time we catch ourselves feeling frustration and shift into curiosity, we increase connection instead of damaging relationships. Through small changes, our very being acts as an invitation to those around us.

We close with Dee Hock's profound insight into the journey: "If you move down this path, there is no reason to be discouraged by shortcomings. Success, while it may provide encouragement, build confidence, and be joyful indeed, often teaches an insidious lesson—

to have too high an opinion of self. It is from failure that amazing growth and grace so often come, provided only that one can recognize it, admit it, learn from it, rise above it, and try again. True leadership presumes a standard quite beyond human perfectibility and that is alright, for joy and satisfaction are in the pursuit of an objective, not in its realization. The only question of importance is whether one constantly rises in the scale" (Hock 2005, 50).

YOUR TURN

- Look at the model for evolutionary learning: How would other people classify where you tend to operate?
- How much awareness do you have around the leadership edges that are limiting your performance and success?
- What might happen if you made a sustained commitment to your personal evolution?

Yesterday I was clever, so I wanted to change the world.
Today I am wise, so I am changing myself.
—Rumi

PATTERN 13.7: FROM CHANGING THE ORGANIZATION TO PEACE WITH THE EGO

KEY POINTS

- The ego is a naturally occurring psychological structure that is the basis for how we perceive and interact with the world.
- Changing the organization will only work to the degree that the leadership has been able to mitigate the damaging behaviors of the ego.

- Any significant effort toward self-evolution will lead one to understand that all personal/leadership growth is ultimately about the ego.
- Many investigations into high-performance leadership and organizations have identified the ego as a key to unlocking effectiveness.
- Applied spirituality can play a role in supporting understanding and coming to peace with the ego.

CHANGING THE ORGANIZATION

Many leaders seek to develop their organizations so that they perform better. In fact, increasing operational effectiveness is part of the core responsibilities of a manager. There is an incredible amount of effort put into tactical and strategic changes: new processes, new ways of working, new organizational structures, and so on. We hear the promise, "Just do this one thing and everything will work out." Or, "Here is a proven, reliable system that will work at your organization." In the end, there is very little in the way of material change.

The more things change, the more they stay the same."
—Jean-Baptiste Alphonse Karr

The primary reason things stay the same is that organizations are failing to address the actual root causes of the issues. Real progress with organizational change requires addressing the underlying issues. To address the root causes effectively requires:

- A willingness to look at the deeper reality of what is happening
- An understanding of the Laws of Organization Dynamics
- The ability to apply this understanding to investigate what is happening
- An understanding of how people play a role in what is happening
- A means to help people evolve so that they operate in ways that align with organizational outcomes

In various patterns it has been shown how people are the problem and that people are the solution. A shift in functioning of people is required to create a shift in the functioning of the organization. Why on earth are there so many problems with people? In this pattern we explore the root cause of the challenges with human beings that limit organizational effectiveness.

PEACE WITH THE EGO

As seen in earlier patterns, the culture of the organization is a reflection of the behaviors of the people. Organizational performance increases with a shift in consciousness where characteristics such as respect, curiosity, humility, courage, and effective emotional self-regulation become the norm. When people operate from a different way of being, there is a wholesale change in behavior. The key insight from earlier patterns is that the consciousness of an organization is a reflection of the consciousness of the leadership. The key question then becomes: What does it really mean to evolve consciousness?

In the From Unaware to Conscious pattern, we explored a basic understanding of what it means to become more conscious. As one begins to examine one's inner world of identity, values, beliefs, and behaviors, there is a discovery that there is a force that is operating that prevents one from showing up as one's best self.

While it is very easy for us to identify how we want to show up as a leader, it's not that easy. Focus on just changing habits and behaviors is insufficient, as this is almost akin to a surface-level treatment of the underlying challenge. Resolving the root cause starts with an understanding of the nature of the ego and its interplay within our consciousness. Fully mitigating the damaging effects only arrives as we come to peace with the ego.

MODEL: IDENTITY IS THE FOUNDATION OF THE SELF

We may understand a person's ego as their sense of self or identity as well as the underlying machinery of the mind that gives us our definition of reality. The ego is a naturally occurring psychological structure that is the basis for how we perceive and interact with the world. We do not take the view that

Figure 13.7: Identity Is the Foundation of the Self

the ego is good or bad but rather focus on the connection between the ego and high-performance leadership.

Earlier we explored the principle, Evolution Is a Shift in Who We Are, as understanding an individual through identity, values, beliefs, and behaviors. As illustrated in figure 13.7, identity is the foundation that values, beliefs, and behaviors are derived from. One's identity is experienced through the thoughts: me, myself, and I. Without me, myself, and I, we cannot identify with thoughts or the body. Ego can be understood as the machinery of experience related to a person's identification with a psychological self. As the ego forms the root of human experience, it is the ultimate leverage point for shifting one's being.

A good first-order approximation of one's inner world is:

Ego = self = identity = me, myself, and I

A thorough explanation of the complexities of a metaphysical explanation will be undertaken in a separate book. The above definition is "good enough and safe to try." The work is to become conscious (aware) of one's inner experience and the functioning of the ego.

PRINCIPLE: THE EGO IS THE ROOT CAUSE OF PERFORMANCE ISSUES

The ego is responsible for both positive and destructive behavioral tendencies inherent in the default mode of operation of a human being. It is the source of our distorted world-

view where everything is filtered from the perspective of "me." How does something affect me? Is it good for me? Do I look good? The ego operates from a constant source of fear, the fear of not existing. The ego is the root cause of one not feeling psychologically safe and the ensuing impairment to brain functioning. The ego is focused on survival. It's the mechanism that creates cognitive bias and inhibits our ability to see situations from others' perspectives.

A particularly striking example of the importance of looking at the deeper implications of our behavior comes from Holacracy (which can be understood as a set of structures designed to support a shift in consciousness): "All of the meeting structures in Holacracy are designed to shine a light on our own stuff, our projections, our ego . . . to make it all just visible, clear and transparent, not judge it but let in naturally dissolve. This is also one of the hard things about Holacracy. My experience is: people love Holacracy when it prevents somebody else's stuff, their ego, their frustrations, their fear, from jumping in and dominating the organization, from derailing the natural process of working together towards a purpose" (Brian Robertson quoted in Laloux 2014, 164).

The ego is the ultimate endgame for personal growth and evolution. Most effective growth techniques are working with aspects of the ego. For example, effective personal coaching increases self-awareness = awareness of the self = awareness of the ego. Most commonly used development techniques address ego challenges at the surface level of behavior and values.

> *You see how much the ego has been denying your own beauty and ignored so much information.*
> —Ram Dass, *The Miracle of Consciousness* (lecture)

PEACE WITH THE EGO UNLOCKS PERFORMANCE

Arriving at peace with the ego is not about destroying or eliminating the ego, since it cannot be eliminated. Instead, it is about creating a shift in identity, beliefs, values, and behaviors that allow us to mitigate the normal damaging effects of egoic consciousness. For example, something as simple as taking responsibility for our behavior requires overcoming the default ego tactics of denial, minimization, justification, and blame (Avery 2015).

As such, high performance, where people act like adults to take responsibility for their behaviors, is fully dependent on coming to peace with the ego.

There is a recognition that many day-to-day behaviors and actions are actually in the service of our ego and not the people around us or the purpose we seek to serve. In pattern 10.5, "From Strengths Development to Self-Development," we started to invite awareness of this topic through the case studies: Bridgewater's "solve you" and NextJump's Better Me.

Laloux found that Teal organizations share patterns of leaders navigating the limitations of their egos. "In Teal, obstacles are seen as life's way to teach us about ourselves and about the world. We are ready to let go of anger, shame, and blame, which are useful shields for the ego but are poor teachers for the soul" (Laloux 2014, 46).

Anderson and Adams's leadership system provides a model for the dimensions of leadership and how they may evolve through stages of letting go of ego. They describe the shift from: ego-centric, reactive, creative, and integral. At each stage there is a letting go of egoic consciousness and a shift to a broader worldview (Anderson and Adams 2015).

We are inviting into our being a state of consciousness where the ego no longer acts as a barrier to taking effective action. When we rest in the truth of who we are, a sovereign conscious being, we experience the highest levels of psychological safety. Our personal sense of safety is what allows us to overcome the fear that usually blocks us from taking the action required in the moment to create success.

Coming to peace with the ego is an essential part of high-performance leadership. Given the overwhelming evidence of the role the ego plays in leadership performance, how can it be that the ego is ignored?

Spiritual Wisdom and Practices Support Self-Evolution

This book is about attaining the highest levels of performance for people and organizations. To accomplish this, it is essential that everyone functions at their highest potential. We are speaking to what shapes one's identity, values, and beliefs that determine how one shows up as a person and that influences how one shows up as a leader. This requires practices and techniques to dissolve the ego and connect to a higher state of consciousness, which activates a person's highest potential. The path of Evolutionary Leadership leads to a shifting of mindset or consciousness through the dissolving of egoic structures that are creating destructive behaviors.

Most spiritual traditions have developed techniques to eradicate the ego on their quest to shift into higher states of consciousness, the journey of enlightenment. The role spirituality plays in self-evolution can't be ignored for anyone serious about high-performance leadership, as it has been independently discovered in too many case studies.

Spirituality is the elephant in the room. It is an uncomfortable truth that will send people from a traditional organizational running. Spirituality is also a highly personal process that has been ridiculed and has caused much conflict. Paradoxically, it is also the elephant in the room due to the enormous power it has to evolve one's inner world.

High levels of performance are only available to leaders who are able to move their egos to the background, where they do not cause as much harm. As people are more conscious of thoughts, emotions, behaviors, and the workings of the ego, they are able to overcome destructive patterns and respond in a resourceful way.

Ricardo Semler also makes the argument that spirituality plays an important role in human performance. There are elements of the ego that need development to reach the highest levels of performance. He writes: "Society and business definition of talent is mostly IQ and it's incorrect. Equation for successful hires: 'IQ + EQ + SQ − EGO.' . . . For decades IQ has created an artificial (and loaded) baseline for intelligence and capability. More recently, evaluating EQ, or emotional content of intelligence, has become popular. Now SQ, or spiritual quotient, has been added to the equation. I mix the three together, and then subtract EGO (I know I would be in trouble with psychologists because ego includes most of the above, but I need a bit of poetic license for this homegrown theory.) . . . As such, it's important to keep egos under control" (Semler 2004, 66).

The logical endpoint of the journey of shifting consciousness is fully dissolving the ego or identity. The very highest levels of performance can be understood through the spiritual terms of awakening into higher states of consciousness and enlightenment. From this perspective, the inclusion of spiritual quotient (SQ) from the Semler equation makes total sense. As we obtain a broader, more conscious perspective on reality, we are able to make more effective decisions. When a person shifts their state of consciousness, the egoic behaviors are no longer exemplified. One behaves in ways that are in connection with people: stable, compassionate, emotionally clear, empowering others, and so on.

In addition to Semler's SQ, other thought leaders have identified spirituality in high-performance leadership and organizations. Anderson and Adams align with our understanding that enlightenment or unity consciousness is the logical endpoint on the journey away from the ego (Anderson and Adams 2015, 295). They have applied a "spiritual boot camp" to support a shift in consciousness and outline some of the practices (239).

In his exploration of extremely high-performing Teal organizations, Laloux found spirituality: "Often the shift to Teal comes with an opening to a transcendent spiritual realm and a profound sense that at some level, we are all connected and part of one big whole" (Laloux 2016, 48). While the main part of *Reinventing Organizations* avoids this topic, we found it buried in appendix 2, "Beyond Evolutionary-Teal." Laloux identifies spirituality as a way to understand what lies beyond Teal to achieve the higher levels of performance (Laloux 2016, 315–317).

In contrast, our contradictory view is that applied spirituality is needed at the start of the journey. It is an essential tool for normal people to evolve their leadership to the point where they can create high-performance evolutionary organizations.

SELF ENCODES SPIRITUAL WISDOM

The SHIFT314 Evolutionary Leadership Framework is the key to successful outcomes and is specifically designed to overcome the limitations of the ego, the identity with the self. In simple terms, we point to an understanding that you are the problem, you are the solution, and then we unlock your ability to evolve and achieve results. The acronym for our framework is SELF—it points to the central role one's *self* and people play on the journey to high performance.

As designers of SELF, we use the knowledge of the ego and its nature to create principles, models, and tools to penetrate the defensive structures of the ego. The SELF technology is an integration of ancient wisdom to shift consciousness and our own unique practices to create an accelerated evolutionary path.

This isn't about religion or some new age mumbo jumbo—it's about acting as an empirical scientist to run experiments and use what actually works in practice. Michael calls it "the weird stuff that works," and we both agree we are speaking to universal laws and principles. It's about using any means to create successful outcomes, no matter how weird or unconventional. Resistance to new ideas is itself the low-consciousness conditioning that keeps people trapped.

One way to understand the SELF system is a practical business-oriented way to integrate spiritual teachings to create results. We measure the effectiveness of any principle, model, or tool—spiritual or otherwise—in terms of its ability to help create a shift toward the reality we desire.

All spiritual practices were created to improve the life of a person and their environment. The challenge with many traditional spiritual practices is that people are unable to effectively integrate or apply the teachings and practices to improve their lives. Many are not seeing the full benefits in their life that these practices promise.

In contrast, the SELF system is a step-by-step guide that applies an integrated approach of business practices and Evolutionary Leadership behaviors to achieve results and improve one's life. Graduates and clients that use the SELF principles and tools report a greater sense of peace, deeper authentic connections alongside results of sustainable success within their organizations.

In our training worldwide, we have been told numerous times by people of various faiths that we have successfully embedded deep spiritual teachings into our work. It was never our intention to crack the code on integrating business and spirituality—instead, this was a surprising and emergent outcome of our work. In hindsight it makes perfect sense that spiritual practices are used to create a more effective way of being in the world (possibly its original intention).

We observe that each step taken toward being and acting in accordance with Evolutionary Leadership incrementally leads to higher levels of performance. It becomes a road less traveled for those leaders who have the courage to become aware of their egoic behaviors and choose to do the work required to shed these unproductive behavior patterns to lead in this more evolved new way. It's a choice to become an Evolutionary Leader.

YOUR TURN

- How comfortable are you looking at the destruction caused by your ego?

- Is your interest and readiness for your own evolution more surface level, or are you ready to dive into your inner reality?

- How comfortable are you with using what might be called "spiritual practices" to shift your leadership?

PART THREE

INTEGRATION AND APPLICATION

14 ■ LEADING

Your Evolutionary Journey

It was at this point that Bilbo stopped. Going on from there was the bravest thing he ever did. The tremendous things that happened afterward were nothing compared to it. He fought the real battle in the tunnel alone, before he ever saw the vast danger that lay in wait.

—J. R. R. Tolkien, *The Hobbit, or There and Back Again*

The Future Is in Your Hands
It's simple to remember facts and information. Yet, this book is not an ordinary book. It has the potential to shift your consciousness. The hardest part with integrating this work is to stay open and have awareness of your behaviors that create damage. Awareness alone is the technology to shift you into higher states of consciousness.

We are inviting you to a very confronting and paradoxically liberating place: you are both the problem and the solution. It is your choice for all that you hope to create in the world. It can be confronting because we are conditioned to focus on the external world—the problem is out there and we just need the right tools to change what's happening.

As human beings, we hold the possibility for self-evolution. It all starts with a desire and a choice. The sense of liberation and empowerment comes from the understanding that we can create anything we want by working on ourselves. And we can do so without authority, power, or a budget.

The whole of this book is to help the part of you that wants to achieve and succeed, to show you that the most rapid and direct means to create success is through self-evolution—the doing and being.

The Choice to Lead

Evolutionary Leadership is a journey to embody the ability to lead an organization into new ways of working. This is the leadership that inspires and invites an evolutionary response in a system. It comes from the wisdom gained through personal transformation. This journey will bring people and organizations along at a pace that is determined by your abilities to dissolve the ego and listen to the voice of the system. It is leadership that turns inward, understanding how the ego and consciousness play a part in creating reality. By looking inward, one can find the blocks that create resistance. The technology for shifting consciousness, while ancient, has been hidden, a best-kept secret, yet it is available to those who are willing to cross barriers. This evolutionary path is for those who have the desire to create impact in extraordinary ways.

It is a choice to go on this journey. It's not a journey for everyone. It is for leaders who want to create profound change. The Laws of Organizational Dynamics integrated with the technology to shift consciousness is available and here to explore and discover for yourself. It takes desire and commitment for transformation. Your "why" can be for yourself, to impact the extraordinary for others, or to unlock your organization's potential for success. The information, the knowledge, and the wisdom must be cultivated by your own experience.

Everything Counts

Leading is an emergent phenomenon. It's about the choices you make. The measure of whether leadership is present in your choices is measured by the outcome. When people are willing to follow you of their own free and clear choice, then you have succeeded in leading in that moment with that specific choice.

Leading Beyond Change is about becoming aware of all the choices—both conscious and unconscious—that you are making. Everything that is happening around you is a reflection of your leadership. Everything that happens in an organizational system is ultimately a reflection of leadership—the organizational structures, the processes, the approach to change, the use of power, the treatment of people, the culture, and so on. All of these aspects of an organizational system reflect the choices of the people who hold the power.

SELF Is about Your Self

The SHIFT314 Evolutionary Leadership Framework (SELF) is a path that consists of models, principles, maps, and tools to ultimately show that you—your self—is the root and foundation of what you may desire or wish to achieve with your organization. SELF is the journey of Evolutionary Leadership. The whole of this book can be seen as an invitation, or perhaps an elaborate trap, to help you realize that you are both the problem and the solution. Success leading and a shift to high-performance organizations depends entirely on your self.

The Evolution of High Performance

What one might call a trap is actually a sophisticated explanation of the path to high performance. It's based on the common-sense laws of cause and effect that we have gathered together under the title The Laws of Organizational Dynamics.

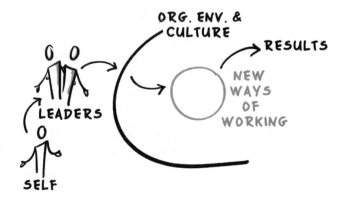

Figure 14.1: Map: Evolution of High Performance

Let's revisit the map, the Evolution of High Performance (figure 14.1), that captures these laws. Results depend on new ways of working, which in turn depend on the organizational environment and culture.

It is only by evolving one's self that one can model an evolved way of working and being to create leaders at all levels. It is the leaders who create the organizational environment and culture through moment-by-moment choices, behaviors, ways of being, and ultimately their consciousness. The key, then, to the evolution of a high-performance organization rests with the evolution of one's self.

Evolutionary Leadership

*Evolutionary Leadership is the **choice** to evolve **oneself** and develop the capabilities needed to evolve an organization.*

Evolutionary Leadership begins with the choice to evolve. Not just with doing but more importantly with our very being to navigate and come to peace with the ego.

There are two dimensions to the choice:

1. *Being:* The ongoing commitment to evolve one's consciousness to a more evolved state of being.

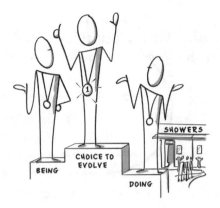

2. *Doing:* The ongoing commitment to understand and apply the Laws of Organizational Dynamics, or SELF, or better evolve people and systems.

Evolutionary Leadership Is the Core of SELF

Evolutionary Leadership is the core of SELF. The entirety of this book gives you the path, with practical maps, models, formulas, tools, and patterns, to support the being and the doing of Evolutionary Leadership.

Key patterns of personal evolution that lead to organizational evolution are:

- *Discovering reality*—An increasing understanding and curiosity around what reality is.
- *Unlearning*—Evolving a greater level of readiness to surrender existing models and beliefs.
- *You are the solution*—An increasing awareness that external challenges are linked with internal ones and that outer victory follows inner victory.
- *Serving purpose*—A deepening sense of interconnectedness and interdependence that leads to moving beyond egoic consciousness.
- *Letting go of control*—The evolving understanding that we operate in complex systems and that release and surrender are far more effective than can be imagined.

- *Increasing freedom*—The increasing recognition that people are sovereign human beings and that operating from this premise is required to fully respect people.
- *Responsibility*—The development of greater levels of personal responsibility, knowing impact, and cleanup in all aspects of our doing and being to act as an impeccable role model.
- *Psychological safety*—Evolving one's own inner sense of psychological safety to operate at the highest levels of functioning and consequently elevate others.
- *Equal voice*—Using listening to demonstrate greater levels of respect and developing others.

Getting Started with Evolutionary Leadership

1. The best starting place is reality. Review and apply the principles and practices in unlearning.
2. Understand your gaps. Read through the various patterns to get a sense of where your leadership edges—your biggest challenge areas—are.
3. Start with your being. Use the oxygen mask and self-awareness to slow down so you can discover the reality around how you are impacting others.
4. Start with your doing. Use the tools outlined throughout the book to explore new ways to interact more effectively with those around you.
5. Observe. Increase the amount of time you spend listening and observing.
6. Learn. Turn all your facts and knowledge about what is going on around you into assumptions to test and validate.
7. Experiment. Run small experiments where you make a different choice than you would have in the past. Notice how it feels for you and how people respond.

Your Evolutionary Journey

Evolutionary leaders take on a personal commitment and embody the personal responsibility of self evolution. There is a direct understanding and application of not only a *desire* to shift behaviors, thoughts, and belief systems that model a new way of being, there is an *actual shift* in consciousness with behaviors that reflect a higher state of being. With a shift in consciousness, there is a permanent actualization of a way of being that is authentic, connected, inclusive, responsible, and unconditional.

This style of leadership has evolved from a deep sense of wisdom gained through the practice of clearing egoic patterns. Simply choosing to be an Evolutionary Leader is not sufficient. Effective progress requires a path for personal transformation. The path includes the practical skills to evolve organizational systems and the technology to shift consciousness. Most important, it requires the commitment of seeing the external world only as a reflection of the inner world and thus taking the responsibility to clear the inner world.

The effects of this type of self-awareness and evolution create an effortless shift in behavior, way of thinking, and conditioning. Evolutionary Leadership then becomes a transmission through the very being of the individual. The metric of this type of evolution and modeled leadership behavior is an impact of a shift in consciousness and evolution within any system they come in contact with, both within the personal life and professional life of an Evolutionary Leader.

 Model: Leadership: Traditional to Evolutionary

Table 14.1 shows the contrast between the key aspects of the journey from traditional leadership to Evolutionary Leadership. We contrast the differing views of key topics related to leadership to highlight the breadth and depth of the shift needed in the worldview of consciousness to make the change. The information in this book is about illuminating the path or the journey. Actually choosing to walk the path is your freedom and choice.

Table 14.1: Leadership: From Traditional to Evolutionary

Belief/Topic	Traditional	Evolutionary
Awareness	Unaware of impact.	Conscious of choices, consequences, and impact.
Focus	Focus on doing.	Focus on a way of being that unlocks the doing.
Modeling	Tells people what to do. View of own behavior as not relevant.	Knows the importance to lead by example, to set the tone for the organization.
Development approach	Traditional leadership development of skills and coaching.	Dedicated to working through one's limiting behaviors to unlock greater impact.
External vs. internal	Focused on changing the external world— the organization.	Focused on changing the inner world first to shift the external world.
Style	Traditional management of objectives and goals.	Evolutionary Leadership with choice for self-evolution and learning how to evolve organization.
Organizational focus	Manages people and organization to deliver on outcomes and goals.	Creating a great environment for people and developing leaders at all levels.
Control	Believes that they have control of the organization and must exercise it to create success.	Recognizes the inherent inability to control a complex system and has developed internal capability of releasing control and surrender.
Use of power	Exercises power and authority to make changes.	Uses influence as primary means in change and authority only when needed.
Sharing power	Limited or oversharing through autonomy.	Sharing power and decisions iteratively and incrementally to develop staff. Uses Advice Process.
Impact	Fear anxiety and low performance, unsustainable success.	Evolution of others and systems, extends beyond professional environment.

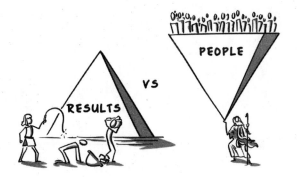

Your Turn

- Where do you see yourself on the leadership journey from Traditional to Evolutionary?
- How invested are you in the choice to evolve yourself?
- What parts of "Getting Started with Evolutionary Leadership" are the most important for you to focus on?

15 ■ BEYOND

Moving into the Beyond

You can't connect the dots looking forward; you can only connect them looking backwards. So you have to trust that the dots will somehow connect in your future. You have to trust in something— your gut, destiny, life, karma, whatever. This approach has never let me down, and it has made all the difference in my life.

—Steve Jobs

From Traditional to Evolutionary

Whether you call beyond the future of work, business agility, or Teal, we invite you to a broader understanding through the term *Evolutionary*. We invite a holistic and integrated view of the beyond. As shown in figure 15.1, all levels of the tree, from understanding reality to results, all are deeply interconnected. (The Laws of Organizational Dynamics express the underlying connection between cause and effect.)

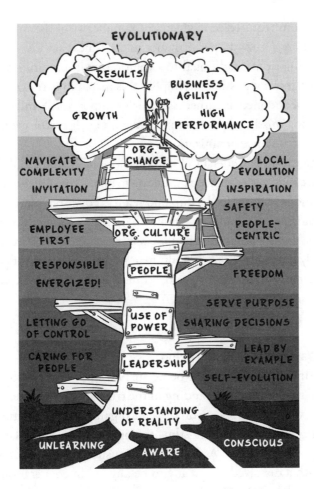

Figure 15.1: Map: Evolutionary (Tree)

Now it is possible to see the connections. As leaders are able to understand and more accurately perceive external reality and inner reality, they will unlock their own Evolutionary Leadership journey to lead by example. Through this process they will learn how to navigate the paradox of power to wield the smallest possible power to let go of control, agenda, and to recognize the inherent sovereignty of every human being. It becomes about their own evolution as responsible, energized cocreators of an organizational culture that truly values people. This evolutionary shift will unlock the local adaptations required to navigate the complexity of the world to create sustained growth, performance and business agility.

Moving from Traditional to Evolutionary is a multidimensional journey. It is not possible to simplify this map. No part of this model can be abandoned as unnecessary or unimportant. Similarly, there is nothing missing: it is a complete map to navigate the evolution of high-performance organizations.

One can now understand all books, models, rules, and theories on increasing performance as speaking to one of the dimensions. Radical candor is about leadership and reality. Focus on relationships is not really about people, it is about the understanding of our reality and the reality of our leadership. Creating psychological safety is ultimately not really about the culture or people or even use of power— it's diving into the depths of our inner reality to unlock safety in our own being.

New Ways of Working and Being

The principle "a new way of being enables a new way of working" is not a fancy slogan, it is standing in the truth of what it takes to work with new ways of working or Teal-like organizational structures. The maturity of the people and thus the organization is the key factor for high performance. A shift in consciousness enables one to "show up" with a dissolved ego, ready to be aligned in cooperation, motivation, collaboration, engagement, and intelligence. This creates an organization filled with leaders at all levels—people who have a passion and desire to create great outcomes.

We believe there is an opportunity to change the world of work—to create systems where people are motivated, happy, and operating as their best selves. The outcomes are organizations that create products and services that change society and build relationships that support the brilliance of others. We believe there is an opportunity for organizations to model high-performance cultures with new ways of working. And perhaps the new world of work will show humanity that it can overcome and reach new heights of human potential.

There is no way for people to fully embody the highly evolved new structures and new ways of working without an evolution into higher states of consciousness. The new structures and ways of working that will create high-performance organizations can be only achieved when there are behaviors that function in alignment with new ways of working.

For example, transparency of payroll throughout the system will not feel safe or be tolerated by those who function as Theory X workers, a type of thinking and behavior that comes from a lower state of consciousness. This produces resentment, jealousy, and can be the activator of behaviors such as demotivation, backstabbing, or noncooperation. Another example would be, Do you or your organization trust people? Are there open budgets and expense accounts? Do people manage their own leave days and vacation days?

Model: Organizational Culture: Traditional to Evolutionary

We can see organizational culture as a clear way to understand an organization's journey into the Beyond. The two definitions of culture from the SHIFT314 Culture Model clarify why culture serves as a key indicator of evolutionary progress:

- Culture is the dynamic emergent cocreation of the unifying fabric of organizational reality.
- Culture is the wibbly-wobbly thing that connects everything.

Table 15.1 highlights the key indicators of a shift in organizational culture from Traditional to Evolutionary.

We offer a free survey that allows you to take a pulse on the culture of your organization by sensing various factors that lead to organizational performance. You can access the survey here: https://www.comparativeagility.com/capabilities/organizational-performance-assessment/.

Table 15.1: Organizational Culture: From Traditional to Evolutionary

Belief/Topic	Traditional	Evolutionary
Reality	Challenging information is ignored or denied.	Openness and curiosity to discover new information.
Learning	Limited learning.	Unlearning.
Evolution	Status quo is acceptable.	Evolution is needed for ongoing adaptation.
Focus	Profit first or customer first.	Employee first.
Management	Traditional management structures and concepts are sufficient.	The responsibility of management is to unleash people's capabilities.
Employees	Theory X. Resources to be managed.	Theory Y. People are the organization.
Culture	Culture is an afterthought.	Culture is the basis for success.
Psychological safety	Fear, stress, blame, cover-ups.	Support, caring, openness, equal voice
Equal voice	Management controls agenda.	Everyone can contribute.
Engagement	Low, partial, and mixed levels.	High. It's an important topic.
Development	Strengths and skills.	Personal growth.

Your Turn

- Where do you see your organization on its journey from Traditional to Evolutionary?
- How much desire do you sense in your organization to evolve from the current organizational culture?
- What beliefs or topics are more open to discussion and growth?

16 ■ CHANGE

Evolving Your Organization

For want of a nail, the shoe was lost.
For want of a shoe, the horse was lost.
For want of a horse, the rider was lost.
For want of a rider, the battle was lost.
For want of a battle, the kingdom was lost,
And all for the want of a horseshoe nail.

—Anonymous

Beyond Change

We hope that at this point any notion of linear, ordered, systematic change has completely left your system. The understanding that change is really about emergence is happening simultaneously on many levels and aspects of organizational systems.

Evolutionary leaders embrace the complexity and surrender to the emergence of what is coming. No one is in control. We are all co-creating the future together. It's a messy, organic, nonlinear, unfolding with ups and downs, twists and turns. All we can do is expect the unexpected.

A growth in consciousness is required to lead and fully participate in such a journey. Leaders need to have enough inner psychological safety to stay the course and let go of control. It is important to understand the paradox of power to such a degree that they can uplift the safety of others while still creating a space for them to grow and contribute (we call this mastery).

History shows us that only a handful of leaders worldwide have been able to lead organizational evolution to such a degree that they have been able to create evolutionary organizations. The truth is that all the powerful tools for the evolution of organizations shared in this book will only unlock for you to the extent that you progress on your leadership journey.

SELF Core Principles

This book presents a rich tapestry of integrated insights important for navigating the inner and outer journey of evolution. The SELF Core Principles are the key principles that summarize the whole book.

The core principles can serve as a kata or practice to guide your own journey as you apply this work. We invite you to slowly read each core principle two times and pause to reflect what it feels like in your being.

Question Your Assumptions

The biggest trap for change is that leaders will interpret all the maps, models, tools, and principles in this book from their current level of consciousness. What this means is that one's existing way of perceiving reality limits the ability to fully understand the meaning of what is shared here. While we may assume we understand, it's more likely to be a partial or distorted understanding to fit with existing worldviews.

Our best advice is to assume that you don't fully understand any part of this book so that you stay open to discovering deeper meanings. The

SELF Core Principles

1. Create an engaging workplace: psychological safety is the cornerstone of high performance.
2. Unlearning is the most powerful form of learning: the ego is the root cause of performance issues.
3. Discover reality to unlock success: listen to the voice of the system.
4. Culture follows leadership: the consciousness of the leader is the limit of an organization.
5. All resistance is created by you: ability to navigate complexity depends on consciousness.
6. Organizational evolution follows leadership evolution: production capability = your future.
7. Put the oxygen mask on first: your own evolution is the most direct and rapid means to create high performance.
8. Employees first: believe in people.
9. Go with the energy: focus on local evolution.
10. Structures follow consciousness: a new way of being enables a new way of working.

astute reader will realize we are simply reminding you of a key to getting started with Evolutionary Leadership:

> *Learn. Turn all your "facts" and "knowledge" about understanding organizational change into assumptions to test and validate.*

Of course, there are likely some very practical changes you can make with your current level of evolution. However, the full benefits and ability to unlock evolutionary change will only come as you grow and evolve yourself.

Let the Maps Guide You

At the start of a journey, it's a good idea to study maps to see what route to take. Take the time to familiarize yourself with each dimension or level in the Traditional and Evolutionary maps. If you haven't already done so, this is a good time to connect each of the patterns to the levels in the map. Take note of what parts of the maps are more comfortable for you and what parts are less clear.

Put the Oxygen Mask on First

The Reality Matrix Map (figure 16.1) shows the connection between cause and effect. So of course the best starting place is with you. Your understanding of reality. Your leadership. You can be the lynchpin—the horseshoe nail—that can save the kingdom. Any hope of evolution rests with your evolution. So your work is to put the oxygen mask on first. The level of evolution of your leadership will determine the upper bound for you to help anyone else.

Go with the Energy

Remember, the most important advice is to go with the energy. Who are the early adopters? Where can local change take place? What dimension or level of the Jenga/tree is more open to invitation at this time? What do people want?

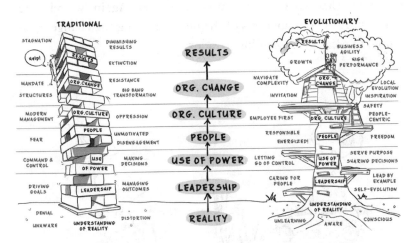

Figure 16.1: Maps: Traditional to Evolutionary with Reality Matrix

How Long Will It Take?

Following a specific time frame is a guaranteed way to destroy any hope of real change. The rate of evolution of an organization is a reflection of the rate of evolution of the people in it.

Once one has made the choice to be an Evolutionary Leader, the emergence of an evolutionary organization around you is a matter of simple physics: progress is a function of your rate of evolution and time. As time is a fixed variable, the only factor that you have control over is your rate of evolution. This is why increasing your evolutionary capability—your rate of evolution—is the most important thing to focus on.

Model: Organizational Change: Traditional to Evolutionary

In table 16.1 we offer a contrast between Traditional and Evolutionary views of organizational change. The table is useful in highlighting challenges with an existing approach to organizational change and points to the possibility of evolving new approaches. Simply copying an Evolutionary approach to change is not going to work. That actually falls into the Traditional approach to "Solution Location." Instead, what is needed is to find an approach to change that works in your unique context. Again, we reiterate that a shift in consciousness of the people leading the change is essential to escape this seeming paradox.

Table 16.1: Organizational Change: From Traditional to Evolutionary

Belief/Topic	Traditional	Evolutionary
Goal	Define the target *state* that can be achieved.	Create a "star on the horizon"—an *ideal* to be strived toward.
Complexity	The workings of the organization can be *modeled and understood*.	The organization is a very *complex system*—we can only have a limited understanding.
Organizational nature	The organization is a *mechanical system*.	The organization is a *complex system*.
Model of change	The organization can be mechanically *changed* from one way of functioning to another.	It's an *emergent journey*, not a destination.
Time frame	It is possible to plan and achieve a shift in organizational functioning in a *fixed time horizon*.	The future will *emerge over time*.
Solution location	It is possible and practical to *copy solutions* from other organizations.	Our organization applies internal and external information to find *solutions that work in our context*.
Control	The change process can be *controlled*.	The change process is emergent, and we see how to *influence* it.
Approach	*Transformation* program.	*Everyday work.*
Choice	Change is *mandatory*.	Change is *invited*—people grow at a rate they can handle.
Leadership	Role is delegate responsibility and to *support* change.	Role is to assume responsibility and to *model and inspire* change.
Scope	*Everyone* needs to change.	Sustainable change happens *locally*.
Motivation	Focus is on mandating change and ignoring or squashing resistance.	Invitation and inspiring change. Creating space and time to integrate people and groups.
Culture awareness	Strategy and tactics dominate agenda.	Culture is considered the foundation of all change.

Your Turn

- Where on the spectrum from Traditional to Evolutionary is the approach to organizational change where you work?
- What assumptions do you have about what effective organizational change should look like in your environment?
- What is your personal rate of evolution?

17 ■ Application Tips and Traps

In theory there is no difference between theory and practice, while in practice there is.

—Anonymous

Your Turn = Your Truth

If you have read this book and taken time to answer all the Your Turn questions, then you will likely have created a shift in how you see yourself and how you see the world around you. This new awareness itself is the shift in consciousness this whole book is speaking of.

It may be the case that you have skipped over the Your Turn questions either by just reading them or answering them in your head. If you have skipped writing out answers, it may be a clue about your level of investment in your leadership journey. If you did skip them, don't worry—it's never too late to go back. You can go back now to the start of the book and answer all the questions. If this activity feels like too much work or you will "do it later," you might want to question your commitment to your own evolution.

In our experience, from our own evolutionary journey and from training and consulting worldwide, we can tell you that the understanding and insights that are fresh in your mind are likely rather fragile. What is crisp and clear in your mind right now may start to fade off as the world around you pulls you toward Traditional, low-consciousness ways of operation, and your own conditioned behavior patterns will disrupt the clarity.

In this chapter, we will discuss putting this work into practice so that you can keep an evolved perspective in mind and start the journey of putting this work into practice.

Invitation to the Extraordinary

Reading books or learning concepts is of no value unless you are putting it into practice. Information is to put thoughts into form or "information." You are the one who runs the experiment of application. Apply theories, ideas, and concepts into your own situation for validation. Things do not change if there is no action.

From here you will not only have an experience of how the concepts work, you will have an opportunity to shift your organizational and personal performance. As you explore the patterns of this work, you will also find there are deeper learnings to be discovered through practical application.

We invite you to begin the experimentation and validation of the concepts. Please, do not take our word for it. The ultimate journey is to go deep into the experience of applying the concepts within this book. You will discover that some concepts are easy and are approachable for quickly shifting your organization, and some will be more difficult to put into practice.

You may find that at times you fail to get the expected outcome. Our advice is to get up and try something different. More important, take time to reflect on what you have learned, what you have gained in perception and experience, and how you grew. In the context of your evolutionary journey, these are actually more important than a single success in the moment. There is no such thing as failure, only learning and growth. These concepts, when applied correctly, will direct you to the pathways that flow into successful outcomes.

Truth is found in the paradox of experience. You may not like what you find, go into denial, or just flat out believe that what we have given in this book is of no value. Again, we have given you the patterns of confirmation bias, hidden truth to organizational realities, and how your leadership behaviors can block your success.

All of the concepts and patterns within this book have been proven out. Many students, including ourselves, have used these patterns and techniques to gain vast amounts of success within organizations and with our own personal evolution. This work is proven, and many have experienced sustainable success. The truth is only that you stop the success of applying the patterns and techniques laid out here. These are the Laws of Organizational Dynamics—only you can break yourself against these universal principles.

Enjoy the journey and take what you need; our only ask is that you remain open to explore and discover this work's potential. Try going to your leadership edges and thinking beyond the box toward the organizational change you have been hoping for. Find places where there might be a hidden reality, or perceptions that have been blocking your success.

Go beyond what makes you comfortable because these are the experiences where you will find the most growth. To achieve the biggest wins, both for you personally and for the organization, the answers are not "out there." To find the truth, seek an inward focus.

The Way You Do One Thing Is the Way You Do Everything

While there may be safe places in your organization to test out elements of this book, we invite you to explore a potentially much more profound opportunity for growth: your home. Your private life offers many small organizational systems to use and apply the information in this book. This may be the environment where it is safe to try. You and your life partner/spouse form an organizational system. Your immediate and extended family are also an organizational system. You may want to impact the organizational system of the community or volunteer groups in which you participate.

Each of these organizational systems are places for you to explore your leadership, your approach to change, and reflect on the unique cultures. Opportunities to work through your leadership edges and evolve as a leader are everywhere, in every situation.

To quote Buckaroo Banzai, "No matter where you go, there you are." We invite you to set aside the traditional organization's fiction of a mask: one for work, one for home, one for friends, and so on. There's just you. Since there is just you, learning in one context will help you in other contexts since the way you do one thing is the way you do everything.

Use any and all environments to explore who you are and how you show up for yourself and for others. Your life partner or your kids may be your greatest allies—not because they will directly help you but because they will reflect back to you exactly how you are showing up as a leader. Yes, your inability to navigate issues at home is just there to show how you are the problem and how you can be the solution (affectionate smiles from authors here).

Traps to Avoid

It takes consistent effort to shift out of the conditioned thoughts and behavior patterns of a Traditional way of doing and being. To support and accelerate your journey, we identify the key traps that our training graduates and clients tend to fall into.

Trap #1: Telling People about Information from This Book

It's totally fine to tell people about this book and how it has helped you to grow and be more effective. If they ask, you can tell them. Use the Green List and wait for a pull signal. The trap is that people fall into the Red List to sell or convince people to do things differently.

Tip: There is a simple rule to follow: never mention this book unless someone asks about what you are doing differently and how you learned it. Otherwise, it's a push into the system, and it will create resistance that will block the actual change you hope for. It's all about desire. Have patience to wait for the pull signal. You will be glad you did.

Trap #2: Noticing Other People's Behavior

This is a really tough one. Once you have read this book, you are going to see Traditional behavior everywhere. It will especially be easy to spot it in other people's behaviors. It may be very tempting to just point it out to help them grow. Unless you have a coaching contract or agreement with that person to give them feedback and they are open to feedback in that moment, sharing any information about their behavior will do more harm than good.

Tip: There is a simple rule to follow: only apply the information in this book to yourself. Don't look at or worry about anyone else's behavior. Instead, focus on your own growth. There is a simple saying: "If you spot it, you've got it." That's right—any annoying behavior you see in others means that you also have that same behavior. Focus on your own irritation or frustration with how they are showing up, and work through that. Once you are clear, then you may be able to help them.

Trap #3: Teaching This Information

There are two challenges people tend to encounter when attempting to teach the information in this book. The first challenge is that they think the book is about knowing and doing. Helping people evolve is simply about sharing knowledge and developing skills. This is the trap of Traditional thinking.

The whole point of this book is that a shift in consciousness or mindset is needed to unlock new ways of doing and being. Once we shift our being, we act as a living transmission for an evolved state of being. It is only from this state of being that we can truly impact people. Once we make the shift in our consciousness, we can teach from our experience so that it really lands in people. Only then will our teaching have the impact we may hope for.

Tip: The simple rule to follow is to focus on your own mastery of this work. You must be a practitioner before you can be an effective

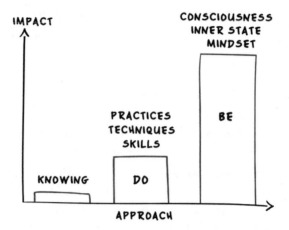

teacher. The way you will know you have developed mastery with your own leadership practice is that you will see people around you copying your evolved behavior patterns.

Your Turn

- What percentage of the Your Turn exercises in the book have you completed in writing?
- What personal context feels important for you to evolve your leadership so you can get better results?
- Which of the three traps do you think you are likely to fall into based on your history?

18 ■ Continuing the Journey

The journey of a thousand miles begins with one step.

—Lao Tzu

Leading Beyond Change is an invitation to start the journey to Evolutionary Leadership. We have developed this path to support your evolution. The whole of your journey lies ahead. Without clarity and determination to evolve, additional tools and capabilities are of little use.

The SHIFT314 Evolutionary Leadership Framework (SELF) provides an integrated system to encapsulate and make accessible the Laws of Organizational Dynamics. It serves as a powerful foundation and starting place for a renewed cycle of growth and evolution for those who are ready to step away from the constraints and limitations of earlier models and systems of thought.

SELF Extensions

The book you have just read, *Leading Beyond Change*, is just one small part of a body of knowledge that constitutes the Evolutionary Leadership evolution path through the SELF. In this book, we have curated the most important foundational elements to support your success. Below we outline some elements that are the continuation of *Leading Beyond Change*.

1. SELF Application Toolkit

We have developed an extensive toolkit that provides the models, maps, principles, and tools to increase one's evolutionary capabilities both at a personal and organizational level. It's an integrated understanding that connects doing with being. This specific path of SELF has been created as an accelerator for evolution.

Personal tools include increasing self-awareness, rapid behavior change, laser listening, and so on. Organization tools include playbooks for high performance, creating alignment, system diagnosis and awareness, developing psychological safety, and so on. Below we introduce two examples that are the SELF foundational pieces of Evolutionary Leadership.

The SELF 4A's Leadership™

The SELF 4A's Leadership is a model, tool, and practice that unlocks rapid shifts in behavior patterns. These are needed to support the shift in behavior needed to move from Traditional to Evolutionary. The 4A's model comes from the technologies to shift consciousness. It includes universal principles that are cultivated to accelerate the dissolving of even the toughest behavior patterns. The model itself is very simple: Awareness, Acceptance, Aspiration, and Ask for help. It is such an important tool in evolution, we have included free access to it via our website: https://shift314.com/leading-beyond -change.

SHIFT314 Playbook for High Performance

The SHIFT314 Playbook™ is an integrated step-by-step guide to invite organizational evolution based on the evolved consciousness

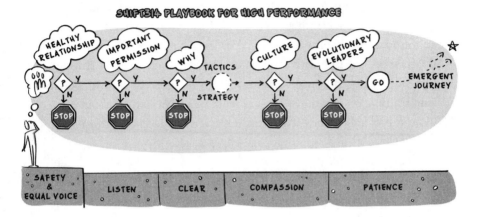

Figure 18.1: SHIFT314 Playbook for High Performance

principles identified in this book. It is a technology for listening to the voice of the system to understand its readiness for evolution. The playbook is a foundational aspect of SELF.

The SHIFT314 Playbook is used to understand how to navigate your organizational system. It is also a guide to see if an organization or group is ready to start an evolutionary journey. There are two aspects to the playbook. The upper SHIFT314 Playbook is the "doing," and the bottom or foundation of the playbook is the "being." The foundation serves as a reminder of the state of consciousness needed to operate this playbook.

The SHIFT314 Playbook is a technology we developed as a foundational personal tool to integrate and apply the patterns and consciousness of Evolutionary Leadership. A simplified version of the Playbook is illustrated in figure 18.1. The SHIFT314 Playbook for High Performance is very specific, and the guidelines for how to use it are only introduced through our leadership training and certified practioner programs.

2. Emotional Science

Emotions run our lives. Emotions trump thinking, analysis, and logic. We were inspired to write the book *Emotional Science* to guide people in discovering for themselves exactly how their emotional system works. We have integrated the techniques in *Emotional Science* as foundational tools within the SHIFT314 Evolutionary Leadership Framework (SELF). This is desperately needed to penetrate through the half-truths and misunderstandings propagated by leading books and training on emotions. Most of what you have learned about emotions is probably incorrect and keeps you at a low level of performance. You need to clear your emotional charge.

People who have read *Emotional Science* use the simple techniques to experience profound shifts in their inner being. Many wonder what the world would be like if everyone knew how their emotional system actually works.

One person reports: "This model is extremely helpful to me as I strive to find constructive ways to deal with my emotions. I have a deliberate method of processing the myriad emotions that surface while I face challenges with my environment and with other people."

As emotional regulation is such a pivotal practice for self-evolution, we have included free access to the Get Clear tool via our website: https://shift314.com/leading-beyond-change.

3. Evolutionary Energetics

Evolutionary Energetics™ (E2) addresses the energetic world that we live in. It explores the quantum field and how to interact within this unseen world. Evolutionary Energetics was founded by Audree and comes from her discovery of an advanced chakra system in 2008. E2 opens a direct access to high-vibrational energies for rapid healing and transformation. Consciousness is directly related to energetic frequencies within the body and the environment. It is prudent for those who want to shift into higher states of consciousness to obtain knowledge about the use of energetic frequencies as they impact the body and the environment. We have integrated the SELF technology and tools into the E2 training to support an acceleration of an evolutionary shift in consciousness.

The Grounding Meditation from E2 is a powerful tool to stabilize your being so that you can be present in the moment and evolve at a faster pace. We have included free access to the Grounding Meditation via our website: https://shift314.com/leading-beyond -change.

For further information on Evolutionary Energetics, we refer you to its website https://evolutionaryenergetics.com.

4. Academy of Leadership Mastery

The SHIFT314 Evolutionary Leadership Framework can be understood at a deeper level as a technology for shifting consciousness. It is a path to support the journey of Evolutionary Leadership, and we have created courses for each level of desire, progress, and evolution. Extraordinary leadership is required to create the very highest levels of performance. As our flagship offering, it is the path we offer for those to become a certified practioner of the SELF.

The Academy of Leadership Mastery is an accelerated Evolutionary Leadership program to shift consciousness. It is grounded in the SELF system to provide integration and application with daily life and work. The academy is an advanced dive deep into the nature of the egoic structures and our sense of identity or self. It's about how we experience reality—the foundation level of the Reality Matrix map. We have designed the academy for all those who have a passion for Evolutionary Leadership in all aspects of life, no certification required.

We offer a fusion of ancient and contemporary wisdom traditions integrated into our own unique Technology of Consciousness. We have nicknamed this Jedi School. This program will change the very fabric of who you are. In a good way.

The academy is a residential Evolutionary Leadership development program. For further information on The Academy of Leadership Mastery, we refer you to the SHIFT314 website: https://shift314.com.

Creating a Better World Together

The journey before you may be the most challenging of your life. What we know from our own experiences and from those we have trained and mentored is that it may also be the most rewarding. It can be daunting to look at and accept our conditioning and almost-constant self-sabotage that leads to inner and outer conflict.

Perhaps the greatest gift that unfolds is a sense of inner peace. We can only create peace in the outer world—our homes, our workplaces, our society—when we have peace in our inner world.

We appreciate you joining us on the journey to be our best selves, and through that, to create a better world together.

In this appendix, we share the elements of the SHIFT314 Evolutionary Leadership Framework (SELF).

SELF Core Principles

1. Create an engaging workplace: psychological safety is the cornerstone of high performance.
2. Unlearning is the most powerful form of learning: the ego is the root cause of performance issues.
3. Discover reality to unlock success: listen to the voice of the system.
4. Culture follows leadership: the consciousness of the leader is the limit of an organization.
5. All resistance is created by you: the ability to navigate complexity depends on consciousness.
6. Organizational evolution follows leadership evolution: production capability = your future.
7. Put the oxygen mask on first: your own evolution is the most direct and rapid means to create high performance.
8. Employees first: believe in people.
9. Go with the energy: focus on local evolution.
10. Structures follow consciousness: a new way of being enables a new way of working.

Part One: Starting the Journey

Maps	Traditional (Jenga)
	Evolutionary (Tree)
	Traditional to Evolutionary
	Reality Matrix
	The Evolution of High Performance
Models	Evolutionary Leadership
	Being Over Doing
	Integration of Culture, Leadership, and Org Change
	Evolutionary Organization
Principle	Listen to the voice of the system
Tool	Readout

Part Two: Patterns for Leading Beyond Change
Unlearning Reality: Can You Handle the Truth?

Models	Reality Distortion Field
	Unlearning
	Local Optimization Trap
Principles	Discover reality to unlock success
	The brain is designed avoid learning
	Unlearning is the most powerful form of learning
	I play a role in what's happening around me
Tools	Navigate Conflicting Ideas
	Question Your Assumptions
	Keep a Tension Journal
	Investigate Your Self

Getting Results—Beyond Organizational Survival

Models	Navigate Complexity to Survive
	The SELF Evolutionary Culture Model
Principles	Believe in people
	Business as usual = Low performance
	Organizational performance follows consciousness

The Truth about Your Organizational Culture

Models	Virtuous Cycle
	Healthy Ecosystem
	Theory X and Theory Y
	SHIFT314 Culture Model
	Culture Is a Fractal
Principles	Employees first
	Culture follows leadership
	Culture influence varies with power
	The consciousness of the leader is the limit of an organization
Tool	Cocreate Values for Yourself

It's All about the People

Models	Psychological Safety Spectrum
	Equal Voice
	Employee Engagement = Management Scorecard
Principles	Create an engaging workplace
	Psychological safety is the cornerstone of high performance
	Focus on self-evolution
Tools	Listen First, Speak Last
	High-Performance Meeting Protocol
	Use Zero for Neutral in Surveys

The Paradox of Power

Model	Responsibility Spectrum
Principles	Leading is an emergent phenomenon
	Leadership emerges from the responsible use of power
	Control is an illusion
	Embrace emergence
	Cultivate surrender
	Eliminate oppression
	Autonomy follows interdependence

Self-organization follows responsibility

Share power iteratively and incrementally

Tools	Four Karmas
	Boundaries
	Hold Space
	We Not Me
	Decision Cards
	Advice Process

Organizational Evolution

Models	Complexity Spectrum
	Tactics, Strategy, Culture
	Culture Bubbles
	Leaders Go First
	Red List (How to Create Resistance)
	Green List (Leading through Influence)
	Organizational Readiness
	Organizational Temperature

Principles	Ability to navigate complexity depends on consciousness
	The consciousness of the change approach limits the consciousness of the outcome
	Production capability = your future
	Strategy follows culture
	Culture is a dynamic, emergent phenomenon
	Align on the goal
	Culture is a local phenomenon
	Focus on local evolution
	Structures follow consciousness
	A new way of being enables a new way of working
	Organizational evolution follows personal evolution
	Organizational evolution follows leadership evolution
	Culture change is not delegatable
	All resistance is created by you
	Go with the energy
	Get the system cooking

Make time for growth

Exit staff to support a healthy environment

Tools	Safe-to-Run Experiments
	Why Workshop
	Culture Adapters
	Amplify Helpful Attractors
	Dampen Unhelpful Attractors

Evolutionary Leadership

Models	Leaders at All Levels
	Employee Motivation
	Journey to Conscious Competence
	Evolutionary Mindset
	Leadership Edge
Principles	Employee self-interest is the highest form of corporate alignment
	Believe in people
	Develop people's capabilities
	Modeling behavior is the most rapid way to inspire evolution in others
	You can only lead others to the extent that you can lead yourself
	Self-awareness unlocks consciousness
	Being is the foundation of doing
	Your own evolution is the most direct and rapid means to create high performance
	Identity is the foundation of the self
	The ego is the root cause of performance issues
Tools	Oxygen Mask
	Self-Awareness

Part Three: Integration and Application

Models	Leadership: Traditional to Evolutionary
	Organizational Culture: Traditional to Evolutionary
	Organizational Change: Traditional to Evolutionary

References

Robert J. Anderson and William A. Adams. *Mastering Leadership: An Integrated Framework for Breakthrough Performance and Extraordinary Business Results* (Hoboken, NJ: John Wiley, 2015).

Jurgen Appelo. *Management 3.0: Leading Agile Developers, Developing Agile Leaders* (Upper Saddle River, NJ: Addison-Wesley Professional, 2010).

Arbinger Institute. *Leadership and Self-Deception: Getting Out of the Box* (San Francisco, CA: Berrett-Koehler, 2010).

Robert Austin and Lee Devin. *Artful Making: What Managers Need to Know about How Artists Work* (London: FT Press, 2003).

Christopher Avery. *The Responsibility Process: Unlocking Your Natural Ability to Live and Lead with Power* (Pflugerville, TX: Partnerworks, 2015).

Christopher M. Avery. *Teamwork Is an Individual Skill* (San Francisco: Berrett-Koehler, 2001).

Dennis Bakke. *Joy at Work: A Revolutionary Approach to Fun on the Job* (Seattle, WA: PVG, 2005).

Richard Bandler and John Grinder. *Patterns of the Hypnotic Techniques of Milton H. Erickson, M.D.* Vol. 1 (Santa Cruz, CA: Meta Publications, 1975).

Don Edward Beck and Christopher C. Cowan. *Spiral Dynamics: Mastering Values, Leadership and Change* (Hoboken, NJ: Wiley-Blackwell, 2005).

Peter Block. *Stewardship: Choosing Service over Self-Interest* (San Francisco: Berrett-Koehler, 1993).

George E. P. Box and Norman R. Draper. *Empirical Model-Building and Response Surfaces* (New York: Wiley, 1987).

Marcus Buckingham and Curt Coffman. *First, Break All the Rules: What the World's Greatest Managers Do Differently* (New York: Gallup Organization, 1999).

Cambridge Dictionary. S.v. "autonomous, n.d." Accessed March 19, 2021. https://dictionary.cambridge.org/dictionary/english/autonomous.

Kim S. Cameron and Robert E. Quinn. *Diagnosing and Changing Organizational Culture: Based on the Competing Values Framework*. 3rd ed. (San Francisco: Jossey-Bass, 2011).

Jim Collins. *Good to Great: Why Some Companies Make the Leap . . . and Others Don't* (New York: HarperCollins, 2001).

Chip Conley. *Peak: How Great Companies Get Their Mojo from Maslow* (San Francisco: Jossey-Bass, 2007).

Roger Connors and Tom Smith. *Change the Culture, Change the Game: The Breakthrough Strategy for Energizing Your Organization and Creating Accountability for Results* (New York: Penguin, 2011).

Stephen R. Covey. *The 7 Habits of Highly Effective People: Restoring the Character Ethic*, 15th ed. (New York: Free Press, 2004).

Jef Cumps. *Sociocracy 3.0: The Novel—Unleash the Full Potential of People and Organizations* (Belgium: Lannoo Publishers, 2019).

Ward Cunningham et al. "Manifesto for Agile Software Development." Agile Manifesto, 2001. https://agilemanifesto.org.

Ray Dalio. *Principles: Life and Work* (New York: Simon & Schuster, 2017).

Deloitte. "2019 Deloitte Global Human Capital Trends." 2019. https://www2.deloitte.com/ro/en/pages/human-capital/articles/2019-deloitte-global-human-capital-trends.html.

W. Edwards Deming. *The New Economics: For Industry, Government, Education*. 2nd ed. (Cambridge, MA: MIT Press, 1994).

W. Edwards Deming. *Out of the Crisis* (Cambridge, MA: MIT Press, 2000).

Robert Dilts, Tim Hallbom, and Suzi Smith. *Beliefs: Pathways to Health and Well-Being* (Bancyfelin, Wales: Crown House Publishing, 2012).

Peter F. Drucker, *The Daily Drucker: 366 Days of Insight and Motivation for Getting the Right Things Done* (New York: HarperCollins, 2004).

Peter F. Drucker. *Management Challenges for the 21st Century* (New York: Harper-Collins e-books, 2009). Kindle Edition.

Charles Duhigg. "What Google Learned from Its Quest to Build the Perfect Team." *New York Times*, February 25, 2016. https://www.nytimes.com/2016/02/28/magazine/what-google-learned-from-its-quest-to-build-the-perfect-team.html.

Carol S. Dweck. *Mindset: The New Psychology of Success* (New York: Random House, 2006).

Amy C. Edmondson. *The Fearless Organization: Creating Psychological Safety in the Workplace for Learning, Innovation, and Growth* (Hoboken, NY: Wiley, 2018).

Glenda H. Eoyang and Royce J. Holladay. *Adaptive Action: Leveraging Uncertainty in Your Organization* (Redwood City, CA: Stanford Business Books, 2011).

Viktor E. Frankl. *Man's Search for Meaning* (Boston: Beacon Press, 1959).

Héctor García and Francesc Miralles. *Ikigai: The Japanese Secret to a Long and Happy Life* (New York: Penguin, 2016).

Louis V. Gerstner. *Who Says Elephants Can't Dance? Inside IBM's Historic Turnaround* (New York: HarperCollins, 2002).

John Paul Getty. *How to Be Rich* (New York: Berkley Books, 1986).

Sarah Gibbons. *Dot Voting: A Simple Decision-Making and Prioritizing Technique in UX*. Nielsen Norman Group, July 7, 2019. https://www.nngroup.com/articles/dot-voting.

Lisa Gill. "10 Components that Successfully Abolished Hierarchy (In 70+ Companies)." Corporate Rebels, 2018. https://corporate-rebels.com/10-components-k2k.

Robert K. Greenleaf. "The Servant as Leader." In *The Servant as Leader* (Westfield, IN: Robert K. Greenleaf Center, 1991).

Jim Harter. "Dismal Employee Engagement Is a Sign of Global Mismanagement." Gallup (blog). Accessed March 19, 2021. https://www.gallup.com/workplace/231668/dismal-employee-engagement-sign-global-mismanagement.aspx.

Stephen Hawking and Leonard Mlodinow. *The Grand Design* (New York: Bantam, 2010).

Dee Hock. *One from Many: VISA and the Rise of Chaordic Organization* (San Francisco: Berrett-Koehler, 2005).

Jeremy Hope and Robin Fraser. *Beyond Budgeting: How Managers Can Break Free from the Annual Performance Trap* (Boston: Harvard Business School Press, 2003).

Tony Hsieh. *Delivering Happiness: A Path to Profits, Passion, and Purpose* (New York: Grand Central Publishing, 2010).

Richard Kasperowski. *The Core Protocols: A Guide to Greatness* (n.p.: With Great People Publications, 2015).

Ellen Kaufman. "Zen Koan #1: Parable of a Cup of Tea—Buddhist Teaching on Spiritual Bankruptcy." The Talkative Man (website), June 19, 2017. http://www .talkativeman.com/zen-koan-cup-of-tea/.

Robert Kegan and Lisa Laskow Lahey. *An Everyone Culture: Becoming a Deliberately Developmental Organization* (Boston: Harvard Business School Press, 2016).

Doug Kirkpatrick. *Beyond Empowerment: The Age of the Self-Managed Organization* (Woodland, CA: Morning Star Self-Management Institute, 2011).

John P. Kotter. *Leading Change* (Boston: Harvard Business Review Press, 1996).

Frederic Laloux. *Reinventing Organizations: A Guide to Creating Organizations Inspired by the Next Stage in Human Consciousness* (Paris: Diateino, 2014).

Frederic Laloux. *Reinventing Organizations: An Illustrated Invitation to Join the Conversation on Next-Stage Organizations* (Paris: Diateino, 2016).

Nelson Mandela. *Long Walk to Freedom: The Autobiography of Nelson Mandela* (New York: Little, Brown, 1994).

David Mann. *Creating a Lean Culture: Tools to Sustain Lean Conversions.* 2nd ed. (New York: Productivity Press, 2010).

L. David Marquet. *Turn the Ship Around! How to Create Leadership at Every Level* (Austin, TX: Greenleaf Book Group Press, 2012).

Joanne Martin. *Cultures in Organizations: Three Perspectives* (New York: Oxford University Press, 1992).

Douglas McGregor. *The Human Side of Enterprise* (New York: McGraw-Hill Education, 1960).

Will McInnes. *Culture Shock: A Handbook for 21st Century Business* (Hoboken, NJ: Wiley, 2012).

Merriam-Webster.com Dictionary. S.v. "empowerment," n.d. Accessed August 13, 2020. https://www.merriam-webster.com/dictionary/empowerment.

Merriam-Webster.com Dictionary. S.v. "fear," n.d. Accessed March, 19, 2021. https://www.merriam-webster.com/dictionary/fear.

Daniel Mezick. *The Culture Game: Tools for the Agile Manager* (n.p.: FreeStanding Press, 2012).

Geoffrey A. Moore. *Crossing the Chasm: Marketing and Selling Disruptive Products to Mainstream Customers* (New York: Harper Business, 2002).

Vineet Nayar. *Employees First, Customers Second: Turning Conventional Management Upside Down* (Boston: Harvard Business Review Press, 2010).

Harrison Owen. *Open Space Technology: A User's Guide* (San Francisco: Berrett-Koehler, 1997).

Joseph Pelrine. "Turning Up the Heat—The Basic Model." Joseph Pelrine (website/blog), June 15, 2009. http://josephpelrine.com/turning-up-the-heat-the-basic-model.

Niels Pflaeging. *Organize for Complexity: How to Get Life Back into Work to Build the High-Performance Organization* (Wiesbaden, Germany: Betacodex Publishing, 2014).

Daniel H. Pink. *Drive: The Surprising Truth about What Motivates Us* (New York: Riverhead Books, 2011).

Pete Reilly. "Gandhi Story." The Teacher's Path: A Journey of the Mind, the Body and the Heart, July 19, 2008. https://preilly.wordpress.com/2008/07/19/gandhi-story.

Eric Ries. *The Lean Startup: How Today's Entrepreneurs Use Continuous Innovation to Create Radically Successful Businesses* (New York: Crown Business, 2011).

Brian J. Robertson. *Holacracy: The New Management System for a Rapidly Changing World* (New York: Henry Holt and Company, 2015).

David Rock. *Your Brain at Work: Strategies for Overcoming Distraction, Regaining Focus and Working Smarter All Day Long* (New York: HarperCollins, 2009).

Oliver Sacks. *The Man Who Mistook His Wife for a Hat and Other Clinical Tales* (New York: Touchstone, 1985).

Audree Tara Sahota and Michael K. Sahota. *Emotional Science: The Key to Unlocking High Performance* (Toronto: Awakened Press, 2018).

Michael K. Sahota. "Real-Time Intelligent Behaviour in Dynamic Environments: Soccer-Playing Robots (master's thesis, University of British Columbia, 1993).

Michael K. Sahota. "Reactive Deliberation: An Architecture for Real-Time Intelligent Control in Dynamic Environments." In *Proceedings of AAAI-94* (Seattle: Second International Conference on Artificial Intelligence, 1994).

Michael K. Sahota. "Personal Transformation Is the Heart of Organizational Transformation." Shift314, 2013b, https://shift314.com/2013/02/personal-transformation-is-the-heart-of-organizational-transformation.

Michael K. Sahota. "'WHY Agile?' Workshop." Shift314, 2014. https://shift314.com/2014/06/agile-is-not-the-goal-workshop.

Michael K. Sahota. "Organizational Behaviour Follows Leadership Behaviour." Shift314, 2016. https://shift314.com/2016/08/organization-follows-leadership.

Jenny Santi. "The Secret to Happiness Is Helping Others." *Time*, August 4, 2017. https://time.com/collection/guide-to-happiness/4070299/secret-to-happiness.

Edgar H. Schein. *Organizational Culture and Leadership*. 4th ed. (San Francisco: Jossey-Bass, 2010).

William E. Schneider. *The Reengineering Alternative: A Plan for Making Your Current Culture Work* (New York: McGraw-Hill Education, 1999).

Ricardo Semler. *The Seven-Day Weekend: A Better Way to Work in the 21st Century* (New York: Portfolio, 2004).

Peter M. Senge. *The Fifth Discipline: The Art and Practice of the Learning Organization* (New York: Crown Business, 2006).

Simon Sinek. *Start with Why: How Great Leaders Inspire Everyone to Take Action* (New York: Portfolio, 2009).

Dave Snowden. *Cynefin: Weaving Sense-Making into the Fabric of Our World* (Singapore: Cognitive Edge, 2020).

Marc Solow. "Culture and Engagement: The Naked Organization." Deloitte (website). February 27, 2015. https://www2.deloitte.com/insights/us/en/focus/human-capital-trends/2015/employee-engagement-culture-human-capital-trends-2015.html.

Frederick Winslow Taylor. *The Principles of Scientific Management* (New York: Harper & Brothers, 1911).

Valve Corporation. *Valve: Handbook for New Employees* (Bellevue, WA: Valve Press, 2012).

Rick Wartzman. "America's Top CEOs Say They Are No Longer Putting Shareholders before Everyone Else," *Fast Company*, August 19, 2019. https://www.fastcompany.com/90391743/top-ceo-group-business-roundtable-drops-shareholder-primacy.

Gerald M. Weinberg. *The Secrets of Consulting: A Guide to Giving and Getting Advice Successfully* (New York: Dorset House, 1986).

C. Westfall. "Leadership Development Is a $366 Billion Industry: Here's Why Most Programs Don't Work," *Forbes*, June 20, 2019. https://www.forbes.com/sites/chriswestfall/2019/06/20/leadership-development-why-most-programs-dont-work/#68055d2761de.

Wikipedia. S.v. "Dunning-Kruger effect," last modified August 4, 2020 (2020a). https://en.wikipedia.org/wiki/Dunning%E2%80%93Kruger_effect.

Wikipedia. S.v. "Knowledge Worker," last modified May 30, 2020 (2020b). https://en.wikipedia.org/wiki/Knowledge_worker.

Wikipedia. S.v. "Strategic Planning," last updated December 22, 2020 (2020c). https://en.wikipedia.org/wiki/Strategic_planning.

Wikipedia. S.v. "Responsibility Assignment Matrix," last modified January 9, 2021 (2021a). https://en.wikipedia.org/wiki/Responsibility_assignment_matrix (accessed August 13, 2020).

Wikipedia. S.v. "Self-Fulfilling Prophecy," last updated February 8, 2021 (2021b). https://en.wikipedia.org/wiki/Self-fulfilling_prophecy.

Wikipedia. S.v. "Management," last updated February 27, 2021 (2021c). https://en.wikipedia.org/wiki/Management.

Michael

Reaching the place I am in now has been an unplanned, unexpected, and surprising journey. There have been many influences and hundreds of people have helped me on my journey of discovery of how people and organizations really work. I am filled with gratitude as I think about all the experiences and people. Here are some toppers:

- My coach, partner, soul mate, and wife Audree Tara Sahota who has supported me through what at times has seemed like insurmountable growth challenges.
- My father Sarwan Sahota for acting as a role model and challenging me to show up fully.
- My brother Paul for always wanting the best for me.
- My children Scarlett, Cliff, and Sean for giving me the opportunity to evolve my leadership in my role as a father. Sorry, it's a little messy at times.
- My friend Olaf Lewitz for sharing a journey of discovery and evolution. And most importantly showing what it means to have a big heart.
- The organizers of Play4Agile Unconference in Germany for creating an amazing chrysalis for learning.
- Luke Hohmnann for sharing his gift of Innovation Games with me and the world. But more surprisingly modeling extraordinary facilitation for me.

- The Lego Technology of Serious Play for forever changing how I understand listening and cocreation.
- Frederic Laloux for creating an extraordinary book that clarified messages about organizations and inspired my own evolutionary journey.
- Edgar Schien for his foundational work on organizational culture.
- Siraj Sirajuddin for his passion and inspiration to help people evolve through his Temenos workshops.
- Lee Devin who helped me understand flow and working through edges.
- Master John Douglas for upgrading my energetic anatomy.
- Sri Amma Bhagavan for supporting my evolution in consciousness through Oneness University. Much gratitude for the guides who were patient with us with our "minds jumping around like monkeys."
- Jean Marc Stroud for inviting me into a view of reality that transcends understanding with Waking Up to the Movies.

Audree

My vision to work with executives and world leaders to create real change for humanity has taken me on a surprising and profoundly impactful journey—one that I could never have imagined or have planned. It seems as though every experience I have had in my life and every person I have met has been an influence and part of the puzzle pieces that have brought me to this profound work. The most significant shift in my consciousness, perceptions, and transformation has been through Oneness University, Sri Amma Bhagavan, and the guides who have dedicated their lives in service of awakening humanity. It is where I met Michael and this incredible manifestation of my audacious desire to change the world found the space to be birthed.

To my husband, Michael K. Sahota, for your sword of truth that slices through the ego and brings me into another level of my brilliance, your profound love for me that allows me to soar into the highest states of consciousness. I would also like to thank my children and their father for their sacrifices, allowing me the space and freedom to bring this work to the world, I love you beyond, beyond. To my mother Roberta who encouraged the artist in me, who taught me to see the world very differently. To my father Marshall and stepmother Evelyn, to my sisters and my friends who have watched me travel strange and unusual roads to find my voice and develop my work, thank you for believing in me. To my grandfather Sandford Jaffee, who taught me the value of hard work, to find the best of the best teachers, and how command-and-control leadership never works.

To Joel Goldsmith, Ramana Mareshi, Maharishi Mahesh Yogi, Master John, John Mark Stroud, and Mooji for your passion to share, to connect into the transmission of higher consciousness and transfer that state to me.

To Dr. Mitchell for your passion to bring energetic healing into the medical profession, giving me the ability to practice my craft and develop the skill that has taken my work beyond extraordinary. To Barbara Brennan, Tricia Eldridge, Shabad Kaur Khalsa, and Shiva Singh for standing as great teachers who lead through the example of holding space and taught me the importance of being a clear channel to serve a teaching.

To David Morelli, my first coaching teacher who inspired me to lead with passion and heart, who taught me how to hold my clients on a bigger plane, and where I had my first glimpse into who I am today. To my relationship coaching community who taught me to stay connected no matter what and where I learned how to penetrate through the ego and to see the truth of my own self in every experience.

To David S. for seeing the truth of my power, noticing I have a passion for business, and inspiring me to bring my work into the world. To L. Allison and the Awakened Press for bringing my thoughts into manifestation.

To all those who have taught me to follow my dreams, think outside the box, and create from the purpose to serve, I have the most profound gratitude for the deep lessons and sometimes uncomfortable experiences that have propelled my vision to change the world.

Page numbers in italics indicate figures.

About the Authors

Michael K. Sahota is an international keynote speaker, trainer, and consultant on evolving people and organizations. Together with his business partner and wife Audree, they have trained thousands of leaders around the globe on the SHIFT314 Evolutionary Leadership Framework™ (SELF).

Photo by Ron Laudadio

As an Agile thought leader, in 2012 he published the ground-breaking book *An Agile Adoption and Transformation Survival Guide: Working with Organizational Culture*. In 2018, he coauthored *Emotional Science: The Key to High Performance* with Audree.

Michael is the cofounder of SHIFT314 Inc.—a boutique training and consulting organization that specializes in the organizational culture and leadership shifts needed to unlock success with Agile, Digital, Lean, and other new ways of working.

While Michael holds a bachelor of engineering, masters in computer science, and a partially explored PhD in artificial intelligence, he has been trained in the esoteric technologies of shifting consciousness through a variety of wisdom traditions. Michael has three grown children and loves to bicycle in nature.

https://shift314.com/michael-k-sahota/

Audree Tara Sahota, B.Msc., is a high-level initiate with the ability to create permanent neurobiological shifts into high states of consciousness. She is the chief metaphysics officer and cofounder of SHIFT314, Inc., specializing in Evolutionary Leadership development and organizational evolution through a powerful framework SELF™ that enables very rapid changes in the evolution of people and organizations.

Photo by Ron Laudadio

Audree is founder of Evolutionary Energetics™, an advanced energy system to accelerate human potential. She has created various meditations for transformation and shifting consciousness. She has published several books; *The Authorities: The Evolution of Consciousness for the Entrepreneur* (2013), *Emotional Science, The Key to Unlocking High Performance* (2018), *The Truth of a Naked Soul* (2019), *The Fairy Princess* (2020).

Since 1994 Audree has held advanced professional certifications in energetic healing, meditation, and yoga, including five years as an energetic healer on a medical team. Audree holds professional designations from the University of Metaphysics (B.Msc.), Brennan Healing Science, EnergyTouch Practitioner. Along with her ten years of formal training in energy medicine, including meditation and yoga, she is professionally trained as a traditional coach, holds a CSM designation through the Scrum Alliance, Breatharian Pranic Healer, and is an advanced trainer & chamber facilitator, OU. India. She is working toward her PhD in theocentric psychology.

With her husband Michael K. Sahota, they achieve their vision of transforming humanity through their thought leadership on the importance of shifting consciousness of business leaders for sustainable success.

About the Illustrator

Marc Hundleby passionately illustrates to visually express ideas that uncover insights within the hearts and minds of his clients. Marc's creativity lives in his DNA, as he comes from a lineage of artists. His expression manifests as a keen adventurer and sailor. Marc is an avid free diver and has circumnavigated the globe in the Clipper Round of the World Yacht Race (2015).

Marc is the founder of The Humble PM, a freelance consultancy specializing in visualisation, training, and coaching to help people SEE, FEEL, and THINK differently. He is a certified Bikablo® global trainer, Agile leadership coach, and an accredited PMP, CPPD, CAL, CSM, Scrum@Scale practitioner.

In 2018, Marc attended a Certified Agile Leadership Course hosted by the authors, which had a profound effect that shifted his consciousness—starting an inner journey to find his life's purpose. That deep inner journey led to a career change and an invitation to illustrate this book.

Marc lives in Sydney, Australia with his partner Renee; his Hungarian Vizsla, Floyd; and his seafaring passion, a classic wooden boat in Tasmania called *Jacaranda*–aka *The Mistress*.

https://humblepm.com/

Dear reader,

Thank you for picking up this book and welcome to the worldwide BK community! You're joining a special group of people who have come together to create positive change in their lives, organizations, and communities.

What's BK all about?

Our mission is to connect people and ideas to create a world that works for all.

Why? Our communities, organizations, and lives get bogged down by old paradigms of self-interest, exclusion, hierarchy, and privilege. But we believe that can change. That's why we seek the leading experts on these challenges—and share their actionable ideas with you.

A welcome gift

To help you get started, we'd like to offer you a **free copy** of one of our bestselling ebooks:

www.bkconnection.com/welcome

When you claim your **free ebook**, you'll also be subscribed to our blog.

Our freshest insights

Access the best new tools and ideas for leaders at all levels on our blog at ideas.bkconnection.com.

Sincerely,

Your friends at Berrett-Koehler

Certified

Corporation